Passport to Reprieve

THE AZRIELI SERIES OF HOLOCAUST SURVIVOR MEMOIRS: PUBLISHED TITLES

Maxwell Smart, *Chaos to Canvas*
Gerta Solan, *My Heart Is At Ease*
Zsuzsanna Fischer Spiro, *In Fragile Moments*/ Eva Shainblum, *The Last Time*
George Stern, *Vanished Boyhood*
Willie Sterner, *The Shadows Behind Me*
Ann Szedlecki, *Album of My Life*
William Tannenzapf, *Memories from the Abyss*/ Renate Krakauer, *But I Had a Happy Childhood*
Elsa Thon, *If Only It Were Fiction*
Agnes Tomasov, *From Generation to Generation*
Joseph Tomasov, *From Loss to Liberation*
Leslie Vertes, *Alone in the Storm*
Anka Voticky, *Knocking on Every Door*
Sam Weisberg, Carry the Torch/ Johnny Jablon, A Lasting Legacy

TITRES FRANÇAIS

Judy Abrams, *Retenue par un fil*/ Eva Felsenburg Marx, *Une question de chance*
Molly Applebaum, *Les Mots enfouis: Le Journal de Molly Applebaum*
Claire Baum, *Le Colis caché*
Bronia et Joseph Beker, *Plus forts que le malheur*
Max Bornstein, *Citoyen de nulle part*
Tommy Dick, *Objectif: survivre*
Marian Domanski, *Traqué*
John Freund, *La Fin du printemps*
Myrna Goldenberg (Éditrice), *Un combat singulier: Femmes dans la tourmente de l'Holocauste*
René Goldman, *Une enfance à la dérive*
Anna Molnár Hegedűs, *Pendant la saison des lilas*
Helena Jockel, *Nous chantions en sourdine*
Michael Kutz, *Si, par miracle*
Nate Leipciger, *Le Poids de la liberté*
Alex Levin, *Étoile jaune, étoile rouge*
Fred Mann, *Un terrible revers de fortune*
Michael Mason, *Au fil d'un nom*
Leslie Meisels, *Soudain, les ténèbres*
Muguette Myers, *Les Lieux du courage*
Arthur Ney, *L'Heure W*
Felix Opatowski, *L'Antichambre de l'enfer*
Marguerite Élias Quddus, *Cachée*
Henia Reinhartz, *Fragments de ma vie*
Betty Rich, *Seule au monde*
Paul-Henri Rips, *Matricule E/96*
Steve Rotschild, *Sur les traces du passé*
Kitty Salsberg et Ellen Foster, *Unies dans l'épreuve*
Zuzana Sermer, *Trousse de survie*
Rachel Shtibel, *Le Violon*/ Adam Shtibel, *Témoignage d'un enfant*
George Stern, *Une jeunesse perdue*
Willie Sterner, *Les Ombres du passé*
Ann Szedlecki, *L'Album de ma vie*
William Tannenzapf, *Souvenirs de l'abîme*/ Renate Krakauer, *Le Bonheur de l'innocence*
Elsa Thon, *Que renaisse demain*
Agnes Tomasov, *De génération en génération*
Leslie Vertes, *Seul dans la tourmente*
Anka Voticky, *Frapper à toutes les portes*
Sam Weisberg, *Passeur de mémoire*/ Johnny Jablon, *Souvenez-vous*

Passport to Reprieve

Sonia Caplan

THE AZRIELI FOUNDATION · www.azrielifoundation.org

Cover and book design by Mark Goldstein · Interior map by Deborah Crowle · Endpaper maps by Martin Gilbert · Biblical text and translation on pages 221–222 reproduced from the *Tanakh: The Holy Scriptures* by permission of the University of Nebraska Press. Copyright 1985 by The Jewish Publication Society, Philadelphia · Article on page 235 courtesy of City of Ottawa Archives/MG011 Ottawa Journal fonds · Article on pages 236–240 courtesy of www.wartimecanada.ca and The Ley and Lois Smith War, Memory, and Popular Culture Research Collection, Department of History, The University of Western Ontario · Document 2 on pages 249 & 252 courtesy of Arolsen Archives, ITS Digital Archives.

LIBRARY AND ARCHIVES CANADA CATALOGUING IN PUBLICATION

Passport to Reprieve/ Sonia Caplan.
    Caplan, Sonia, 1922–1987, author. Azrieli Foundation, publisher.
The Azrieli series of Holocaust survivor memoirs; XIII
Includes bibliographical references and index.
Canadiana (print) 20210360941 · Canadiana (ebook) 20210360992
ISBN 9781989719169 (softcover) · ISBN 9781989719275 (ebook) ·
ISBN 9781989719282 (PDF)
LCSH: Caplan, Sonia, 1922–1987. LCSH: Holocaust, Jewish (1939–1945) — Poland — Tarnów (Województwo Małopolskie) — Personal narratives. LCSH: Holocaust survivors — Canada — Biography. LCGFT: Autobiographies.

LCC DS134.72.C35 A3 2021   DDC 940.53/18092—dc23

MIX
Paper from responsible sources
FSC   FSC® C004191
www.fsc.org

PRINTED IN CANADA

The Azrieli Foundation's Holocaust Survivor Memoirs Program

Naomi Azrieli, Publisher

Jody Spiegel, Program Director
Arielle Berger, Managing Editor
Catherine Person, Manager and Editor of French Translations
Catherine Aubé, Editor of French Translations
Matt Carrington, Editor
Devora Levin, Editor and Special Projects Coordinator
Stephanie Corazza, Historian and Manager of Academic Initiatives
Marc-Olivier Cloutier, Manager of Education Initiatives
Nadine Auclair, Coordinator of Education Initiatives
Michelle Sadowski, Educator
Elin Beaumont, Community and Education Initiatives
Elizabeth Banks, Digital Asset Curator and Archivist

Mark Goldstein, Art Director
Bruno Paradis, Layout, French-Language Editions

Contents

Series Preface:
In their own words. . .

In telling these stories, the writers have liberated themselves. For so many years we did not speak about it, even when we became free people living in a free society. Now, when at last we are writing about what happened to us in this dark period of history, knowing that our stories will be read and live on, it is possible for us to feel truly free. These unique historical documents put a face on what was lost, and allow readers to grasp the enormity of what happened to six million Jews — one story at a time.

David J. Azrieli, C.M., C.Q., M.Arch
Holocaust survivor and founder, The Azrieli Foundation

Since the end of World War II, approximately 40,000 Jewish Holocaust survivors have immigrated to Canada. Who they are, where they came from, what they experienced and how they built new lives for themselves and their families are important parts of our Canadian heritage. The Azrieli Foundation's Holocaust Survivor Memoirs Program was established in 2005 to preserve and share the memoirs written by those who survived the twentieth-century Nazi genocide of the Jews of Europe and later made their way to Canada. The memoirs encourage readers to engage thoughtfully and critically with the complexities of the Holocaust and to create meaningful connections with the lives of survivors.

Millions of individual stories are lost to us forever. By preserving the stories written by survivors and making them widely available to a broad audience, the Azrieli Foundation's Holocaust Survivor Memoirs Program seeks to sustain the memory of all those who perished at the hands of hatred, abetted by indifference and apathy. The personal accounts of those who survived against all odds are as different as the people who wrote them, but all demonstrate the courage, strength, wit and luck that it took to prevail and survive in such terrible adversity. The memoirs are also moving tributes to people — strangers and friends — who risked their lives to help others, and who, through acts of kindness and decency in the darkest of moments, frequently helped the persecuted maintain faith in humanity and courage to endure. These accounts offer inspiration to all, as does the survivors' desire to share their experiences so that new generations can learn from them.

The Holocaust Survivor Memoirs Program collects, archives and publishes select survivor memoirs and makes the print editions available free of charge to educational institutions and Holocaust-education programs across Canada. They are also available for sale online to the general public. All revenues to the Azrieli Foundation from the sales of the Azrieli Series of Holocaust Survivor Memoirs go toward the publishing and educational work of the memoirs program.

$\sim$

The Azrieli Foundation would like to express appreciation to the following people for their invaluable efforts in producing this book: Adam Bartosz, Doris Bergen, David Caplan, Judith Clark, Mark Duffus (Maracle Inc.), Jan Grabowski, Janusz Kozioł, Aliza Krefetz, Gloria Kushel, Tilman Lewis, Meg Lipstone, Susan Roitman, Arthur Roskies, Andrea Schwartz-Feit, Agnieszka Wierzcholska and Second Story Press.

Editorial and Research Note

The following memoir contains languages, terms, concepts and historical references that may be unfamiliar to the reader. English translations of foreign-language words and terms have been added to the text, and parentheses have been used to include the names and locations of present-day towns and cities when place names have changed. The editors of this memoir have worked to maintain the author's voice and stay true to the original narrative while maintaining historical accuracy. The detailed research on Tarnów in this memoir would not have been possible without the generous assistance of Adam Bartosz from the Muzeum Okręgowe w Tarnowie (Regional Museum in Tarnów), Janusz Kozioł from the Muzeum Historyczne Miasta Krakowa (Historical Museum of the City of Kraków) and scholar Agnieszka Wierzcholska, whose book *Nur Erinnerungen und Steine sind geblieben. Leben und Sterben einer polnisch-jüdischen Stadt, Tarnów 1918-1945* [Only memories and stones remain. Life and death of a Polish-Jewish town, Tarnów 1918-1945] will be published by Schöningh | Brill : Paderborn in 2022.

General information on major organizations, significant historical events and people, geographical locations, religious and cultural terms, and foreign-language words and expressions that will help give context to the events described in the text can be found in the glossary beginning on page 223.

Introduction

In one of the final chapters of her Holocaust memoir, Sonia Caplan (née Roskes) describes her feelings on the eve of her arrival in Montreal, Canada.[1] After three years of living in Nazi-occupied Poland, and another two years in a German camp for foreign nationals, after enduring forced labour, malnutrition, continual fear of death, after losing neighbours, friends and relatives, Sonia writes, "Unlike so many whom I had known and loved, we were given a second chance. Would I do it justice? Would I deserve my incredibly good fortune? Would my life, wrenched from murderous attacks, have real meaning?"

Sonia Caplan's memoir, *Passport to Reprieve*, is a compelling account of the unlikely survival of three women: herself, her younger sister, Hela, and their mother, Ida. It is also a deeply personal account, recalling the experiences of a young woman, rich with memories of emotional ties and sexual encounters, some of which enabled her to improve the material standing of her family and their chances of finding hiding places in the ghetto. These vignettes add important texture to the intimate story of one family's survival in Nazi-occupied Poland.

---

1 The Roskes family in Canada changed the spelling of their name to Roskies, as reflected in the Afterword written by Sonia's son, David Caplan.

The experiences of young women like Sonia and their role in the survival of Jewish families had long been largely ignored by historians. However, a growing number of scholars are examining the experiences of Jewish women in the Holocaust.[2] In her review essay on women and gender in the Holocaust, historian Marion Kaplan summarizes why this is important: "Without women's memories we missed not only familial and domestic aspects of the Holocaust but also gendered public behaviors and humiliations and gendered persecutions in ghettos and camps."[3] Sonia's memoir helps us pose new questions about and allows for a more nuanced discussion of women's sexuality and the survival strategies of women at the helm of their families during the Holocaust.

For many young Jewish women, economic status and family relations, particularly between parents and daughters, was a crucial aspect shaping their experiences during the Holocaust. The longer families stayed together, the longer parents could attempt to exercise their parental responsibilities, even if internal family dynamics underwent transformation. Sonia's agency and power to define and redefine her coming-of-age experience in Eastern Europe during the Holocaust was limited under the Nazi regime, but not completely shuttered — her gender and class shaped her adolescence in the Tarnów ghetto.

---

2 See Dalia Ofer and Lenore J. Weitzman, eds., *Women in the Holocaust* (New Haven, CT: Yale University Press, 1998); Marcia Sachs-Littell, ed., *Women in the Holocaust: Responses, Insights and Perspectives (Selected Papers from the Annual Scholars' Conference on the Holocaust and the Churches, 1900–2000)* (Merion Station, PA: Merion Westfield Press, 2001); Anna Hájková, "Sexual Barter in Times of Genocide: Negotiating the Sexual Economy of the Theresienstadt Ghetto," *Signs* 38, no. 3 (2013): 503–33; Natalia Aleksiun, "Gender and Daily Lives of Jews in Hiding in Eastern Galicia," *Nashim* no 27 (fall 2014): 38–61; and Zoë Waxman, *Women in the Holocaust: A Feminist History* (Oxford, UK: Oxford University Press, 2017).

3 Marion Kaplan, "Did Gender Matter during the Holocaust?" *Jewish Social Studies* 24, no. 2 (2019): 39.

Sonia had a happy childhood attending school, discussing books and current events with her peers as well as making plans for the future. This life changed dramatically in the spring and summer of 1939, a change augured by a moving and vivid account of a trip to her parents' native city of Białystok to attend what proved to be the last Passover they celebrated together. Then came the rushed departure of her beloved father, who went abroad to prepare for immigration to Canada for himself and his family, followed by the outbreak of World War II. Sonia would never again be a lighthearted teenager. Her father's absence forced her to take on a new role in the family.[4] Sonia describes this time with her mother and sister Hela:

Mother seemed near collapse and could not think. All she did during those few fateful days was groan repeatedly, "Izak, Izak, what should we do?" and "Why have you left us alone?" Hela, though perky and bright, had, at her age, only a dim view of our predicament. And so, almost against my volition, the leadership of the family had passed on to me. I felt that I was ill-fitted to be cast into the role of a leader in a precarious life situation, for underneath my outer layer of sophistication and certain cerebral endowments I was still very much the child — unsure of myself and badly in need of mature guidance. However, as it was to be so often in the nearly six years to come, I had no choice.

While dealing with the separation from her father, Sonia's account remains the story of a family struggling to stay together through the coded, yet heart-wrenching, letters they sent and received, and the brave strategies she adopted in Tarnów to avoid getting separated. Sonia's story is in many ways unique, not only because she, her mother

---

4   I write about this tension between childhood and adolescence, which other memoirists have expressed, here: "Girls Coming-of-Age during the Holocaust: Gender, Class, and the Struggle for Survival in Eastern Europe," in *Jewish Women's History from Antiquity to the Present*, eds. Federica Francesconi and Rebecca Lynn Winer (Detroit: Wayne State University Press, 2021), 273–295.

and her sister survived together. Her story also stands out because of her unusual trajectory during the war and her ability to leave Europe before the end of the war. This trajectory — ghetto, prison, internment camp and eventual journey to North America — resembles one other well-known account of a young woman two years Sonia's senior. Mary Berg, born Miriam Wattenberg (1924–2013) had kept a diary under the Nazi occupation, written between October 10, 1939, and March 5, 1944, which, as one of the earliest published accounts to emerge before the end of the war, became a touchstone for scholars studying diaries and their immediacy in expressing wartime experiences. [5] Interestingly, Sonia, too, published an early account, in May 1945 — reproduced here in the documents and photographs section of this memoir — detailing her time in the Liebenau civilian internment camp in Germany, which remains one of the rare English-language sources on the camp.

Where Mary and her family were at first held in the Warsaw ghetto, Sonia and her family were trapped in the ghetto in Tarnów. Mary's mother held American citizenship, and she, her parents and her sister were detained in Pawiak prison in July 1942, prior to the liquidation of the Warsaw ghetto. Sonia's father, in a feat of epic proportions, managed to become a citizen of Nicaragua while still living in Canada, and sent Sonia and her family the passports he had managed to obtain for them. In late 1942, it was those passports that led to Sonia, her mother and sister being transferred to a prison in Krakow.

In January 1943, around the same time that Sonia and her family were sent to the Liebenau internment camp in Germany, Mary

---

5 Mary's memoir, *Warsaw Ghetto*, was first serialized in New York's Yiddish newspaper *Der morgen Zshurnal* in 1944, and soon after appeared in other newspapers, translated into English and other languages. *Warsaw Ghetto* was published in English in February 1945. After going out of print in the 1950s, the memoir was revised and republished in 2007, 2009, 2013 and 2018 by Oneworld Publications as *The Diary of Mary Berg: Growing up in the Warsaw Ghetto.*

and her family were transferred to Vittel, an internment camp in France for British and American citizens and others who thus escaped death, often only temporarily. On March 1, 1944, they boarded a train for Lisbon. After their departure, many of the Jewish inmates of Vittel were deported to Auschwitz, a tragedy that Sonia recalls, having known some of the victims and hearing about it at the time. The Bergs, too, boarded the ocean liner MS *Gripsholm* for the voyage to America, albeit the year before the Roskes family.

Like Berg, Sonia Caplan experienced a relatively carefree life before the war. Born in Białystok in 1922, she was raised in Tarnów, a city located about ninety kilometres east of Krakow, Poland, where her parents had moved because of her father's successful career in textile manufacturing and commerce. She felt at home there and enjoyed a childhood shaped by her parents' middle-class social status and their intellectual aspirations, participating in social, religious and political activities, surrounded by Jewish friends. Her family was part of the internal migration in the aftermath of the Great War, when many citizens of the newly reborn Polish state crossed the borders of the former partitioning Russian and Austrian empires. The Roskes family moved from industrial Białystok, which had been an important textile centre in the Russian Empire, to a city that contained the fourth-largest Jewish community in Galicia, after Lwów (now Lviv, Ukraine), Krakow and Stanisławów (now Ivano-Frankvisk, Ukraine).

Among the major towns of the province, Tarnów had the highest percentage of Jews in the total population. The census taken on September 30, 1921, a few years before the arrival of the Roskes family, records 35,347 people living in Tarnów. Most (19,217 or 54.4 per cent) were Roman Catholic, but Jews formed a sizable group, with 15,608 (44.1 per cent) declaring themselves to be of the "Mosaic" faith. Other religious groups were present, but in much smaller numbers. Within the Jewish population, 10,223, or about two-thirds, also declared their nationality to be Jewish. The remaining third joined the Roman

Catholics in declaring their nationality to be Polish, forming a combined majority of 24,589. The other, much smaller, national groups included 440 Ruthenians (Ukrainians), 27 Germans and 68 others.[6]

By December 9, 1931, the date of the next census, Tarnów's population had grown to 44,927 out of which 19,330 were Jews. There was little change in the percentage ratio of the two main religious groups, Roman Catholics and Jews. The new census avoided the thorny question of nationality and instead asked about language (*język ojczysty*), with about 64 per cent declaring Polish as their first language, and 35 per cent declaring Yiddish or Hebrew. Only 0.3 per cent declared other languages.[7]

Over the next several years, Tarnów's population continued to grow — by 1938, it numbered close to 55,000 — and the number of Jewish citizens was also growing.[8] The last head of the Jewish community in Tarnów, Abraham Chomet, published a detailed history of the local community in 1954, based on his personal knowledge, documents and newspaper reports. He noted that by 1939, before the war, the Jewish community had reached approximately 25,000, about 45 per cent of the total population. He also pointed out that in 1938, the Jewish community administration was supporting more than one thousand refugees from Nazi Germany, and continued to support waves of newcomers during the war, opening a community kitchen to assist them.[9]

---

6 Główny Urząd Statystyczny Rzeczypospolitej Polskiej, *Skorowidz miejscowości Rzeczypospolitej Polskiej: opracowany na podstawie wyników pierwszego powszechnego spisu ludności z dn. 30 września 1921 r. i innych źródeł urzędowych.* Tom XII: *Województwo Krakowskie, Śląsk Cieszyński* (Warszawa 1925), p. 34.

7 Główny Urząd Statystyczny Rzeczypospolitej Polskiej, *Wyniki ostateczne opracowania spisu ludności z dn. 9.XII.1931 r. w postaci skróconej dla wszystkich województw, powiatów i miast powyżej 20 000 mieszkańców Rzeczypospolitej Polskiej* (Warszawa 1935), table XIV 16b.

8 Polska Agencja Telegraficzna, *Rocznik polityczny i gospodarczy* (Warszawa 1932–1939).

9 Abraham Chomet, "Towards a History of Jews in Tarnow," "The Annihilation of the Jews of Tarnow," in *Tarnow: The Life and Destruction of a Jewish City* ed.

Among the important local Jewish institutions in Tarnów was the Tarbut coeducational gymnasium, which belonged to a network of 270 such modern secular Jewish educational institutions in the Second Polish Republic. Focused on educating the young generation of Polish Jews to be fluent in Hebrew and committed to Zionist nation building in Palestine, Tarbut institutions in interwar Poland included kindergartens, elementary schools, high schools and teachers' seminaries.[10] Sonia belonged to a generation that was being shaped by these new educational projects, whose ideological commitment differed from that of her parents and who found among their peers a source of emotional support and intellectual stimulation. "If our parents were at times uneasy about the heavy dose of secularism and active Zionism disseminated by the school," she writes in her memoir, "it was because they were caught between the old and the new ideologies. Unable to stem the tide of intellectual and psychological progress washing over their young, they could do little more than acquiesce to the inevitable. A new Jewish identity was being forged in the school, and there was no turning back." Sonia's activities in the Zionist youth movement represent just a glimpse into the political activism of her generation and more broadly into the modern Jewish politics that played out locally in Tarnów in the interwar period.[11]

Abraham Chomet (Tel Aviv: Associations of Former Residents of Tarnow, 1954), 1–186, 808–870 [in Yiddish]. See the demographic data on pages 75–76, 158, 167, 818. For an ongoing English translation project of the book see JewishGen, Yizkor Book Project, Tarnow, https://www.jewishgen.org/yizkor/tarnow/Tarnow.html.

10 See Adina Bar-El, "Tarbut," *YIVO Encyclopedia of Jews in Eastern Europe*, https://yivoencyclopedia.org/article.aspx/Tarbut (accessed October 1, 2021). For an interesting discussion on Jewish education at this time, see See Kamil Kijek, "Was it possible to avoid 'Hebrew assimilation'?: Hebraism, Polonization, and Tarbut schools in the last decade of interwar Poland," *Jewish Social Studies* 21, no. 2 (2016): 105–141.

11 See Agnieszka Wierzcholska, "Relations between the Bund and the Polish Socialist Party from a micro-historical perspective: Tarnów in the interwar period," *East European Jewish Affairs* 43, no. 3 (2013): 297–313. On the political activism of the young Polish Jews, see Kamil Kijek, *Dzieci modernizmu. Świadomość, kultura i*

~

Tarnów came under German occupation as early as September 7, 1939.[12] The community was taken by surprise by the advance of the German army. In his account, Abraham Chomet noted with some pathos, "The autumn of 1939 was warm, wonderful and sunny, as though in league with Hitler's troops, helping them advance across Polish highways and roads to despoil the Polish land."[13]

As in other towns of the newly established General Government, a quick succession of antisemitic decrees followed, which forced the Jews to wear a Star of David and to mark their businesses with a white Star of David. Their bank accounts were frozen, and Jewish institutions and schools were closed. Jews aged fourteen to sixty had to register for forced labour. During these initial weeks and months, many Jews — especially young men — escaped to areas occupied by the Soviets. Indeed, among these refugees were Sonia's friends.

Tarnów was established as the centre of a *Kreis*, a district, and was at first administered by Ernst Kundt and his deputy, Walter Heinrich. In December 1940, Ludwig Stitzinger succeeded Kundt, who in January 1942 was replaced by Dr. Kipke. In November 1939, a Judenrat was formed under the former chairman of the Jewish community, Dr. Józef Offner, and operated at first in the old building of the Jewish community, at Nowa Street 11. Offner, whom Chomet described as "the pride of the judicial profession in Galicia," soon resigned from the Judenrat. The new Judenrat leaders appointed in 1940, Dr. Szlomo

_____

socjalizacja polityczna młodzieży żydowskiej w II Rzeczypospolitej (Krakow: Austeria, 2021).

12 Joanna Śliwa, "Tarnów," *The United States Holocaust Memorial Museum Encyclopedia of Camps and Ghettos, 1933–1945*, ed. Geofrey Megargee, vol. II, part A: Ghettos in German-Occupied Eastern Europe, ed. Martin Dean (Bloomington: Indiana University Press, 2012), 584–587. Chomet and other survivors give September 8 as the beginning of the German occupation of Tarnów. Chomet, 808.

13 Chomet, 808.

Goldberg and Dr. Wolf Schenkel, who — as Chomet emphasized — had tried to protect the Jewish population, were sent to Auschwitz-Birkenau.[14] The last head of the Judenrat, Artur Volkman, appears in the testimony of survivors in a rather positive light because of his efforts to organize assistance for the Jews in Tarnów when the Judenrat was forced to provide labour and respond to social issues. Chomet, however, stressed that those who saw the Judenrat as a continuity of the Jewish communal representation were naive. Burdened with implementing German orders, the Judenrat struggled to organize forced labour in order to minimize abuse, but roundups accompanied by beatings continued.[15]

While Sonia mentions the role of the Judenrat only in passing, the Jewish police (Ordnungsdienst), established in Tarnów by the Germans in October 1941, came to play an important role for her and her sister because of their personal contacts. The memoir offers a personal insight into the police force and a testimony to the role that Israel Schmuckler, Hela's boyfriend, played in the family's survival. He appears to be one of the "rare exceptions" Chomet described, among the policemen who otherwise were a "plague on the Jewish population," one of those "who did not forget that they were Jewish. They would warn the Jewish population of every misfortune and in many cases exhibited [their] humanity."[16]

Sonia chronicles the difficulties her family faced during the early weeks and months of the occupation and the ways she was trying to make ends meet. Although she was unable to obtain significant supplies, her family was able to sustain itself with the assistance provided by their father from abroad, as well as through the help of Zosia, a Polish gentile who, risking the consequences for aiding Jews, smuggled food to them when she could. Sonia's account of life under

---

14 Chomet, 813, 819.

15 See Archive of the Jewish Historical Institute in Warsaw (Archiwum ŻIH, henceforth AŻIH), 301/436, testimony of Renia Froelich, 1-2. Chomet, 811.

16 Chomet, 811.

the German occupation in Tarnów is remarkable in revealing how little contact she seems to have had with the Polish inhabitants of the town. Aside from Zosia, Sonia had encounters only with a Polish taxi driver, whom she paid to arrange a secret trip to Krakow. Considering the previous census data, one might question the dynamics between Polish gentiles and Jews living under Nazi occupation. Scholar Agnieszka Wierzcholska, who has focused on the social processes between Jews and gentiles in the microcosm of Tarnów, writes of "shifting social norms," "rivalry for social and material benefits among the gentile Polish population" and that the "extreme terror [that] prevailed severely affected relations between Jews and gentile Poles." The shift in relations between neighbours came well before the war — antisemitic acts in Tarnów increased between 1935 and 1939, and the polarization of society was well in place before the arrival of the Germans.[17]

Though Sonia considered trying to go into hiding with Zosia, her efforts centred on obtaining exit visas for herself and her mother and sister to join her father in Canada. In the fall of 1940, thanks to the Nicaraguan citizenship her father had been able to secure, her family received official exemption from having to wear armbands. She describes the changing urban space of her town, as Jewish apartments had to accommodate Germans moving in and as Jews were restricted from entering districts north of Krakowska and Wałowa Streets and west of Brodziński Street, as well as from public parks. Gradually, they were even prohibited from looking out of their windows onto

---

17 Agnieszka Wierzcholska, "Beyond the Bystander. Relations Between Jews and Gentile Poles in the General Government," in *The Holocaust and European Societies: Social Processes and Social Dynamics*, eds. Frank Bajor and Andrea Löw (London: Palgrave Macmillan, 2016), 267–287. For a further discussion of interethnic relations in German-occupied Tarnów, see Agnieszka Wierzcholska, "Helping, Denouncing, and Profiteering: A Process-Oriented Approach to Jewish-Gentile Relations in Occupied Poland from a Micro-Historical Perspective," *Holocaust Studies* 23, no. 1–2 (2017): 34–58.

certain streets. Jews were also forced to work clearing streets of snow and garbage. Their life was regulated by a curfew imposed in April 1940, which required them to be indoors after 9:00 p.m. Jews were forced to pay a ransom of 500,000 złoty, Jewish homes were plundered, Jewish religious books destroyed and Jewish Orthodox men tortured and humiliated in public.[18] The situation for religious Jews was particularly dire, as ritual slaughter was illegal and Jewish men were prohibited from wearing beards and sidelocks.

A formal ghetto was established only in 1942. Before this, in August 1940, Jews living in the more elegant apartments on Krakowska and Wałowa Streets were compelled to move to the eastern part of Tarnów, known as Grabówka, and given only twelve hours to do so. As more streets became forbidden to Jews, more were forced to move into this neighbourhood. In June 1941, with the Germans invading and declaring war against the Soviet Union, the circumstances for Jews in Tarnów deteriorated further, with a shortage of food and the spread of epidemics. In the winter of 1941, the Germans ordered the Jews to surrender all fur clothing, a measure Sonia recalls in her memoir. Her family was particularly affected by the ban on receiving food packages introduced in December 1941.

When the ghetto was established, it was at first an open one with four entrances. Random violence and shootings in the ghetto became a daily occurrence, in particular following the arrival of SS-*Sturmscharführer* Wilhelm Rommelmann. Rommelmann appears on the pages of Sonia's memoir and also in other survivors' testimonies as a sadistic and unpredictable murderer.[19] One child survivor from Tarnów, Marlena Lilith Mittler, recalls how news about mass shootings and deportations brought depression and resignation, so much so that even the sight of terrified relatives became unbearable.

---

18 Chomet, 818.

19 See AŻIH, 301/3432, testimony of Leon Leser; AŻIH, 301/3433, testimony of Józef Korniło; AŻIH, 301/3434, testimony of Izaak Izrael; AŻIH, 301/3437, testimony of Łucja Rauch.

She wrote in her postwar testimony that her life in the ghetto was equivalent to being "sentenced to death and awaiting execution at any moment."[20] Among those murdered were Jews who had returned from Lwów after the Germans had invaded and occupied the area previously held by the Soviets, a tragedy that profoundly affected Sonia.

What her memoir only alludes to, however, is the adoption and implementation of the "Final Solution," the Nazi-orchestrated mass murder of all European Jews, beginning in the late summer and fall of 1941. Although the first killing centre began operating in December 1941 in Chełmno, the plans for the mass murder of Jews in the General Government were initiated earlier in the fall of 1941 and then intensified after the Wannsee Conference in January 1942.[21] As part of the Nazi Operation Reinhard, which aimed to murder Polish Jews in the General Government and which began in March 1942 with the deportation of Jews from Lublin to the killing centre in Bełżec, the turning point in the history of the Tarnów ghetto occurred on June 10, 1942.[22] After the completion of the registration of the Jewish population, Tarnów Jews were informed of the impending "resettlement" from which only the hospital staff and Jews with stamped identification cards were to be exempted. On the following day, the Jews were ordered to stay at home while their houses were searched. What became known as the first *Aktion* lasted until June 18, under the command of Rommelmann with the assistance of the German and Ukrainian auxiliary units. Around 6,000 Jews, mainly the sick, the elderly and children, were murdered in the Buczyna Forest at Zbylitowska

---

20 AŻIH, 301/3703, testimony of Marlena Lilith Mittler, 1, who was born in Tarnów on September 18, 1933.

21 See Christopher Browning, *The Origins of the Final Solution: The Evolution of Nazi Jewish Policy, September 1939–March 1942* (Lincoln: University of Nebraska Press, 2004).

22 Stephan Lehnstaedt, *Der Kern des Holocaust: Bełzec, Sobibór, Treblinka und die Aktion Reinhardt* (Munich: C.H. Beck, 2017).

Góra, and around 3,000 were shot at the Jewish cemetery in Tarnów, while around 3,500 Jews were deported and murdered in Bełżec. Survivors recalled the brutality with which Jews were treated, especially children and the elderly, as well as the randomness with which the stamped documents were either honoured or ignored during the searches.[23] Sonia and her family, spared due to their supposed status as foreigners, remained sequestered throughout the seven days of the *Aktion*, hearing gunshots. "For an entire week, Jewish blood ran like a red river in the gutters all around the square," she writes, "forcing its way into adjacent streets."

Jews who remained in Tarnów had to move to a closed ghetto, sealed with barbed wire and guarded on the outside by the Polish "Blue" police while the Jewish police guarded it inside. Administered by SS-*Oberscharführer* Hermann Blache, the ghetto included Jews working both inside and outside it, escorted by either the German or Polish police. The workers received little payment.

On September 11, 1942, another registration of the Jewish population took place followed by the second *Aktion*. Jews were ordered to assemble at the Magdeburski Square and selected for deportation. On September 12–13, 1942, as Sonia and her family stayed hidden in a cellar, around 3,500 Jews were deported to Bełzec; thousands more were murdered in the town.

The third *Aktion* took place on November 15, 1942, when the Polish police surrounded the ghetto while the Germans rounded up 2,500 Jews, who were deported to Bełżec. While Sonia and her mother hid in yet another cellar, Hela was saved only by a last-minute intervention. Afterwards, the ghetto was divided into two sections, separated by a fence: ghetto A (for all Jews with permanent work papers) and ghetto B (for the elderly, children and people without permanent work papers). By November 1942, all the smaller ghettos

---

23 AŻIH, 301/437, testimony of Renia Frohlich, 2–3. Frohlich did not have the required documents but was spared due to the employment of her brother.

in the district of Tarnów had been liquidated. The remaining Jews were forced to clear the area of the former ghettos and were then transferred to the larger ghettos still in existence, including Tarnów, raising the number of Jews in the Tarnów ghetto to 12,000. They were forbidden to leave the ghetto, and were issued new armbands and used as slave labourers.

The Nicaraguan passports that Sonia, her mother and her sister had received in the fall of 1940 eventually proved lifesaving. By the fall of 1942, SS-*Reichsführer* Heinrich Himmler, head of both the Reich Security Main Office of the SS and the Reich Ministry of the Interior, appeared to be willing to respond to the initiatives of exchanging Jewish citizens of neutral countries for German prisoners of war (POWs). Representatives of Jewish organizations in Switzerland, in partnership with Polish diplomats and certain consular officials, provided a large number of forged passports from neutral countries in Central and South America, most notably Paraguay, to Jews in occupied Poland, but most of those for whom such passports were intended were already dead.[24] However, a number of those in the still-existing ghettos who received these passports were transferred to civilian internment camps such as Vittel and Liebenau, as well as the "exchange camps" of Bergen-Belsen; on the exchanges that eventually came to fruition, relatively few Jews were allowed to leave German-occupied Europe.[25]

---

24 See Agnieszka Haska, "Proszę Pana Ministra o energiną interwencję," Aleksander Ładoś (1891–1963) i ratowanie Żydów przez Poselstwo RP w Bernie in *Zagłada Żydów. Studia i Materiały*, no. 11 (2015): 299–309; Mordecai Paldiel, "The Role of Polish Diplomats in Saving Jews," The Jerusalem Post, February 27, 2021, https://www.jpost.com/opinion/the-role-of-polish-diplomats-in-saving-jews-comment-660425 (accessed November 12, 2021).

25 Less has been written about Liebenau than Vittel, which was a larger internment camp. For a glimpse of the exchange process and Jewish hostages in Vittel see https://encyclopedia.ushmm.org/content/en/article/vittel (accessed November 2,

In December 1942, the family's legal status as citizens of Nicaragua granted them a reprieve. They were led out of the Tarnów ghetto, held in the notorious Montelupich prison in Krakow and then ended up in the Liebenau internment camp in Germany as "exchange prisoners" for two years. Their fate still lay in the balance, and it was not until January 1945, when their names were finally placed on an official repatriation list, that they reached Switzerland and could breathe freely. In February 1945, Sonia and her family were put on a ship that landed on American soil. From there, they travelled to Canada, ending their agonizing wait and culminating in an emotional family reunion.

In Tarnów, those still remaining in the ghetto had been subjected to the final liquidation, which Sonia and her family had so feared. On September 2, 1943, German and Latvian units surrounded the ghetto and removed the internal fence that divided it in two. The Jews were again ordered to assemble on Magdeburski Square. They were notified that they were being sent to the Plaszow camp. Children could not be taken, but mothers secretly smuggled their children with them on the transport. In this final *Aktion*, overseen by Amon Göth, the cruel and infamous commandant of Plaszow, about 4,000 Jews were sent to Auschwitz; 2,000 were sent to Plaszow; and a group of 300 young and strong Jews were selected to clean out the ghetto and afterwards transferred either to Plaszow or to the Szebnie forced labour camp. The last transport of the remaining 150 Jews from Tarnów left for Plaszow on February 9, 1944.

Ahead of the long-awaited reunification with her father, Sonia reflects on her commitment to becoming a witness to the destruction

---

2021); on the Bergen-Belsen camps that held "exchange Jews" see Rainer Schulze, "Keeping Very Clear of Any 'Kuh-Handel'": The British Foreign Office and the Rescue of Jews from Bergen-Belsen," *Holocaust and Genocide Studies* 19, 2 (2005), 226–251; and on Liebenau see Reinhold Adler "'Da waren lauter Jüdinnen...' Das Internierungslager Liebenau im Zweiten Weltkrieg" in *Leben am See* (Bodenseekreises: Verlag Senn, Tettnang), XXIII (2006), 36–48.

of the Jewish community in her hometown of Tarnów: "Deeply in my wounded psyche, I vowed once again to tell anyone who would listen, and those who would not, all I knew about the Holocaust. There were to be many broken promises in my life, but this one I fulfilled consciously, talking to individuals, lecturing and reporting to dozens of groups and organizations, and willingly giving interviews to the media for many years." In the light of this youthful promise, her powerful memoir emerges as the last act of bearing witness.

Dr. Natalia Aleksiun
Professor, Graduate School of Jewish Studies
Touro College
2021

The author would like to thank the editor Arielle Berger for her insightful comments as well as Antony Polonsky and Yehoshua Ecker for their helpful feedback.

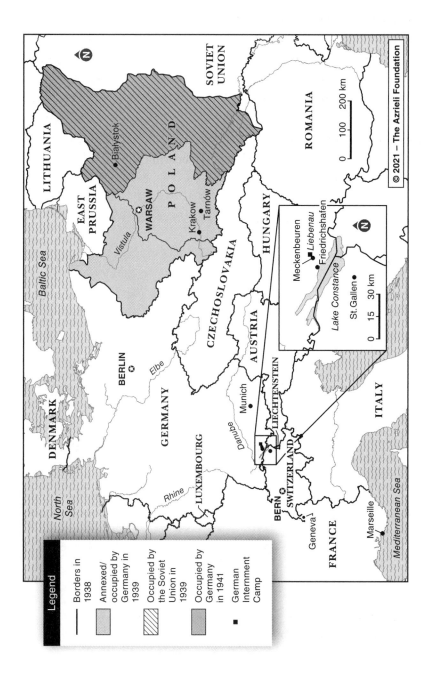

Legend

— Borders in 1938

Annexed/occupied by Germany in 1939

Occupied by the Soviet Union in 1939

Occupied by Germany in 1941

■ German Internment Camp

North Sea

DENMARK

Baltic Sea

LITHUANIA

EAST PRUSSIA

Białystok

SOVIET UNION

BERLIN

Elbe

Vistula

WARSAW

P O L A N D

Kraków

Tarnów

GERMANY

LUXEMBOURG

Rhine

Danube

Munich

CZECHOSLOVAKIA

AUSTRIA

LIECHTENSTEIN

HUNGARY

ROMANIA

0   100   200 km

BERN

SWITZERLAND

Geneva

FRANCE

Marseille

ITALY

Mediterranean Sea

Meckenbeuren

Liebenau

Friedrichshafen

Lake Constance

St. Gallen

0   15   30 km

© 2021 – The Azrieli Foundation

An Idealistic Youth

Spring came early to Poland in 1939. My hometown, Tarnów, in the southern part of the country, nestled in the foothills of the Carpathian Mountains. It was a night's train journey from Białystok, in the northeast, a much larger city in which I was born and from which my family had moved south when I was four years old.

The fields that surrounded Tarnów on three sides were an expanse of young green wheat dotted with crimson poppies and blue cornflowers, shimmering like opalescent garlands in the spring sun. The mountain to the south of it, St. Martin's, beckoned with its many crisscrossing trails over which the trees in their delicate bloom formed undulating canopies of light and shadow as the spring breeze gently caressed them.

Tarnów, with its fifty thousand inhabitants of whom nearly twenty-five thousand were Jews, was emerging from its winter slumber. In the affluent neighbourhoods the shutters of the houses had been scrubbed and were thrown open, the billowing curtains in the windows revealing an abundance of green plants, and here and there, a finely polished piece of furniture that reflected the pale golden light. The wide streets, broad sidewalks and the grassy squares in the parks were teeming with maids and nannies pushing baby carriages and leading by their hands young children dressed in their spring sailor outfits. The stores along the business district revealed varieties of new merchandise in their display windows. Their owners lingered in their shirtsleeves on the steps or gathered in groups, engaged in animated discussions about business deals. Elegantly clad women promenaded in threes and fours or sat outside the open-door cafés, carefully arranging their finery, to be seen and admired. The solitary streetcar, Tarnów's claim to modernity, clanged its way along the town's three principal streets, Krakowska, Wałowa and Lwowska, full, for the most part, of noisy high school students, happy at the prospect of Easter and the welcome school break.

In its munificence, the warm sun also shone on the poor quarters of the town, the areas in the east, around and behind Lwowska Street, where most of the residents were Jews. The small and shabby houses, some of them downright ramshackle, seemed to have shed their winter squalor to greet the year's new and brilliant season, their rough-hewn walls almost white under the bleaching power of the sun's rays, and their wooden stoops waxed and polished to a mirror-like shine. The grey cobblestones of the narrow streets and winding alleys, their rivulets of snow now melted, looked white too, the occasional fragments of quartz among them sparkling like diamonds in the translucent light. A holiday mood and an air of pleasant anticipation enveloped the whole city.

The Jews of Tarnów were a mixed group. A rather small number of them, mainly the wealthiest members of the middle class such as industrialists, mill owners and bankers, proud of their nouveau riche status, thought of themselves as emancipated. Some of these, a generation or two removed from their shtetl origin, managed to break into the middle and even the upper circles of the Polish society, spoke Polish with the right pronunciation, and, if not yet totally assimilated, emulated their gentile acquaintances enough to shun the company of other Jews and to break with the observance of all Jewish traditions. They invariably sent their children to Polish schools in the hope that the next generation would complete the assimilation process and become indistinguishable from the Poles.

At the other end of the scale were those who were pious and adhered to all religious precepts. Strictly Orthodox, they guarded their ranks closely against any dissenters. Their children were receiving their education in one cheder or another. It was the rare father among them who, hoping perhaps that some familiarity with the Polish language and with the ways of the world would help his offspring compete for a better financial status, reluctantly enrolled his son — never a daughter — in Tarnów's secular Hebrew school.

Most of the Orthodox lived along the cobblestone alleys behind Lwowska Street and earned their living as tradespeople, store clerks and workers in Tarnów's dominant textile industry. Through their open windows one could hear singsong voices chanting prayers or reciting passages from the Torah and the Talmud. It was not an unusual sight to meet men with their look-alike sons walking to and from the synagogue in the streets on the Sabbath and the Jewish holidays, wearing the traditional long black coats, or kapotes, and large fur hats, or *shtreimels*, their faces bearded and their sidelocks bobbing rhythmically with each step.

There were some staunch adherents to Orthodoxy among the wealthier Jews as well. They were distinguished from their poorer counterparts by the fine silk of their traditional garb, their more luxurious *shtreimels*, their spacious and better located homes and, above all, by their more desirable seats in the synagogue, close to and facing the east wall. Ironically, although as businessmen they often had the religious poor in their employ, the two groups remained far apart socially, the rich avoiding contact with those whom they considered beneath them. Snobbery, a pervasive and particularly tenacious trait among the Polish Jews of the 1930s was, in the scheme of things, only a peg or two below piety.

Somewhere between those two extremes, there was by far the largest, if the most heterogeneous, group of Jews, which consisted of both businessmen and members of the professions — the intelligentsia. They had remained committed to Judaism but had sought to change the thrust and nature of their involvement and thought that they had found a viable compromise for the vexing question of their Jewish identity. They firmly believed that their transformation into true modern Jews had been motivated, perhaps for the first time in Jewish history since the beginning of the Diaspora, not by a blind wish to escape antisemitism in Poland, but by rational and positive considerations. They were in the process of what was then known, on a clue from the most widely read of the new Hebrew writers, Leon Pinsker, as auto-emancipation.

And yet, they had remained ambivalent about the fledgling ways they were beginning to practise. On the one hand, in order not to offend their aging parents, they retained some vestiges of Jewish rituals, even if in a diluted form; on the other, they prided themselves on being enlightened, treating religion as moral philosophy rather than metaphysical faith, and professing to have insight into the changes being wrought by the renaissance of the Hebrew language and the growth of secular Zionism that was sweeping Central Europe.

My own parents were perhaps an apt example of this new phenomenon among the East European Jewry. When visiting their families in Białystok, they adhered to the ways of the households there — speaking Yiddish exclusively, attending the synagogue whenever expected to do so, observing the strict kashrut in both my grandparents' homes, and, in my father's case, often participating in the daily prayers with concomitant external accoutrements, tallith, phylacteries and all. My grandparents were fully aware that this show of religiosity was put on for their benefit. My paternal grandfather, in particular, was too wise and, at the same time, too tolerant to either fool himself or resort to recriminations over matters he knew he could not control.

It was different in our home in Tarnów. Father and Mother spoke Yiddish to each other, for it was the language of their childhood and they knew it best, but they both used Polish when addressing me and my younger sister, Hela. Their observance of Jewish traditions was reduced to attendance at the synagogue on the High Holidays, the substitution of matzoh for bread at Passover and my mother's mechanical lighting of the Sabbath candles. Mother hardly knew any

Hebrew, and Father had a smattering of the language, with its old Ashkenazi pronunciation, which he had learned while attending cheder as a young boy.

Although less given to philosophizing about the new trend than some of their friends, my parents had followed the example of members of their social class and enrolled first me, and later Hela, in a private Tarbut school, one of the many that were springing up all over the cities and towns of Poland. The school was coeducational and bilingual and what in that era could be termed progressive. Consisting of both elementary and high school grades, it was aptly called Safah Berurah, or "clear language," as mastery of Hebrew was one of its main educational goals. It had a strong secular Zionist bias. The Hebrew in which all Judaic subjects — Hebrew language and literature, the Bible, religion and Jewish history — were taught was with the newly emerged Sephardic pronunciation, the one recently revived by contemporary Jewish writers who had exchanged it as a vehicle of their creative work for their former Yiddish. This revised form was also spoken by successive waves of emigration, or *aliyot*, in Palestine.

It was common for the school's graduates, myself among them, to read, write and speak Hebrew fluently, to have a good grasp of the Rashi commentary on the Bible and to be familiar with the Aramaic of sizable portions of the Talmud.

In addition to the regular and state-required matriculation at the end of Grade 12, the school held a Hebrew matriculation. Educational standards in both were scrupulously equal and high. A student could be prevented from graduating as easily for failure in Latin, Polish literature or maths as for that in Hebrew grammar or Jewish religion. If our parents were at times uneasy about the heavy dose of secularism and active Zionism disseminated by the school, it was because they were caught between the old and the new ideologies. Unable to stem the tide of intellectual and psychological progress washing over their young, they could do little more than acquiesce to the inevitable. A new Jewish identity was being forged in the school, and there was no turning back.

Besides attending the school, my friends and I, on reaching adolescence, had become members of one or another of Tarnów's Zionist organizations that complemented and advanced the ideas garnered in the classrooms. It was there that theoretical and practical Zionism had been forged into the central ideal of our lives. In frequent discussions, during field trips and during those rousing times when we abandoned ourselves to Hebrew songs and dances, we sought to reconcile the theories we had gleaned from our voracious readings of the world's great minds — Spinoza, Hegel, Marx, Freud — and our favourite authors, like Dostoevsky, Kafka, Mann and Shakespeare, with our admiration for Herzl, Ahad Ha'am and the Hebrew writers of the Enlightenment.

With the enthusiasm and idealism of youth, we swept aside all contradictions. We were supremely eclectic. It was easy, we felt, to press the intellectual giants of the world into the service of our practical aim to rebuild Palestine. Most of us were convinced that ultimately, leaving the stifling and antisemitic Polish milieu behind us, we would settle and work in our liberated version of Herzl's *Altneuland* or Ahad Ha'am's "spiritual centre." We would test our acquired learning against pragmatic reality and would, we were convinced, shape a revolutionary phase in Jewish history. Our eclecticism would fall on new and fertile ground where it would herald the end of all the woes of a two-thousand-year-old dispersion and bear fruit in the creation of a model and free Jewish society.

By that spring I had turned seventeen. I had graduated from Safah Berurah a year earlier, and, like a number of my schoolmates, had applied to and been accepted to a university outside Poland. Some of the graduates had already gone — my childhood boyfriend, Milek Korn, who was spending the year at the University of Glasgow studying engineering, among them. Zygmunt (Zyga) Flaum, a tall, lanky youth, perhaps the best read and the most intelligent of our tightly knit group, was going off to Padua in Italy to study the humanities. I felt secretly drawn to him, attracted both by the analytical and ironic cast of his mind and his burgeoning masculinity, but was on my guard in order not to fan the flames of Milek's notorious jealousy.

Jurek Bayer, a stockily built but shy and sensitive boy, whose na-ïveté and propensity to daydream were the butt of our frequent jokes, had enrolled in a pre-medical course in Prague. Meyer Taub, the soft-spoken but tough newcomer to our group and academically less en-dowed than some of the others, thought of studying textiles in Liège, Belgium. Resia Goldberg, our blond beauty queen, a close friend with whom I had shared a desk since Grade 1, was studying the arts at the Józef Piłsudski University of Warsaw, but, discouraged by the minus-cule number of Jewish students — for whom the Polish universities had a stringent quota — she was examining syllabuses of colleges abroad, hoping to transfer in the fall. Lusia Maschler, Regina Feigen-baum and my very best friend, Klara Chaikin, were as yet undecided, enjoying the freedom from the school routine while half-heartedly selecting and rejecting half a dozen places. A few others had decided not to enter university at all but to get work instead, preferably in some of the countries known for their fair degree of tolerance toward Jews. Whatever our individual plans for the immediate future might have been, we were all propelled by a common dream: at the end of our studies, we would all go to Palestine where we would live on a kibbutz, or found one of our own, and work toward reclaiming the land.

I was heading for the famed Sorbonne in Paris to embark on the study of journalism. The thought of putting what was generally con-ceded my considerable writing talent to a test was as elating as my hope to spend a few years in the bohemian Cité internationale uni-versitaire de Paris, where life was said to be quite free from formal social restrictions, unstructured and brimming with the intriguing student activism of the late 1930s. The awareness that I would be sep-arated from my intimate friends did not cause me — or any of us — much concern, for we were convinced that our separation would be temporary and that, when we got together again, we would be better than ever equipped, by acquiring knowledge and wide expertise, to put our ideals into practice.

I felt that I had more reasons for wishing to leave home than most of my friends. My relationship with my mother had been unhappy and badly flawed since my childhood. Except on rare occasions, she had treated me, and less so Hela, for whom I had borne some of the brunt, as a nuisance and a burden. A woman of rare beauty, she liked to think of herself as a purely decorative object; motherhood, to her, was some sort of a flaw or, at best, the price she had to pay for her attractiveness.

She was critical of my academic achievement even though my teachers and friends had consistently regarded me as the best student of my class. She found fault with my appearance which, admittedly falling far below hers, abounded in good features, a fact that the mirror tended to confirm to my doubting mind. She disapproved of my Zionist activities, which she found not genteel enough for a girl of my social status, and of my choice of friends, some of whom came from lower-class families and, as an added mark against them, lived in the poor section behind Lwowska Street. She restricted my movements by setting up stringent rules, such as forbidding me to join my Zionist group for their country hikes, enforcing bedtime at 7:30 p.m. until I was well into Grade 12, or nagging me to do homework right after school even when there was no homework to do.

At times, I sullenly submitted to the criticism and the maltreatment, but at others I rebelled and sought escape. At the risk of corporal punishment (for she readily resorted to the slapping of hands and face), I would join my friends heading for St. Martin's or a bike ride to a country inn, would occasionally sneak out, aided by the Polish maid as my co-conspirator, to a Zionist meeting at 8:00 p.m. after my parents had gone out for their evening entertainment, or would defiantly let myself be seen with a group of young people whose social standing was not up to Mother's standards.

The tug of war between Mother and I would probably have been a source of greater unhappiness to me had it not been for the compensation I amply received from my highly developed sense of group identity and from my father. With these two intimate presences in my life — and with my grandparents whenever I visited them — I knew that I belonged. There was enough love and closeness in all those relationships to make up for the inadequate mothering I felt I received.

Father was a brilliant, self-educated man. Among his business associates and all those who knew him, his opinions and judgment were highly respected. He was an innovative and expert businessman and had built a successful textile mill in Białystok and just as successful a store for his own wollen garments in Tarnów. However, what mattered to Hela and me most was that he brought into and practised at home an attitude diametrically opposed to that of Mother's. He was affectionate and gentle, taking our side whenever he felt that we were unjustly punished, comforting us when we felt hurt and most importantly, treating us as desirable, much-wanted children. We felt that we were a source of pride and happiness to him, for he let us know it at every opportunity and was lavish in his praises. We admired him for his diplomatic talent of quiet persuasion — one which he used, often successfully, to mediate between Mother and us. Although he was deeply in love with his wife and strongly attracted to her, in his tenderness toward us he would argue our side unobtrusively but firmly, winning for us, over and over again, welcome concessions. Unfortunately, his business required him to divide his time between Tarnów and Białystok so that he was not always there when we needed him. Still, he brought love into the home whenever he came, and we loved him deeply in return.

In spring 1939, I felt euphoric enough about my close ties of friendship and about what I thought was my imminent departure for Paris to put my problems with Mother into the background. And yet, my good mood was marred and the general feeling of elation among my friends was overcast by deepening shadows. Although we continued holding endless discussions on intellectual topics on which we were self-proclaimed experts, our Socratic debates about Marxism versus anarchism, psychoanalysis versus existentialism, and other equally ill-digested isms had lost some of their lustre under the as yet guarded but increasingly sinister threat of Nazism.

The real world had encroached on the idyll we were spinning for our future. We could not disregard the plight of our fellow German Jews next door even if, in our moments of levity, we ridiculed them as the pompous, stuffy *yekkes*, nor could we ignore the inroads that the Nazis had made into some of our adjacent countries. We could not silence Hitler's hysterical speeches and the thunderous "Sieg Heil!" (Hail Victory!) from his ever-swelling mass audiences. Looking at the map of Poland, we began to realize that the country was vulnerable, as so many times in the past, to armed invasion, and the most recent push for the annexation of Danzig filled us with foreboding. We recoiled in fear whenever we watched films displaying seas of waving swastikas, and we could not close our ears to reports about a growing number of concentration camps for Jews and others in Germany. Besides, all of us had read *Mein Kampf* and were familiar with its proposed solution to the Jewish question; we no longer could, as we had done earlier, dismiss it as the mere ravings of a maniac.

In our adolescent drive toward the ideal, we put our psychic defence mechanism to work: we simply tried to evade the issues. Some, Zyga among them, argued that Hitler would not invade Poland as it provided a natural buffer zone between Germany and the communist Soviet Union; little did he, or any of us, know what was soon to become of that argument. Resia, who had taken some courses in political science while at the University of Warsaw, waxed eloquent about Hitler's reluctance to risk open warfare with England, France and possibly the United States. Each of us knew of many reasons why we personally were not in any danger. The Polish radio was our natural ally for it kept broadcasting encouraging news about the might and invincibility of the Polish army. In our stubborn wishful thinking, we believed every report. Perhaps it was a sign of our sheltered youth and immaturity that in the spring of 1939 we lived quite comfortably the paradox of the golden dream and the black nightmare.

The Last Seder

Passover was approaching. Spending the holiday at the home of my paternal grandfather, David Roskes, was a family tradition. Aside from those annual pilgrimages, I had spent much of my time in Białystok throughout my twelve years of school. It was a large and lively centre of the best in Jewish culture, and I had friends there. I had gone to Białystok for many summers, visiting alternately with my mother's and my father's parents, and had continued my visits after my mother's father and, later, my father's mother, had died. Whenever I was there, I had felt myself blossoming under the loving care of all my relations. My grandparents' homes had offered an escape from Mother's constant nagging into a cozy nest where I was accepted and loved. Sometimes I would go to a summer camp nearby and visit my Białystok family on weekends. At other times I would spend the entire summer on Grandfather Roskes' dacha, deep in the pine woods surrounding the city, where I would bask in the tranquility of the sylvan landscape and in the accolades of my uncles, aunts and cousins. Of all the grandchildren, I was the closest to our Białystok roots.

The coming Passover had all the makings of becoming a milestone in my life. For the first time in many years, almost the entire family on my father's side — even those living outside Poland — would be there. My eldest uncle, Owsej, whom I had always remembered opening and closing windows, inspecting his throat in the mirror, and taking his pulse at regular intervals, would come from Budapest, where he had one of the largest textile mills in Hungary. He would be accompanied by his equally eccentric wife, my aunt Malcia, who delighted in taking stock of the contents of other people's cupboards, but who could also recite from memory lengthy passages of Russian, Polish and German poetry. They would be accompanied by two of their sons, Nat, whom I knew, and Arthur, whom I had not met yet. Then there would be my favourite uncle Enoch, a true intellectual who was equally at home in Jewish and secular culture, and who had recently given up his post as the principal of a high school in Warsaw to become a businessman in Romania (a *melamed* turned *secher* — a teacher turned merchant — according to my mother's scornful barb). He had just married, after years of bachelorhood, an accomplished young Viennese woman, Mandy, whose beauty and elegance were matched by her brilliant mind. They would come from Cernăuți in Romania (now Chernivtsi, Ukraine), where Enoch, in partnership with his younger brother Leo, another academic turned industrialist, had founded and was running a rubber mill. Leo, the youngest of my uncles, had, prior to becoming a *secher*, graduated in chemistry from the university in Vilnius — one of a handful of Polish Jews who had reached that high a level of education. He would be almost literally led by his wife, Masza. She eschewed all languages to rule her husband in her loud but flawless and highly articulate Yiddish, and their two young children, Benjie and Ruth, would be trailing behind her. The family would be complete with the addition of my father's only sister, my charming and bright aunt Pola, her husband, Moishe — another textile merchant — and two little daughters whose names I no longer remember. Aunt Pola and her family lived in Grandfather's spacious house of which Pola had become the gracious *châtelaine* after my grandmother's death.

I was looking forward to seeing them all for, despite their assorted foibles and idiosyncrasies, they were warm-hearted, witty, articulate and well informed on subjects ranging from the Scriptures and Jewish history to modern philosophy and current political issues. It would be a treat to answer their questions directed to me, as I was very sure I would surprise them with the accuracy of my answers. In my teenage arrogance, I was eager to show off and parade my presumably great learning for one so young.

Then there would be the added fun of spending time with my maternal grandmother, Rose, her widowed daughter, Rebecca, my uncle Jacob, an apothecary, and his wife, and my mother's youngest sister, Golda, her husband, and all the children of those families, my cousins on the Onin side. Although they did not have the intellectual brilliance of the Roskes family, they were all so hospitable, warm and giving that I longed to be enveloped in their flowing love. I had never ceased to wonder at the puzzling difference between my mother and the eminent humanity of the other members of her family.

There was yet another, perhaps the most exciting, element in my anticipation of the visit — I knew that I was my grandfather's favourite granddaughter and one of whom he was deeply proud. Whenever I had been with him in the past, I would take him to the synagogue or, since he was blind, would read for him biblical passages in Hebrew and portions of the Gemara in the Aramaic. Many a time, sitting across the table from him and looking affectionately into his sightless eyes, I would answer his questions or engage with him in one of his favourite Talmudic debates on the arguments and pronouncements of ancient Jewish sages. I would cast loving glances at the snow-white beard of that true Jewish patriarch and at the unseeing sky-blue eyes covered by heavy glasses and would thrill at the suggestion of his inner spiritual visions. I enjoyed his many visitors — Jews from far and wide who, when faced with problems they could not solve themselves, had come to seek his advice and encouragement. In my exalted view, he was one of Israel's true wise men, a latter-day King Solomon. People had heeded his suggestions and had accepted his judgment in matters of religion even as my father and his brothers had done in matters of business. A keen observer of human nature, he also offered pertinent comments and gave sound guidance on intimate personal matters.

During the ride to Białystok I remembered with nostalgia and affection all the previous seders we had spent with Grandfather. They had always been visually splendid, with a white damask cloth spread over the huge dining room table, the glitter of fine china, crystal and silver, prismatically reflected by the lights of the large chandelier, everybody in festive finery, and, grandest of all, Grandfather reclining in his big chair in a white, silk-embroidered robe. My thoughts that kept interrupting my sleep on the train berth were tinged with sadness, too, for I felt this might be my last such seder for a long time to come. After all, I would not be coming first from France and then from Palestine at this time of year. This knowledge made the visit I was heading toward all the more precious.

On the morning of the seder, bedlam reigned in Grandfather's house. My cousins had come a day or so before, and Hela and I played with them noisily indoors and outdoors, running now and again into the kitchen where the specially hired cook was baking a cake for each grandchild, following a ritual initiated by my grandmother some years earlier. I stole away for a few hours to my mother's family where some delectable morsels had been spread out for my consumption and where I relaxed quietly with my grandmother Rose and my aunt Rebecca, the two women I loved profoundly. When it was time to go back and get ready for the seder, I hugged everyone in sight and dashed over to the Roskes family home where I scrubbed myself clean and gingerly put on a brand-new dress created by a skilled Tarnów dressmaker specifically for the occasion.

When I came down to the dining room to join the family at the seder table, expecting my uncles to greet me, as usual, with jokes and banter, I was startled to find the older faces showing tension and distress. There was no time to dwell on this unexpected sight as everybody had to be seated right away, and Grandfather, resplendent in his white robe, gave a motion to the housemaid that the seder was about to begin. From the time she brought in the basin for the ritual handwashing to the time when the Haggadah calls for a break in the proceedings and heralds the arrival of food, my cousins, Hela and I had a rare good time alternating between joining in the prayers and kicking one another under the table. I had already answered a few of Grandfather's questions about the interpretations of certain Passover legends and was looking forward to meeting more such challenges after the seder resumed. Over supper, and initially at least, I was not listening to what the adults were saying. I continued chattering with my cousins when, casting a quick glance at the grown-ups' faces, I caught a glimpse of what I had earlier recognized as a look of unexpected concern. Sensing that something unusual and significant was going on, I abruptly ceased the play and began to listen intently to the obviously serious conversation. It was conducted mainly in Yiddish, with a liberal sprinkling of Polish and Russian, but I had no difficulty following the linguistic mixture.

At first, I made out single words like *Anschluss*, Sudetenland, Austria, Danzig, Dachau, Buchenwald, words that had already become a part of my vocabulary before my arrival in Białystok, but which I had kept on the periphery of my mind. Something about the emotional intensity of what I heard made me realize immediately that what was taking place around the table was no ordinary political discussion, such as I had heard often in Grandfather's house. The talk sounded deeply personal and the voices of the men and women who were trying to outargue one another bore the mark of unrelieved seriousness.

Somehow, it was at that very moment that I realized, with something of a violent jolt, how childish I had been, hiding as I did in the world of vague ideologies inside my thick adolescent cocoon. It was time to shed it and face the facts of the Nazi menace, as the adults around me were doing; it was time to grow up at last. The impact of this sudden self-revelation was so strong that I know I turned pale, and my right hand, guiding the soup spoon into my mouth, began to shake. Mother, who was sitting beside me, nudged me with her elbow, causing my spoon to overturn and stain the tablecloth. "Act like an adult," she hissed at me through half-closed lips, "or else you'll go upstairs."

She must have been surprised at how quickly I obeyed and managed to compose myself, but she was never to know that it was not her remark that made me regain my equilibrium. I simply did not want to miss a word of what was being said, for I sensed intuitively that the outcome of the heated discussion would somehow change my familiar world and affect my future.

I saw Grandfather raise his hand to command some quiet and heard him say after the several voices had died down: "What would you all think about getting out of Europe while there is still time? I would like you to consider a move to Canada. From what I hear, and from what Pola has been reading to me, it is a good country in which to live and to build up textile industry. It is also a free country, one which has flexible immigration laws and which, I am sure, would receive you warmly for it needs your capital and your know-how. You would be desirable immigrants there. And remember, old as I am, I want to go too. I don't want to stay here while Hitler is readying his army for a war which, I am sure, will be against Poland. It is the next country on his list to be invaded. Hungary and Romania will be gobbled up too. And I don't think I need to tell you what all that means for the Jews."

After Grandfather's initial address, a momentary hush fell on the room. I looked around me for any sign of cheer or good humour, but all I saw was faces deep in thought, showing signs of strong inner struggle. In a few moments, all my aunts and uncles raised their voices again, each trying to present a personal view, and again the situation gave all signs of becoming a chaotic verbal battle. Grandfather listened to the shrill individual opinions as though taking stock for a while but then tapped his hand on the table. When the talk subsided he spoke once more, this time turning in the direction of my father and addressing him. "Izak, despite some noisy differences of opinion, I sense that there is general agreement with my proposition. The question I heard raised is not whether we should go, but who should go first and explore the opportunities. Well, I think it should be you, for you are our textile expert. And take Henry with you. He understands textiles, too, and besides, he speaks some English." Henry was my eldest Budapest cousin, twenty-four years old at the time, who had not been able to come with his parents and his brothers to the seder.

Father, his brow knitted together as always when he was worried, answered with a mixture of bravado and tension, "Why me? How can I liquidate my business in Tarnów and in Białystok on such short notice? Why should I uproot my family for something as uncertain and unknown as Canada? For all I know, it may be all wilderness out there."

The rest of his argument was drowned out by another cacophony. The discussion was long and heated, with my father trying to defend himself against everybody's obvious desire for him to initiate the general move, but at the end, it was clear that all would be willing to emigrate if he went first and explored the opportunities.

They are making him a Joshua and a saint, I thought to myself, hoping that he would refuse. My eyes had been riveted on him ever since Grandfather had singled him out, and I watched his strong inner conflict gradually turn into acceptance. I knew then that the seder of 1939 had indeed marked the end of the only kind of life I had known. My carefree mood had disappeared altogether, leaving me trembling with a sense of menace and, above all else, the fear of separation from my father.

The reading of the Haggadah was then resumed, and a semblance of normalcy reappeared around the table. And yet, despite a show of better spirits among my elders, the joyful chants associated with the Exodus from Egypt and the return of calm to Grandfather's face, I continued to be uneasy. I tried to catch my father's eye, and when I finally succeeded, he gave me his usual affectionate smile. A little reassured, I nevertheless began to brood about how long our separation might last and what such a violent uprooting would mean to me.

What would happen to my university studies? Would I be permitted to go to Paris when my new home would be an ocean away? What would I tell my friends in Tarnów? How would they take the news? Question after question kept sweeping over me like a torrent, leaving no time for reasoned answers. Later I would have to make some order of the sudden chaos I had been thrown into. At the moment I could do little more than acquiesce, at least on the surface, to what now seemed a firm consensus.

After the holiday was over, it was time for everyone to return to their homes. I made a brief and tearful visit to my mother's family to say goodbye. My grandfather, led by Aunt Pola, took us to the station. I cried bitterly over what I thought was the ruin of my life and so did all the others for reasons of their own, until Grandfather, wiping his eyes and arranging his glasses on the bridge of his nose, said in a resonant voice, "Enough of that nonsense. We act as though we are mourning when we should be rejoicing. We are about to enter a new and exciting chapter of our family history. You are young and have great skills. I want to sense some smiles all around. The children, too, will study again." (There he squeezed my hand, which had been holding his all along.) "You will be safe. And don't forget, you will relocate an old Jew who, at his tottering age, is still eager for adventure. Be of good cheer."

After another round of lingering kisses and tight embraces, we boarded the train. It started to move away from the platform. On it we left our Białystok family members, looking smaller and smaller. We were never to see them again.

Waves of Confusion

On the train back to Tarnów I tossed and turned restlessly, unable to sleep. My thoughts were confused, and I was overwhelmed by the turn of events that had taken place. Hela, sleeping in the berth below me, kept poking at my mattress, saying crossly that I was disturbing her. I did not think that my twelve-year-old, red-haired and freckle-faced sister could possibly have grasped the implications of the decision made at the seder as fully as I had.

After our return, Father busied himself immediately with preparations for the trip. He tried to set his financial affairs in order, which necessitated commuting more frequently between Tarnów and Białystok. He also travelled back and forth to Warsaw to obtain an immigration visa for Canada from the British High Commissioner (who then represented the Dominion of Canada in Poland) and a temporary visa for the United States, which he thought his business would require him to visit.

On the surface our life returned to normal. Mother resumed her social activities, which included her daily promenades on Krakowska and Wałowa streets and the frequenting of her favourite clubs and cafés. Hela rejoined a group of her friends and, judging by her constant state of excitement, was having a good time. To my relief, she no longer had to be accompanied and watched by someone older, which put a virtual end to my reluctant babysitting and left me free to spend time with my own friends, whose company I now craved more than ever before.

In the meantime, Milek had come back home from Glasgow for his summer vacation. I spent much of my time with him, talking to him about my father's impending trip to Canada and wondering aloud in his presence what changes it would cause in my life. Milek seemed unperturbed by the news. Always a pragmatist, he argued that my father, brilliant man that he was, knew what he was doing; as for the two of us, he felt confident that if I were to give up Paris and enroll at McGill in Montreal, as my parents wished me to do, he could join me in a year or two, after getting credit for his studies in Glasgow. "That is," he would add with his mischievous, impish smile that had always endeared him to me, perhaps sensing the cooling off of my earlier ardour for him, "if you don't change your mind and still want me to come." Perhaps he was giving me a chance to tell him of my so far platonic infidelity, but with more important things on my mind, I passed up the opportunity. Anyway, I still had not made up my mind whether I preferred Zyga to him. For now, I clung to Milek's happy-go-lucky outlook on life. We walked for hours in the sun-drenched golden fields of wheat, climbed the grassy slopes of St. Martin's, and spent time kissing and touching indoors in our apartments during our parents' absences. His presence, if only until the fall, helped calm my misgivings and was a source of comfort to me.

The situation was more complex with my other close friends. On hearing the news, they, like myself, had to face squarely the gravity of the political events affecting us, and were sobered by new and pervasive reflection. We still did our best to enjoy our former activities of highbrow discussions, Zionist meetings and nature hikes, but the euphoria that had permeated all these had gone, not to be retrieved again. My own predicament seemed to have a direct effect on the entire group; unwittingly, I bore a serious message for all my friends, and, willing or not, they were all forced to wonder how it applied to each of them personally.

I sensed that the attitude of a few of them toward me had changed. While some, Zyga, Meyer and Klara among them, voiced their approval of what they considered a clever plan, I noticed that others began to look upon me with envy and even avoid my company. I was no longer just their bright and devoted friend, a good sport and a future journalist. Instead, I felt that I had become almost an outsider: either somebody who would soon abandon her friends in distress, however reluctantly, or, worse, one who was lucky enough to be given an opportunity denied to them. Even though I felt such views were unjustified and illogical, I myself, just as illogically, felt that I was about to betray them, a feeling that added guilt to my already perturbed mind.

My parents' friends and acquaintances were as divided among themselves on the subject as were my own peers. While some expressed the opinion that my father was acting impulsively on the basis of insufficient evidence, others agreed that there was a pressing need for Jews to flee the threat of Hitler. I often overheard remarks like "Izak, you are being foolish," or "Izak, you have lost your sense of proportion and you are spreading needless, uncalled-for fear. Why the sudden panic?" Just as often, however, opposite views were expressed. "Izak," some said, "we have always trusted your judgment, and now you have given us proof that you are indeed more far-sighted than the rest of us," or, "I wish I could follow your lead, but I haven't got your courage and determination to take such a gigantic step." The opinions of the adults did nothing to dissipate my confusion or clear my concerns.

In our own apartment, Father's approaching departure cast a heavy gloom upon us. Without thinking for a moment that our separation might last longer than the eight weeks allotted to it, and without really knowing, despite our ostensible preparation, how close to cataclysmic events we were, Mother, Hela and I were nevertheless seized by unfamiliar anxiety as the intervening weeks rushed by. Whenever the four of us spent time together, the conversation centred invariably around the details of the trip, which was scheduled for very soon — the beginning of May. Could Father possibly make it in less than eight weeks? When would he get the immigration papers for us? Was he reasonably assured that he could establish himself quickly in that strange and faraway country, Canada? Father answered those and other queries with his customary optimism and calm reassurances, although I sensed that he, too, had some misgivings about the venture. However, having committed himself this far and being basically convinced of the necessity of the move, he was not going to reconsider or back out.

On his last return from Warsaw, Father had all his papers in order. He would travel by train to Gdynia, one of Poland's main seaports, from where he would sail on the Polish ship *Batory*. The ship was scheduled to dock in New York, where he intended to spend a few days visiting Mother's American relatives. He would then proceed to Montreal, where he would join our cousin Henry, contact prospective business connections and apply immediately for our visas.

The day of his departure arrived. Since he was to travel to Gdynia overnight, we had the entire day to spend together. We stayed home and busied ourselves with mechanically packing and repacking his things, trying not to show him our gnawing heartache. That evening, we went to see him off at the station. I had always had a phobia of railway stations, which to me signified a violent tearing apart and were the epitome of loneliness. Yet nothing that I had experienced when witnessing other departures had prepared me for the sinking sense of loss that gripped me and held me fast during our last moments together.

There was nothing left to say. There was only a dull ache, and, at least on my part, an almost uncontrollable desire to cry out, "Daddy, please, don't leave us! We can't live without you!" However, biting my lips and holding back my childish impulses, I did not cry out. Instead, I put my head on his shoulder for the last time and let him hold me and kiss my hair. I then averted my eyes as he said goodbye first to Hela, who was clinging to him as though she would never let go, and then to Mother, whose loud sobs filled and echoed in the high-vaulted, empty station. As Father boarded the train, waving goodbye to us, Mother continued to cry and wail. Feeling pity for her for the first time in my life, and surprisingly empty of all my accumulated hostility toward her, I tried, with Hela's help, to quiet her somewhat and to lead her away. As soon as her sobs turned into whimpers, we took her home. In the tram, we murmured assurances in her ear that all was for the best, although we ourselves were filled with pain and foreboding. It was in our apartment that we gave vent to our pent-up sense of abandonment, and went to bed for an uneasy, restive sleep, with our tears still wet on our cheeks and our eyelids swollen from hours of crying.

From then on our countdown began. Convinced that we would see Father again in several weeks as had been arranged, the three of us made another attempt, just as we had done upon our return from Białystok, to normalize our lives. Mother's worries gradually diminished, and she began sharing with her friends her fantasies about her future home in Montreal where she was sure she would enjoy the same — and perhaps even a higher — social status than she did in Tarnów. Her attitude toward Hela and I softened considerably. If Father's departure had been a rude shock, it had the unexpected but welcome side effect of kindling in her a spark of positive, accepting motherhood. Hela and I responded in kind, for the trauma had matured us, too, and we dimly sensed the need for a more harmonious relationship among the three of us than we had known in the past. If not exactly joyous, life at home was, at least for part of that summer, better than tolerable.

Feeling uneasy that my time with my friends was running out, I was spending almost all of my days with them, and especially with Milek, who was going back to Glasgow at the end of his vacation. The topics of our group and tête-à-tête discussions had shifted irrevocably from pondering abstract themes to practical considerations. As reality was making inroads into our earlier idealizations, we began devouring the daily papers and listening to all available radio broadcasts. Our opinions about the imminence of the Nazi danger to us personally were now sharply divided, the lines of reasoning having shifted and being drawn differently than they had been earlier in the spring. Milek and Jurek persisted in feeling that our fears were exaggerated because Hitler had had his fill of territorial conquests. Zyga, with his probing mind, had changed his views after my return from Białystok; Resia had abandoned the theories gleaned from her political science class. Klara and I interpreted what we saw and heard around us that Hitler was preparing for an all-out war with Poland.

My friends seemed to pay careful attention to my opinions, expecting me to be better informed than they were. I felt uneasy in the role of arbiter, which had been thrust upon me. I was as ignorant and confused as they were, and all I wanted was to belong as one of them, not as someone who perhaps had access to secret sources of information, and so I shunned many of the questions and spoke to no one except Milek, and occasionally Zyga and Klara, about the changed and unhappy situation my father's departure had put me into. Yet despite our generally darkened vision of the future and some of the tensions among us, we were all as one in denying that disaster would strike soon. Despite our extensive knowledge of the latest political developments, we continued in our naïveté, and denied — however unconsciously — that each of us could become a potential victim at any moment.

It was at the beginning of July that we received Father's first letter. Mother, Hela and I read and reread his urgent message with heavy hearts. In Father's words, we were in grave danger, as, according to American political experts and public opinion, war was upon us. He pleaded with Mother to start liquidating the business and exhorted all three of us to start packing. In keeping with his original plan, Father was coming personally to fetch us. He and our papers would probably arrive at the same time. The letter ended with expressions of his deep love for us and his confidence that very soon we would be together and safe.

We were stunned by the unexpectedly urgent tone of the letter. It was obvious that Father was more serious about the need for our escape than we had ever known him to be before. The war, on which we had continued to reflect somewhat academically, was closer than we had dared to think. It was equally obvious that we had to obey his instructions without delay; his requests and exhortations had not been lightly conceived nor vaguely conveyed. And so, during the intervening weeks and in the first half of August, we plunged into hectic if somewhat chaotic activities. We started filling some trunks with linens, bedding and clothes, and Mother, who knew little about business, made a few trips to the store where she went through the motions of starting to liquidate it. However, without discussing the matter among us even once, we knew that at some point we would have to stop, as we could not accomplish all there was to do before Father's arrival. We continued our efforts for a while, compelled to perform our tasks by our desire to follow Father's instructions and, subsequently, by our as yet half-conscious sense of being vulnerable and unprotected. Besides, Father's frequent letters strongly encouraged us to persevere.

The last days in August were like an accelerated, animated film, so rapidly did momentous events succeed one another. On the morning of August 23, we woke up to the radio announcement that Germany and the Soviet Union had entered into a non-aggression treaty. We listened to the news with disbelief. Even the most optimistic of Tarnów's residents had to grant that in the event of war, now virtually a certainty, the two big powers would partition Poland according to some pre-arranged plan, probably along the entire length of the Vistula River.

I went out into the streets to ferret out the general mood of the population and found groups of people everywhere, Jews and Poles, their faces drawn, their voices subdued, obviously reeling from the shock of the latest disclosure. I joined a group of my friends, some of whom were saying that they would start right away toward the east.

If war broke out, they would be better off under the Stalinist than under the Nazi regime, they argued. At worst, they might be sent to Siberia where, with any luck, they might either survive or escape, and perhaps make their way through the Balkan countries to the Black Sea, and then possibly to Palestine. My heart fell when I heard that Zyga was among those planning to leave, for I feared that very soon I would lose both him and Milek for an indefinite time.

Less than enlightened by the contradictory news I garnered in the streets, where panic was spreading like wildfire, I decided that I would be better off at home. However, listening to the radio constantly did nothing to allay our fears. It was blaring rousing patriotic music, military marches and announcement after announcement about the might and courage of the Polish army. In our apartment, tight-lipped and moving like robots, we kept packing and waiting for the postman.

On August 24, we received a letter from my uncle Enoch and my aunt Mandy. They had gone in July to the World's Fair in New York and were writing to tell us that they were not returning to Romania but were joining my father and Henry in Canada. We learned from them too that my uncle Owsej and aunt Malcia, who had been vacationing in Vichy, France, were not going back to Hungary. They had left their mill there intact and were also proceeding to Montreal with their youngest son, Arthur. Their middle son, Nat, was joining them from Leeds, England, where he had been studying in a textile institute. We realized with dismay — and not a little bitterness — that only the three of us, our family in Białystok and that of Leo Roskes' in Cernăuți were as yet unable to get out. By that time, our correspondence and telephone contacts with my grandparents had ground to a stop, as services between the south and north of Poland had been disrupted. We were unable to communicate with Uncle Leo and his family either. A year and a half later, we found out that they had stayed in Cernăuți until mid-1940, before Romania allied with Germany; they managed to escape through Bucharest and join the others in Canada.

And so, the large Roskes family in the potential war zone had dwindled, and the three of us were all alone.

As our own, and the general apprehension around us mounted, we were still waiting for Father. At the end of August, we received another letter. "Leave everything as is," he instructed my mother. "Your papers should have arrived in Warsaw and be on their way to you right now. I shall be boarding the *Batory* on August 23 and am coming for you. Be of good cheer; we'll be together within a week of your reading this letter." There followed again a few tender lines of a great outpouring of his love and longing to be reunited with us. I read the letter over and over again, trying to derive some comfort and hope from it, but thought that I had detected desperate overtones between Father's deceptively cheerful lines. The fateful date of August 23 sounded an ominous note, too. For the first time in my seventeen years, I began to fear that, of all Father's undertakings, this, the most momentous one of his life, might turn out to be his equally momentous failure.

In the last few days of August, as the farmers around Tarnów were preparing to harvest their luxuriant golden wheat and as the trees in their orchards and on the lower slopes of St. Martin's were laden with succulent fruit ready for picking, indicating that autumn was upon us, I made a few frantic phone calls to the office of the British High Commissioner in Warsaw. By sheer coincidence, one or two telephone lines to Warsaw were still open. At first I was informed that the office had received an advance notice from London that our papers were on the way to Poland. But on August 30, I was dismissed with the curt announcement that the High Commissioner's office was formally evacuating Poland. To my question whether I should venture a quick trip to Warsaw to retrieve our documents, the answer was that all papers on hand had been packed and that ours had probably not even arrived. On August 31, my ring went unanswered. The same evening, Milek left for Glasgow on one of the last trains to cross the Polish border before the war.

I awakened soon after dawn on September 1, 1939, to the news that the Germans, minutes after their succinct declaration of war, had invaded Poland and were advancing steadily along the entire frontier. Listening to the radio reports which, while downgrading the military successes of the Germans, shrilly extolled the courageous feats of the Polish army, Mother, Hela and I could only stare at one another idiotically. It took us almost the entire day to raise ourselves from our stupor and to become aware with painful lucidity of the fact that we were caught in the grips of war and might never see Father again.

Deciding to Stay

From September 1st until the 6th, Tarnów was in a state of complete chaos and lawlessness. Many of the Polish authorities were preparing to leave, and my attempts to enlist the services of a few officials of the town council to help us retrieve our papers met with not unexpected failure. People were wandering in the streets like uneasy ghosts, their talk having dwindled to whispers. Rumours about the German invasion of town after town, of Warsaw still holding out, the Polish army in disarray, and the Soviet advances in the east were passed from person to person, sowing anxiety and further confusion among the tense population.

For the first two or three days, ruminating on the fact that Father would not be able to come for us and that we would have to fend for ourselves, we sought shelter in our apartment. By the standards of the time, it was spacious, consisting of a foyer, a dining room, a den, two large bedrooms, a kitchen and a bathroom, and afforded us enough room to pace all over it and occasionally to look out the windows at the street milling with people, apparently going nowhere.

Now and again, tired of walking around in circles, we would sit down at the table and wonder aloud whether there would be any opportunity to get in touch with Father before long. Although France and England were already at war, Canada and the United States were not, so that, we mused, was a flicker of hope that we might establish some contact with him and that, if the Germans conquered all of Poland, he might devise new ways to get us entry into a neutral country. All our speculations were based on our utter trust in Father's love for us and on our faith in his creative imagination.

We wondered about our tenuous position. We knew that should the conflagration engulf all of Europe, our chances of rescue would get slimmer, and perhaps even be dashed altogether. I think that I personally had assessed our situation more realistically than Mother and Hela. Mother seemed near collapse and could not think. All she did during those few fateful days was groan repeatedly, "Izak, Izak, what should we do?" and "Why have you left us alone?" Hela, though perky and bright, had, at her age, only a dim view of our predicament. And so, almost against my volition, the leadership of the family had passed on to me. I felt that I was ill-fitted to be cast into the role of a leader in a precarious life situation, for underneath my outer layer of sophistication and certain cerebral endowments I was still very much the child — unsure of myself and badly in need of mature guidance. However, as it was to be so often in the nearly six years to come, I had no choice.

I either sat glued to the radio, listening to the sporadic and contradictory broadcasts, or carefully watched the activities in the city. I concluded that, for the moment and until the situation began to show a discernible pattern, there was nothing to do but wait.

It was to be the first of our countless waiting periods throughout the war. I thought it was ironic that many of my friends, particularly those who not long ago had envied my lot, were among the first civilians to flee east. They, and many of Tarnów's population, Jews and gentiles, had chosen to cling to the fast-retreating, decimated Polish army, heading mainly for Lwów, a large southeastern city.

Yet despite the exodus of some of the native population, the count of Tarnów's residents did not become depleted. Through the vagaries of war, for every person that left there was at least one other to take his or her place, as refugees from Silesia, particularly from the towns that had been conquered on the very first day, had also fled east and, as a result, deluged our town. It was because of the large number of the newcomers who, realizing that it was pointless to go any further, settled in Tarnów to stay, that the number of Jews remained for a time constant.

During those first few days, after it had become certain that the German army approaching Tarnów had begun to surround it, the streets teemed with horse-drawn carriages, large wheelbarrows and all sorts of improvised buggies, laden to the top with a few pieces of furniture, bundles of clothes and bags of food. The scenes below our windows had an aura of black comedy about them and the atmosphere, with all its frenetic activities, seemed carnival-like. There was a lot of shouting, gesticulating and even loud laughter as groups of people, executing steps as though in some phantasmagoric dance macabre, tried to pile the conveyances to the very top, while the children were scaling and sliding down the flimsily tied structures.

Unable to contain my restlessness, I took to the streets in search of some undetermined clues and looking for my friends with whom I was anxious to exchange views on the latest events. I sensed excitement in the eyes and voices of the people. Choosing to become refugees for a while and, based on what I made out of snatches of conversation everywhere, hoping that they would return as soon as the armed hostilities ended, they were starting their treks eastward, mostly on foot and weighed down by the loads and bundles they were carrying.

My search for my friends was frustrating; they were hard to find. Maybe, I thought, they were roaming the streets like myself in an attempt to arrive at some decision by gauging the mood of the crowd. Most doors on which I knocked were locked. Almost ready to give up the search, I wandered into the courtyard of a large building at 4 Lwowska Street where Zyga lived with his parents, when I suddenly felt a tap on my shoulder and heard a familiar voice. I turned around and saw Zyga towering over me, and, next to him, a cart half packed with books and some carelessly tied boxes.

"Don't look so bewildered," he said, a half-sad, half-sardonic smile playing around his lips. "We all have two choices as to by whom we prefer to be wiped out. Personally, I have chosen the Russian guns. There is a chance they will be used more sparingly than those of the Nazis. And," he added, still with his characteristic gallows humour, "let's face it. We are all stuck, but I, for one, wish to postpone the inevitable. About a half of our graduating class is leaving, with or without their parents. I am going alone. How about you?" he asked, his penetrating eyes scanning my face, his cynical banter giving way to concern.

My heart seemed to have stopped beating. Now, I thought, not only my father, but a dozen of my friends were leaving too, and I was going to be totally abandoned by everybody who counted in my life. When I finally found my voice, I muttered something about being still undecided and giving myself twenty-four more hours to make up my mind.

"Whatever I decide," I said, my voice shrill, "I shall never leave Mother and Hela. We've got to stick together whatever happens. Meanwhile, goodbye Zyga, and good luck." I stretched out my hand to shake his, but he, stooping from his great height to put his face close to mine, kissed me and held me in a tight embrace. In a voice choked with suppressed emotions, he whispered hoarsely, "I love you, although, because of my reputation for callousness and cynicism, I couldn't say it before. I want you to know it now for I may never see you again." Unable to respond, I clung to him passionately for a few moments, and then, the tears streaming down my face, gave him one last lingering kiss, wiggled out of his embrace without daring to look back, and darted out of the yard.

On my way home, I bumped into Meyer, but all I could understand him to say was that he was not going away. I greeted his statement with something akin to indifference. I had not counted Meyer among my closest friends, and anyway, after having parted from Zyga, I felt that there were too few of us around to be of real comfort and help to one another. Little did I know that Meyer's decision would have uncommon significance for me and my family in the months and years to come.

In another day or so, I had become as hardened — at least on the surface — as I had been weepy before. My earlier world was collapsing, leaving no room for the luxury of tears and self-pity. By the evening of September 5, it seemed as if the last Polish authorities had abandoned Tarnów. I looked up at the sky ablaze with shooting flames, either from German bombs or fires set by the departing Polish officials, looked down at the street where the last of the refugees were hastily making their exits, and made a decision. We were going to stay. My assumptions were intuitive rather than rational, but I felt that there was no time for long deliberations. My resolve prevailed. I convinced Mother and Hela that by remaining in our home at 11 Sowińskiego Street we would provide Father, if and when the time came, with as definite and steady an address as circumstances would permit. On the other hand, if we were to become refugees and nomads, he would not be able to contact us. The decision sounded weak and hollow as the Germans had started their bombardment of Tarnów, but, hiding in our potato cellar, which served as a pitifully inadequate bomb shelter, I managed to talk myself into the belief that I was right. Incidentally, I was vindicated, at least in the short run, when after a few days news reached us that German planes were strafing both the fleeing Polish army and the civilians, inflicting heavy casualties; many townspeople died within hours of leaving. For the time being, we had managed to stay alive.

Between the evening of September 5 and dawn of September 7 Tarnów was ungoverned by any authorities, and the rule of the mob was rampant. In the anarchic situation people looted stores, broke into the liquor and tobacco warehouses, which had been state-controlled under the Poles and left unlocked, and into bakeries, emptying them all. My good friend Klara, along with her parents, had come to live with us temporarily as their apartment building lacked even a potato cellar to shelter them from the air raids. Klara — who had smoked while still at school in her attempt to lose weight — made several trips to the tobacco warehouse and returned loaded with many sacks of cigarettes, pipe tobacco and cigars. While the bombs were exploding all around us, we descended to our cellar and there, under her tutelage, I became a lifelong smoker. Moreover, we hid large supplies in the hope that they might serve as barter for greater necessities, such as food, on the black market which, we knew historically, would start to flourish very soon as the inevitable by-product of wartime conditions.

Early in the morning of September 7, Klara and her parents returned to their apartment. Somehow we sensed, or perhaps succumbed to rumours, that the German troops would come into town that day. Most of us started lining up on the sidewalks along the main streets to catch sight of the awesome spectacle we expected to see.

We were not disappointed. Minutes after the streets had filled with onlookers, the first armoured divisions began rolling along where we were standing; we had a full view of the heavy guns protruding, followed by soldiers in full military gear marching to the tunes of various German brass bands. I had no idea, nor did I attempt to estimate, how many Wehrmacht battalions passed through Tarnów on their way east. I remember only that for some two days and two nights it was impossible to cross the streets, so never-ending was the procession. I remember, too, and later heard it from others who had a similar experience, that the faces of the young soldiers under their fierce-looking helmets were young and pleasant, and that they blew kisses to the onlookers. Lulled into temporary relief at seeing apparently civilized young people barely older than my friends and I behaving normally, Mother, Hela and I returned home to await further developments.

We did not have to wait long. Over the next week or so, all of partitioned Poland except for Warsaw, which withheld the onslaught for about three weeks, was in the hands of the Germans and Soviets, who easily subdued all resistance. Their occupational authorities began immediate rule of our defeated country.

Rule of Terror

In Tarnów, the new city commissioner, and later chief German administrator, *Kreishauptmann* Ernst Kundt, installed himself in the council chambers of the former mayor and soon set out to prove to the residents that he was the absolute authority in all areas of their lives.

In October, all Jews — men, women and children — were ordered to wear a white armband with a blue Star of David on it on their right arms, effective immediately. Excuses would be of no avail. Those found without it would be shot. Overnight, Jewish women got busy sewing the armbands, and in the bright sunshine of the next morning, a good many people hurrying to and fro in the streets had become instantly visible and readily distinguishable from the rest.

Another step undertaken by Kundt and his cohorts in the early months of the occupation was to seek out and list the more livable homes and apartments of the Jews, and to seize some rooms in them to accommodate the ever-swelling numbers of German officers and civilians. Later on, some homes were confiscated altogether while their inhabitants were turned out into the streets to seek shelter among friends, in order to provide comfortable quarters for German wives and other women who had come with their manager-husbands and were busy sending carloads of valuable furniture and other goods to their homes in Germany.

The three of us, although forced to give up the larger bedroom in our apartment, enjoyed a few weeks of unexpected but welcome respite. Our first tenant was an aging Austrian lieutenant who moved in with his orderly, Karl Kaller, also a Viennese. Kaller was, by his impassioned admissions to us, a tenacious social democrat and filled with scorn of the Nazis, and he did everything in his limited power to alleviate our deteriorating conditions. Under the guise of bringing supplies to his superior officer, he succeeded in scrambling around to get for us sizable portions of food and replenish our fuel for the coming winter. His disgust of the Hitler regime was of such magnitude that he often gave vent to his feelings by spitting into his officer's soup and diluting his meals with water. This exceptional, tender-hearted man did not stay with us for long. After a few weeks, he and his superior were posted closer to the war front. We carried on a sporadic, clandestine correspondence with Kaller for some twenty months and found out from his last letter, written before he was about to be shipped to the battle zone in the Soviet Union in summer 1941, that, in his concern over us, he had been in contact with my father via Switzerland and Portugal. The letter was written from a hospital in Vienna where he had landed after having slashed both his wrists in order not to engage in further combat. After this last communication, we lost all touch with this unique humanist, the only one we had encountered in our wartime dealings with the Germans.

We were less lucky after our first tenants' departure. Our apartment went through a succession of lodgers, at first army personnel and later officers of the SS, all of whom treated us with disdain and icy indifference. The skull and crossbones on the caps of the SS, indicative of their mission in Poland, were enough to fill us with alarm. However, there were certain departures from the prevailing situation when some of the officers, often more than slightly drunk, would make lewd propositions to me hinting that, if I succumbed to their sexual advances, our essential needs would be supplied. Prayer had long ceased to be of comfort to me. Instead, faced with my first real crisis of conscience, I lay awake nights, clutching Father's photo, which I had begun to carry amulet-fashion inside my slip, and childishly begged him for guidance and help.

In my naïveté, I had not connected the frequent deliveries of foodstuffs and fuel to some of our neighbouring Jewish apartments with anything but a passing generosity of another Karl Kaller. When truth struck me in its disgusting implications, I gave up my wishful and ineffectual thinking, permitted myself to be invited to the room of an officer, pretended to enjoy the glass of looted Rhine wine or French champagne, suffered a mostly drunken kiss, and, filled with shame and revulsion, allowed the male hands to explore the curves of my seventeen-year-old body. Yet, for reasons I did not understand then, and which have eluded me since, I succeeded in beguiling my wooers by soothing promises of greater intimacies to come, if only they would see to it that our apartment was supplied with food and fuel. And so, for some weeks, while offerings of the pleasures of flesh were whispered into my unwilling ears, I held off some panting officers' advances by ever sweeter and bolder promises, given in my most charming German. It was by sheer luck and coincidence that those lustful men were successively ordered to move their troops elsewhere, and I was not forced to pay the humiliating price. To add to my good fortune, after a while our young tenants were succeeded either by officers of the paterfamilias variety or fairly decent commissars. All they thought of was how to get rich quickly and paid me scant attention.

When the situation improved, I regained my shaky equilibrium and, freed from the threat of prostituting myself, managed, with the silent support of Mother and Hela, who had stood by me through my period of trial, to let the degrading events sink to the bottom of my consciousness.

Kundt's initial orders followed one another fast and furiously. Before ceding his absolute power to the Gestapo and the SS, whose contingents arrived in Tarnów in November, Kundt had managed to execute a widely dreaded order: In a single day, he ordered that all the synagogues be burned. While flames rose high over the city in the early winter sky, the streets resounded with scuffles, the swishing sounds of whips and cries from every direction where the pious Jews, in vain defending the symbols of their religious faith, first pleaded with their assailants and then, defenceless and beaten, hurried to their homes to mourn their shame.

Around this same time, Kundt, with a Machiavellian flourish, forced new helpers among the most unlikely segment of the population for his dealings with the Jews. He created a Jewish Council (Judenrat) consisting of about fifty men and housed its offices in one of the town's ramshackle houses, with a conveniently large yard, in the Jewish district.

After the arrival of the Gestapo, all Jewish business establishments were appropriated by expelling their former owners from their premises and confiscating the merchandise as the property of the German Reich. In this, they were assisted by German civilians. My father's store was taken over by a middle-aged commissar from Berlin, Walter Tidow. A greedy but not an unkind man, he gave Mother, Hela and me filing and clerical jobs. These turned out to be desirable in more ways than I had expected: they meant that we were "at work," and thus, theoretically and at least for a time, not subject to be seized for forced labour at a moment's notice; and they provided us with stationery, stamps and a typewriter, all of which I hoped we would use in our as yet hypothetical correspondence with Father.

The net to catch men and women for backbreaking labour in the nearby fields and factories was being flung ever wider and pulled together ever tighter. These almost daily orders for forced labour were accompanied by the guards' whip lashes. Many were ordered to work in the military barracks and other war installations in and around Tarnów, often putting in up to sixteen hours of hard labour without food and drink, resulting, sometimes, in disease and even death.

Food rationing had also been introduced. Hela and I had to line up in front of the town's few bakeries as early as 4:30 a.m. to get our meagre daily quota of bread. Sometimes we made it, but at other times we did not, and we had to return home without the precious loaves. Mother, Hela and I, although not suffering from hunger yet, began apportioning our meals carefully and managed to live on soup, cheeses and the occasional supply of milk that our trustworthy milk-maid, Zosia, who used to deliver to us before the war, smuggled into our home from time to time, occasionally providing us also with a feast of fresh, recently harvested fruit and vegetables.

And so, the rule of terror, gathering momentum as the months went by, had begun. Among the people I knew, and especially among my friends who had stayed in Tarnów, there were at first cries of out-rage, coupled with vague plans of self-defence and revenge, and, il-logically, with a tenuous hope that "things will get better" once the Nazis had used their conquest to their complete advantage. Gradu-ally, however, it became clear that the enemy was as devious and de-termined as he was powerful, and that we, the Jews of Tarnów as their primary target, were helpless to stop the all-out assault on us. We had borne the brunt of every carefully conceived and implemented attack of brutality. And yet, powerless to counter the sweeping anti-Jewish atrocities, we were loath to give up our ill-founded fantasy that some unnamed, larger-than-life force would come to our rescue.

"You'll see," Lusia Maschler, a notorious dreamer in our group kept saying during our long discussions on the subject, "the neutral countries will persuade Hitler to send all of us Jews over to them where they will take care of us until the war is over. And he will do it, too, for he obviously doesn't want us." I could see some of my friends' eyes light up when they heard her speak, but Meyer, Klara and I, the three skeptics, disagreed completely with the fanciful tale. Not to dis-illusion the optimists among us, we would just look knowingly and sadly at one another.

First Winter of Captivity

Throughout these first months of German occupation, the three of us, careful not to make ourselves conspicuous, adhered strictly to all the rules. I let no event I knew of pass unnoticed. With my information about every available detail of the Nazi activities in town augmented by frequent reports from Meyer, Jurek, Resia and the others, I lay awake nights trying to figure out primarily how to avoid a bullet, whether stray or intentional, and secondarily, though no less pressingly, how to re-establish contact with my father. My friends and our well-meaning neighbours, to whom I often turned, were as full of nebulous advice as I was of ill-conceived plans.

Mere months after the Gestapo and the SS contingents had arrived in town and had requisitioned two large tenement buildings on Urszulańska, a tree-lined street off Krakowska as their headquarters, I had my first encounter with the icy grip of German forced labour. One frosty February morning, walking to work at our former store, now managed and systematically denuded by Tidow, and keeping to the back streets to avoid the patrols that favoured Tarnów's modern avenues, I was seized by two strong hands, their knuckles white with the strain of their hold on me. Looking up, I saw a cleanly shaven face and an obviously bald head barely visible under the death-head-and-crossbones adorned cap of an SS man, who released me as suddenly as he had clutched me and ordered me to follow him. When we arrived at the wire fence of one of the town's many military barracks, he curtly gave instructions to the sergeant in charge of sanitation, and minutes later I was told to get a pail, a mop and some smelly rags to clean the latrines. My nausea got the better of me; I threw up and retched helplessly, but was lucky enough to be standing then in a dark corner where the man in charge mistook the heaving of my back and shoulders for hard work.

It took till mid-afternoon to clean the twenty-odd filthy latrines allotted to me. My clothes and hands splattered with shit, my throat raw and constricted from vomiting, and my head pounding with a blinding headache, I mopped, scrubbed, washed and rinsed the urinals and the toilets, but their foul odour continued to make me faint and nearly senseless. When I heard a pistol-like voice saying, "Genug, raus!" (Enough, out!), I did not know, at first, that it was I who was being released.

Trying to focus on the man who gave the order, I recognized the SS officer who had brought me to the barracks in the morning. While he conferred for a while in a barely audible voice with the sergeant, I was suddenly seized by fear that I would be shipped to a labour camp in Germany rather than allowed to go home. I swayed on my feet and then my legs gave way so that I was kneeling in front of the two uniformed figures in a position akin to that of supplication. That is how the Germans must have interpreted my posture, for suddenly they burst into jeering laughter. "Look at the Jewess down there," said the SS man. "She is like all the others, unable to do a day's work, they all beg for mercy like dogs. This is what we do to dogs." With those words, he kicked my knees with the tip of his boot while I tried to stifle a scream of pain. "Get out of here, fast," he added, "we'll get you when your time comes."

Unaware that I was to hear the same threat many times in the months and years to come, I do not know how I found my way home that day. I felt bruised all over and totally drained as I finally staggered up the familiar stairs to our apartment, leaving an odour of urine and feces behind me. On seeing me, Mother wrung her hands in despair and Hela cried. It was Hela who was finally galvanized into action. She went to fetch Meyer, whom I dimly recognized. They must have all cleaned and bathed me, for the next thing I remember is resting under a blanket in my bed and Meyer supporting my head, trying to pour a shot glass of vodka down my throat. "Don't worry," I heard him say, in an attempt to sound jocular as I was sinking into sleep, "you have just added another accomplishment to your many others. When you see your father, you can tell him about it. He'll be proud of you." I thought I heard a sob escaping from the direction where he was bending over me, but I was too exhausted to listen. Instead, I dropped off to sleep and remained in blissful oblivion for some fourteen hours. I opened my eyes the next morning, squinting at the bright light that enveloped the room and slowly becoming conscious of my sore and aching limbs. Painfully making my way to the window, I opened it wide and saw the fresh snow, which must have fallen during the night and which now glittered under brilliant sunshine on the roads, sidewalks, railings and rooftops. It brought sharp memories of past winters, the vacations with my parents in winter resorts, sleigh rides and skiing with my friends on St. Martin's, which I tried to blot out as soon as they emerged.

This was no time for reminiscing. It was the first winter of our captivity. I wondered whether we would survive and, if we did, how many more winters we would have to spend separated from my father. I pondered, also, how we would keep warm and whether Zosia would come with her precious supply, risking capture, in the frigid weather. With great effort I tore myself away from the window and forced my jumbled thoughts to store the previous day's incident in some deep vaulted memory bank while I got ready to face another day at Tidow's.

The Gestapo were now firmly entrenched in Tarnów. Their chief was *Oberscharführer* Otto von Malottki, and his closest assistant was *Scharführer* Nowak, a so-called *Volksdeutscher* who was a Czech citizen of German descent. He had probably offered his services to the Germans immediately upon their occupation of the country. He and the other "German-folk" had already established a reputation for their ferocity, particularly in their treatment of the Jews. It surpassed even that of the "real" Germans. The trio of Malottki, Nowak and Kundt started their attacks against the Jews on a steadily increasing scale and began to exact a quota of Jewish blood on a daily basis. Jews were shot for stepping outside city limits, wearing their armband on the wrong arm, failing to salute a German officer, or when caught talking about the shortage of food and fuel. However, most Jews just kept going to work and returning home, still clinging to the belief that if only they managed to be neither seen nor heard, they would not be targeted. The three of us among them still clung to a hope that, even though the Allies seemed to be losing the war and therefore could not be counted on for help, the Germans aimed merely at showing their might by eliminating individuals, but the majority would be, somehow, miraculously spared. In those early months of the Gestapo rule, it was as though the Jews were to be mainly made sport of for the amusement of the superior "Aryan" race, and nothing much more sinister than that.

A strict curfew of 9:00 p.m. had been imposed. After that hour the streets became deserted, their eerie silence interrupted from time to time by heavy thuds of the boots of German patrols looking for marauders or dispatched on a mission of more arrests. The screams of women and the muffled sounds of the arrested men pierced the quiet too, filling those huddled in their homes with dread and foreboding. Our life after 9:00 p.m. became completely confined to our apartment building, where we formed close bonds of friendship with our neighbours. Based on a common threat and the resulting need for togetherness, these connections lasted and deepened throughout the war.

During the spring of 1940, we received a letter written by Father, signed Abe Cohn, with a return address of West New York, New

Jersey, where the actual Abe Cohn, my mother's older brother, had lived for many years. Snatching it from one another's hands, we finally pieced it together, reading and rereading Father's tightly written German lines until we knew every long-awaited word by heart. Flushed with excitement, we ran into some apartments in our building showing the minor miracle — a letter from America — to our neighbours, and then I stuck it into my coat pocket to share the great event in my life with Klara and Meyer. Long after curfew, Mother sat discussing it with the Holoszytz family across the hall, while Hela was with a few of our younger neighbours in the corner of our apartment, from where the sounds were those of merriment and frolic.

Father was well and had begun an all-out campaign to bring us to him. He told us, though succinctly, that he had tried to board the *Batory* on August 23, 1939, but had been held back bodily by relatives until the ship sailed away from the New York harbour. He implored us not to despair but to remember that he was waiting for us and had unshakable faith in our reunion. In the meantime, he had arranged to send us food parcels from Portugal and Sweden, where a couple from Białystok, friends of my parents who had fled the Russians, now lived. He asked us to direct any requests or messages to him through this couple. The letter closed with yet another expression of tender love and hope. It was only in the postscript that father included the most important information of all: while he was not leaving a stone unturned to get us transit and other visas through a half a dozen countries, we were to do our best to get an exit visa, what was referred to as *Ausreise*, from our authorities. He begged us, too, to take the greatest care of our health possible under the circumstances.

I took Father's letter to the den, and there, at his desk, tried to organize and control my unruly thoughts in order to concentrate on what action I had to take. The letter had been opened by a German censor and resealed, so it had passed inspection. It was obvious that Father had deliberately avoided any reference to the war and to Poland's occupation, dwelling only on personal matters. That meant, I speculated, that if we avoided political topics, worded our writing in innocuous diction and couched it in scrupulously neutral tones, some two-way communication via Sweden and the United States might be possible as long as these two countries remained neutral. Then, I thought, there was the thorny matter of the exit visa. As Jews, we were forbidden to leave our town and travel to another city, and the *Passstelle*, visa office, was in Krakow, some ninety kilometres from Tarnów. Supposing, I said to myself, that the various visas Father had mentioned should arrive. How would I ever get to Krakow to plead our case? Since I could not find a workable answer for the moment, I resolved, as so often before and after, to stay put for a while, to continue, with Mother and Hela, to avoid the Germans, to write often to Father addressing him as "Dear Uncle Abe," and try to devise some way to get to the inaccessible institution.

Even as we busied ourselves with writing almost daily letters to Father, and as fairly regular mail began coming in from him and his friend, Mr. Marejn, in Sweden, Malottki and Nowak were devising new ways of getting rid of ever larger numbers of Jews. Every day brought grim news.

Early in the summer of 1940, the two men, aided by Kundt and his assistants, began a thorough search of the homes of Polish and Jewish intellectuals and members of the professions. They let it be known that they were about to root out the Jewish "conspiracy" which, in collaboration with Jewish "menace" elsewhere in the world, was plotting to undermine the victorious German Reich. At the end of this particular "project," many unsuspecting people — doctors, lawyers, teachers and formerly affluent merchants — were dragged out of their homes in the middle of the night and taken to the local jail already full to overflowing.

One of these nights, two stormtroopers, their bayonets fixed, seized a well-known lawyer in our building. We heard his wife and children scream for a short while, but then there was total silence broken only by the ominous sound of heavy boots descending the stairs.

We rushed to a window and by the light of the street lamp caught sight of our neighbour, in his pajamas and slippers, being pushed into a police wagon amid blows to his head, legs and the rest of his body.

We ran down to the neighbour's apartment and were met by a horrifying sight: the neighbour's wife sat slumped in the only chair that had not been overturned, her two young children bleeding from cuts across their cheeks and foreheads crying and pulling at her. If she recognized us, she gave no sign. Gingerly, we straightened out as much furniture as we could, washed and dressed the children's wounds, gave them some food and put them back to bed. It was some hours later, when we were about to return helplessly home, that the lawyer's wife broke into wordless sobs and suffered herself to be put to bed, too.

A few of the new prisoners were sent home, while others were taken daily out of jail to the Gestapo headquarters to be interrogated by Malottki. There they were tortured so that they would confess to their non-existent crime — treason against Germany. One day I saw a small group of the prisoners being taken back to jail after some three hours of interrogation. Escorted by four SS men who whipped them and pushed them along with rifle butts, they walked in the middle of the street. They were all barefoot, their faces were streaked with blood, their clothes in tatters, and their arms limp.

A few nights later, we were awakened by shots so deafeningly loud that we were sure they had been fired close by. I ran across a few deserted streets to find Meyer, who had already developed the reputation for quickly nosing out information. My worst fears were confirmed when Meyer told me that half of the prisoners had been shot in the prison yard. In my mind, I transformed the image of the smiling faces I had seen atop the German tanks at the beginning of the occupation into that of jeering, loathsome masks of murderers.

In June, I spotted a large group, at least several hundred — comprised mainly of Polish gentiles along with a number of Jews — marched under heavy escort to the railway station. That they had proceeded from there to Auschwitz became evident when some of the prisoners' wives and mothers later received telegrams bearing the name of the camp. The wording of all those form messages was identical, with a few modifications: "Your husband (father, son) died suddenly of a heart attack (stroke, pneumonia, etc.) while a political prisoner in Auschwitz."

The name Auschwitz, which I had known in Polish as Oświęcim, was familiar to me from my study of Polish geography and seemed innocuous enough, but the mention of a concentration camp on Polish soil shook me deeply. What before the war had been merely an ugly sound bearing no relevance to our lives had now become a part of our personal realities. Auschwitz, now infamous in our minds, later became known as a death camp. Little did we know then how well it, and many others like it, was to live up to that sinister name.

The Elusive Exit Visa

Living in constant fear that one of Malottki's organized house searches might bring the Gestapo to our own door, I nevertheless persisted
in my single-minded, though as yet formless, plans for our reunion
with Father. Every day at work, where I had managed to convince
Tidow that my German was perfect and that I could translate fluently and was therefore indispensable to him, I spent hours at the
typewriter, a gadget I had never learned to use properly but at which
I was quite fast banging away with my two index fingers and turning
out a fairly presentable copy. As my job was not too exacting, I typed
little for Tidow and a lot for my father. I wrote a letter daily, and I was
pleased to learn both from Father's and Mr. Marejn's replies that my
neatly typewritten print was passing the censor much faster than, as I
imagined, my indecipherable hieroglyphics would have done.

On a cue from Father I adopted our private code language. The
warm winter garments became our central metaphor. "Please, Daddy," I would say with variations in many of my letters, "try to send
us some clothes made of genuine American wool." In their letters,
Mother and Hela would also follow the pattern: they, too, would write
that we had barely survived the winter as we had been catching bouts
after bouts of severe flu, and that only an exchange of good, warm
coats for our shabby, worn-out ones might save us from similar, or
worse, health problems in the winter to come. "And," I would add
frequently, hoping that my words would sound as though in praise

of German efficiency, "many thanks for the food parcels. They have been coming frequently and with minimum delay both from Portugal and from Sweden, and we have been feasting on them, sharing them with our friends and neighbours who also wish to express their gratitude to you." All our letters ended with lofty reassurances of our love and longing to be reunited.

Despite the occasional light tone we tried to assume in our letters to Father, a sense of deepening failure was beginning to engulf us. I had still not devised a workable plan to go to Krakow, although we had already received transit visas through Spain, Portugal and, alternately, through some Balkan countries and Turkey, to travel to the United States. I often spread the polyglotic papers on the table either to study them with fascination at Father's ingenuity or to show them to my friends, who, even as they admired my father's resourcefulness and marvelled at the uncommon documents, had little practical advice to give me.

After a great deal of soul-searching and unable to contain my uncertainty any longer, I had formal German translations made of all the visas and resolved to make an illegal trip to Krakow. I decided to go by train. Early one morning in July, I slipped out of the apartment, took off my armband, and sauntered, my heart beating wildly and the precious briefcase by my side, to the railway station.

Posing as an "Aryan," I pretended a calm and serenity that I was far from feeling. "A return ticket to Krakow, please," I said in my accentless Viennese to the girl at the ticket counter. She handed me a ticket and I boarded a car directly across from me on which a big sign proclaimed it to be "Nur für Deutsche," for Germans only. My decision to travel as a German rather than a Pole had been prompted by my feeling that I did not look Polish enough, but that, with my light-brown hair, blue eyes, slim build, and — most important — my proficient German, I might make it as one of the many civilian members of the German autocracy in Poland. My answers to potential casual questions had been well rehearsed. Now, as I settled in with a copy of a German newspaper in front of me and waited for the train to start, my tensions had begun to ebb. I felt lightheaded and dizzy, but no longer paralyzed by fear.

The trip was a success. I showed the conductor my ticket and my identification as a secretary for Tidow enterprises, and started munching on a piece of chocolate. The few Germans in the compartment were either snoozing or looking over some briefs spread over their knees. One or two addressed me politely and I answered briefly but courteously. A soldier asked whether I would be staying in Krakow long enough to have dinner with him that night. I was ready for this contingency as well. "So sorry," I said, "but I'll be getting a few orders for my boss and must catch the early afternoon train back to Tarnów." I gave him a warm smile, and then got ready to get off as the train was pulling into the station in Krakow.

Falling into a jaunty step, I walked over to the *Passstelle* building. Once inside, I put on my armband and approached the first window, spreading our visas and transit permits in front of the official inside. My heart beat wildly for fear that he would ask me how I had managed to come; I had a few answers ready for that eventuality, but had counted heavily on the possibility that despite their efficiency, Germans in one department would not necessarily be informed on what was happening in others. To my great relief, I was right.

For two and a half hours, I was sent from window to window, and was finally informed that the dossier was incomplete. I was to come again and bring some missing papers that had to be obtained from the local Tarnów authorities before a ruling could be made on our exit visas. The official sounded so convincing that I believed him. What I did not know yet, nor did the official see fit to disclose it to me, was that *Ausreisevisum*, the official term for an exit visa, for a Jew was a myth.

And so, feeling disappointed yet not quite defeated, I slipped off my armband in the washroom and stole back to the train for a quick trip home. Mother and Hela, relieved at seeing me unharmed, besieged me with news and questions. Did I know that Malottki had looted three apartment houses across the street from us and had taken some Jews with him? Had I heard that a number of Father's business associates had been jailed on suspicion of hiding their store's goods and their wives' jewels? And what about our visas?

Suddenly drained of all my precarious strength and emptied of the hope I had still maintained only that afternoon, I shut my ears to all the questions and statements and threw myself, fully clothed, on the bed. We were not going to make it, I thought with mounting panic. It was only a matter of time before they came for us. I had risked my life for nothing. My uneasy sleep that night was shot through with one of the very few nightmares I had during the war years: amid deafening shouts of "Sieg Heil," in front of Hitler and Malottki standing on a raised platform, and to the tune of a military band playing "Lili Marleen," Mother, Hela and I had been brought in wearing torn black gowns to be viewed by a huge crowd. The "Sieg Heil" turned into "Tod den Juden" (death to Jews) and to a rhythmic chant of "Juden-rein, Juden-rein" (free-of-Jews), issuing from thousands of throats to another melody just as we were made to face the firing squad, which had materialized out of nowhere. I woke up with a loud scream, squirming and throwing myself wildly in my bed. It took Mother and Hela a while to convince me that we were alive and that I had had a bad dream.

Listlessly, I made the rounds of a few authorities to obtain the documents required by the *Passstelle*. The Polish administrative offices, which had about the same latitude as its Jewish Council counterpart, furnished me, after many delays, with records of birth, domicile, schooling and similar particulars. A difficult document to obtain was an acknowledgement from Kundt's office that there was nothing suspicious about us or our belongings. I went from one German official to another until I could finally add the report from the civic authorities to our dossier.

The most formidable task we had yet to overcome. In front of a Gestapo officer, I had to swear on behalf of the three of us that, if we were granted an exit visa, we would take absolutely nothing with us. Fearful to venture into the Gestapo quarters myself, I sought help from Israel Schmuckler, who had been going out with Hela and was her regular boyfriend by that time. One morning, he brought me to the town square near the Judenrat where, pacing the steps of what used to be a display area for farmers' wares but was now an empty shell, a broad-shouldered Gestapo officer, whip in hand, addressed me without any preamble: "So, you are the Jew who doesn't like it here under our benevolent protectorate. You want to leave, yes?"

"Yes," I said feebly, with downcast eyes, "but not because we are suffering any privations. It is simply that we wish to be reunited with my father from whom we have been separated since the war."

"You all have excuses," he answered angrily. "There will be no peace until the world is rid of you once and for all. By the way, how is it that your father has so many connections and got you so many visas? He must be active in the Jewish international conspiracy against the Aryans, no?"

"No, Herr Hauptmann (captain)," I answered faintly. "He is a very simple man with no aspirations other than to see his family again."

"Jewish lies," he hissed scornfully as he held out a folded sheet of paper in his gloved hand. "Here is your precious document. I have signed it as required by the Passstelle. But mark my word, it will do you no good. Weg!" (Go!) he shouted as he motioned me away. As I turned to walk, I had a sinking feeling that he would shoot me in the back, a trick I had seen performed on many others. When we were a safe distance away, I thanked my escort and ran home to put my papers in order for the second round.

I kept working for Tidow and arranging our documentation while the Gestapo stepped up their harassment of the Tarnów Jews. It now seemed as though they were working with a list from which they were crossing off, one by one, the deeds they had already committed and those yet to come.

After a particularly vicious incident when Malottki and Nowak, to show off their prowess before some German women who accompanied them, had shot three teenage Jewish boys who were on their way home from work, my friends gathered in my house where, unwilling to discuss the episode and to speculate again on when and how the next blow would fall, we sat in stony silence for a while. Meyer was the first to speak. He contended that more atrocities and greater degradation were in store for us and that none of us were clever enough to anticipate or outguess the diabolical trickery of the Gestapo and the SS. "I, for one, am going to find out how one goes about forging Aryan papers. Hitler is winning the war and there is no help for us from anybody. It may not do much good, but I can think of no better solution. If the war lasts much longer, we'll all be dead." We bandied the subject around for a while, and after discussing details, I asked Meyer to try to get such documents for us, too. Resia, the most "Aryan-looking" of us all, warmed up to the idea quickly, and everybody followed suit. "I'll find out," said Meyer, whose stereotypically Jewish nose, I thought sadly to myself, would give him away in no time. Even as I "signed up" Mother, Hela and myself for the "Aryan" papers, I explained to my friends that I was going to continue my efforts to emigrate officially with the aid of the visas that Father had sent us. If they had any adverse reactions to my statement, they did not show it. Unlike in the days right after my return from Białystok, we were now acutely conscious that, faced with the possibility of death at any moment, it was each person for themselves.

A few days later, I approached a Polish taxi driver, Bolek, whom I vaguely knew. Before the war, Tarnów had been sufficiently motorized to support five taxis; after the occupation, all five drivers were forbidden to operate their vehicles and their cars were confiscated. "You are in luck," said Bolek. "I told the Germans that I had scrapped my car, but I still have it hidden. But," he added, "your suggestion is dangerous and you'll have to make it worth my while to risk my neck." "Don't worry," I replied hastily, "I'll pay you in American dollars."

A few months earlier, Father had mentioned in a letter that we might get a visitor, a friend of the Marejns, from a small town near Lodz. At the time, we had thought that he meant someone who would bring an additional food package or perhaps some clothing. It had turned out, however, that the middle-aged Jew who had knocked on our door one early afternoon had been instructed to get a hundred American dollars on the black market, where he had connections, and to bring the money to us. I remember that we had then felt another surge of gratitude to my father, who ceaselessly, while living in freedom himself, was so attuned to our precarious lot that he was racking his brain for any possible way to help us. Not knowing what to do with the acquisition, we had hidden the American money and had not given it much thought. And now Bolek was asking for twenty dollars, payable in advance. Blowing an imaginary kiss to Father, I gave Bolek the money and we arranged to meet before dawn the following day.

It was 4:00 a.m. when, slipping out of our apartment with the Jewish armband in the pocket of my jacket, I scurried as quietly as a cat to the junkyard where Bolek kept his car. Without speaking, he started the engine, and we began to move. Since we were worried about patrols on the main highway, we took many back roads, watching in silence the trees and the scattered farmhouses as the small headlights illuminated them in the pre-dawn light. After an hour, I saw Bolek's hands tighten on the wheel. "I think there is a patrol up ahead," he whispered. "I am going to stop the car and turn off the lights. Get out as soon as I do."

Five minutes later, we were both crouching in a ditch, the car invisible under a clump of trees. Now I, too, discerned voices becoming louder. A group of German soldiers seemed to be coming closer. With bated breath and racing pulse, I stretched out in the ditch, voicelessly telling myself that my hour had come. The icy terror slowly gave way to the mournful thought that I would never see Father again. *Please, Daddy, help*, I prayed childishly without moving my lips. *Help all three of us as you have always done*, I kept silently repeating, totally unaware of the irrationality and ineffectualness of my wild entreaties. Just then, as I clutched Father's photo more tightly to my chest, the voices began to fade away and there was silence once again, interrupted only by the rustling of the leaves in the trees. Cautiously, Bolek crept out of the ditch and, after looking in all directions by the faint light of the dawn, motioned for me to follow. We were both stiff from our half-hour sojourn in the ditch and from the tension, but so glad to have gone undetected and to be on our way again that we babbled and laughed hysterically all the way to Krakow.

At 9:00 a.m. sharp, my armband firmly in place, I confronted the *Passstelle* officials once more. They examined my papers, asked a few questions, took some notes, and then handed me back the thick envelope telling me that all was in order, but that I still had to get exit permission from all the three branches of the city police: the Gestapo, the SS and the Schutzpolizei, an ordinary branch who were in reality a rubber stamp for the other two. Completely deflated, I gathered all my documents and, blinded by my rage, was about to tear them up in the bathroom where I rushed after the interview. After I had taken a few deep breaths, some force, the identity of which I was uncertain of, restrained me from executing the destructive act. The decision to keep the documents was almost mechanical and not fully conscious. I angrily stuffed the envelopes into my briefcase, found Bolek in a small café where we had arranged to meet, took off my armband to masquerade as being Polish while in the car, and we left.

Studying my face, Bolek knew better than to ask questions. He kept his eyes on the winding side roads and interrupted his silence only once, to offer me a sandwich. My throat was too constricted for food, but I took a few gulps of strong coffee from his thermos. Our return trip went without a hitch. We drove inconspicuously into the junkyard where I slipped my armband back into place and held out my hand to Bolek to say goodbye.

"Don't give up," he said, looking at me gently. "I know it hurts like hell, but don't let them get you down. You have a father to go to when you leave all this. Most of us have nobody." I threw my arms around that friendly Pole's neck and mumbled amid my sobs, "Thank you, Bolek. It was worth it if only to find a friend." Unable to say more, I went home. Mother and Hela met me at the door, anxious to hear the news. All I could do was shake my head to indicate no.

A Temporary Triumph

To counteract events we did not dare to face fully, we formed a true underground subculture. People banded in close-knit communities, almost like extended families, in the buildings in which they lived. Mother, Hela and I, cut off completely from our relatives in Białystok and keenly feeling our isolation, continued to develop very warm relationships with our neighbours. While the raids were going on all over town and we were not certain whether we were on one of the lists, we visited or were visited by our new friends almost nightly. Over a cup of weak tea or ersatz coffee, we would speak for a while mournfully of those who had fallen victim to the Nazi bullets, but, almost invariably, would set our heavy burdens aside to engage in a game of cards, exchange information on where to get black-market food and even indulge in the frivolities of a little gossip. The three of us had attained a limited sort of fame as "that Roskes family with the exotic victuals," for we often brought to our nocturnal escapades sardines, cheeses, packaged cookies and other locally unobtainable delicacies we were receiving regularly in the food parcels from Sweden and Portugal.

I was friendly with the Holoszytz family across the hall, a young couple with two little boys, and the Kleinhandlers, one storey below us, who had two teenage girls, but struck up a closer friendship with a young married woman, Irene Oberlander, on the ground floor. She was a black-eyed, raven-haired beauty. Her husband, a gynecologist, had joined the Polish army as a colonel and had been reported missing. Irene, only six years my senior, was considerably younger than her spouse and did not act the sorrowing widow. She read avidly and was an accomplished pianist. Rumour had it that, in return for favours granted, she was getting all her needs supplied by German officers. We never talked about it. Instead, we discussed literature, our plans for after the war if we happened to survive it, and sometimes, in a lighter vein, even the pretty clothes we used to have. At my request, she played the piano for me often, and I would sit on her sofa in a trance, lulled, for a blissful music-filled hour or so, into a sense of temporary peace.

I was therefore shocked one evening when I went down for my customary visit to find Irene's door ajar and her apartment empty. At first, I was filled with dread that the Gestapo had taken her away. It was only on the following day that I learned from Meyer, my constant and reliable source of information, that Irene had gone into hiding on her "Aryan" papers. I never saw her again. By evening, the Germans requisitioned the apartment for a few SS officers and took the opportunity to raid all the floors. As they were the Schutzpolizei rather than the Gestapo, they did not shoot anybody. I suppose they had no such orders; they merely beat most of our male neighbours and dismissed the others with the now familiar phrase, "We'll get you later." This is what they apparently decided about Mother, Hela and me when, after entering our apartment, directing us with their rifle butts to the corner of one room and stuffing their pockets with the contents of our food parcels, they left as suddenly as they had come. As this was our first such experience on our own premises, we shook uncontrollably for a long time after they had left and took almost the entire night to calm down.

In late fall 1940, we received what was to become Father's most significant and crucial letter during the entire period. In it, he told us that he had become a Nicaraguan citizen and that, according to the laws of Nicaragua, the same citizenship had been conferred on us, his family. "Be of good cheer," he wrote, "for your new passports are on the way, and, as foreigners, you will be permitted to join me."

Our first reaction was that of utter disbelief. In our boldest dreams of rescue, such an esoteric, unique possibility had never occurred to us. It bordered on magic and the supernatural. How did Father manage all those miracles? We marvelled at the constant, unrelieved thinking about our plight that he had been engaging in to come up with such mind-boggling ways to be useful to us. We could almost physically feel his presence, despite the distance separating us, for in his heart and mind he was not really away at all.

After our initial sense of wonder and exultation had subsided, I did some serious thinking and began to worry all over again. While it was true, I mused, that we might have a better chance of getting an exit visa as neutral aliens, how were we going to convince the Gestapo that the whole thing was genuine? After all, everybody knew that we had been living in Tarnów for many years, and that Father had gone to Canada, not to Nicaragua. I argued with myself that the Gestapo did not know it, and our friends were not about to enlighten them. Worn out from our endless talks all starting with, "Wonderful, but what if...?" the three of us finally decided to cross this newest of bridges when we came to it.

We came to it soon enough. Toward the end of 1940, the Polish postman brought us a thick manila envelope, covered with stamps and official-looking seals on both sides, on which the return address read: The Consulate General of the Republic of Nicaragua, New York, U.S.A. We were practically falling over one another to have a look when the contents began to emerge. Finally, while we held our breaths, Mother took out three light-blue folders. Even though Father had alerted us to their imminent arrival, it was still beyond belief to discover that they were actual passports, one for each of us, with recent photos of ourselves (which we had sent to Father earlier on his request) staring at us from the page, with unmistakably Spanish print listing the usual passport particulars, and with a highly conspicuous, large stamp of the Republic of Nicaragua across the printed information. We realized that the passports had been issued in New York and were definitely genuine; we had enough experience, by now, to spot forged documents.

I had practically given up all efforts to obtain the elusive exit visa, but I was now catapulted into action once again. First, I discussed the new situation with my trusted friends, Meyer, Jurek, Resia and Klara. They handled and studied my passport with reverence approaching awe. My father, whom they had all liked and respected, rose in their estimation to almost God-like proportions. He seemed to be able to accomplish what nobody else could or dared imagine — the impossible. Later, on sober reflection, they all counselled me that if I wanted to turn the extraordinary documents to our advantage, I had to register our new status with the puppet Polish authorities as well as with the Gestapo. At that point, I began to feel as though the exchanges between Father and us were like some carefully staged game of volleying a ball back and forth. The ball was now in our court. It was our turn to act.

My friends' advice confirmed the decision I had already made but on which, at least for the moment, I was too frightened to act. All the "what ifs" haunted me, robbing me of my sleep, and making me go robot-like about my daily chores. I thought of the murders, tortures and hastily dug graves I had both seen and heard about, and feared that we three would become added drops to the huge bloodbath as soon as we came near anyone wearing a cap with a skull and crossbones on it. But I also knew that I could not delay much longer what was obviously necessary to do. Besides, if I did not take all possible steps, it would be tantamount to the betrayal of Father, who, thousands of miles and a whole battered continent away, was watching over us, never stopping his attempts to perform the miracle of our reunion. As inaction was unthinkable, I plunged in.

We went to the Polish offices first. We knew that it was no more than a formality, but the law required that everybody be properly registered with the Polish administration authorities. In a small office, a haggard-looking man scrutinized our passports, looked up at us with great astonishment, and got up to confer with two of his colleagues seated at another table. After a few minutes, he came back and began writing something I could not make out. He then turned to us, handed us the passports and some pink forms, and told us to come back after we had filled them out. His voice, when he finally spoke to us, was friendly, though with a trace of concern in it. He faced Mother and said, "Mrs. Roskes, your husband is obviously a very resourceful man. But tell me, how did he manage to become a Nicaraguan citizen so soon? It isn't all that long since he left." Mother muttered something unintelligible about the laws of the country, but he was either not listening or pretending not to hear. I was reassured that the man had empathy for us and would not give us away. Before we reached the door, he added in a louder voice, "Remember to register with the Gestapo, too, if you want your passports to do you any good."

The first round won, we returned home to study and fill out the pink slips. The heading stated that they were "Certificates of the Registration of Foreign Persons Residing Temporarily in Tarnów." They looked official enough and seemed to have been left over from the pre-war period. Savouring the irony, I filled out all the questions but had to think for a while when we came upon two tricky ones: the first asked through which port we had entered Poland, and the second how long we intended to stay in Tarnów. We searched for plausible answers and then, fusing the two, stated that we were permanent residents of Tarnów but were Nicaraguan citizens by virtue of Father's citizenship of that country. I knew that the answers were inaccurate but banked on the assumption that the Poles were quite indifferent, and perhaps even kindly disposed, toward the whole procedure. And so I took the forms, duly signed, to the Polish offices, where the same man looked them over cursorily, countersigned them, and stamped them in two places. He then gave me the detachable bottom parts, which were the receipts, with an admonition that we were to have those on us at all times.

We were now bracing for round two. We knew that our success with the Poles was meaningless to the Gestapo. Since there was no way to make an appointment, we had to venture right into the Gestapo headquarters and pray that they would not shoot us for daring to enter their sanctuary. The day we felt that we must not delay any longer, we went and, shaking all over, faced the heavy door on which a sign read "hinein" (enter). I surmised that no knock was required and pushed the door wide enough to allow us to go in. Once inside, we found ourselves in a large, sparsely furnished room where the only objects that drew our attention were an oversized portrait of Hitler on the wall, a large flag with a swastika perched in one corner, and a rifle resting against the wall in another. We positioned ourselves in a straight line a few yards in front of a massive desk behind which a Gestapo official sat reading, as I discovered with my legs buckling under me, *Der Stürmer*, Julius Streicher's infamous newspaper full of programs to eliminate the world's most inferior and most loathsome race. When the man finally glanced at us over the top of the newspaper, I noticed, as I had on previous occasions, how ordinary he looked without his fearsome helmet and martial gear. He was wearing a drab civilian suit, and his smoothly shaven, youngish face was of the same hue.

He looked at us, up and down, for what seemed like an eternity but was in fact only seconds, and barked in clipped German that we should approach the desk. With our passports and Polish receipts held shield-like in front of us, we stepped closer, expecting him either to take out his handgun or reach for the idling rifle. All our muscles tightened, but he did neither. Instead, he asked curtly, speaking to us in the third person, "What do the Jewesses want?"

Mutely, I took the papers from Mother and Hela, added them to mine, and placed them gingerly on the desk. After scanning them for a minute or so, he raised his head and hissed, "I don't understand either the Spanish or the Polish gibberish. I repeat for the last time: what do the Jewesses want?"

Recovering my speech, I launched into a long and rapid recitation about Father being away and living in Nicaragua, about us having been prevented from joining him by the war, and about his becoming a Nicaraguan citizen. As he had not interrupted me that far, I continued, my words tumbling over one another, that the passports were designed to permit us to get *Ausreisen* from the *Passstelle* and were supposed to give us, according to the Geneva Convention, certain immunity.

Afraid that I had talked too long, I stopped abruptly. Again, agonizingly long seconds passed and, again, I began to wonder when he would take out his gun. To my surprise and relief, he did not, at least — I thought — not yet. Instead, he spoke. "The papers seem genuine enough, but" (here he turned to face and glower at me) "I don't want to hear another word about Geneva Convention and all that crap. We shall register you as foreigners, but remember, you are still, and always will be, Jews first and foremost. We shall keep your file in case there is an Austausch" (an exchange of Germans for Allies, a phenomenon we had vaguely heard about). "Take it from me, you'll be dead long before there is one." He then ignored us, took three pieces of paper and started typing on them quickly, looking up at us once or twice as though to verify certain particulars. Having finished typing, he affixed a large Gestapo stamp to each of the documents. "Read it!" he barked. I looked at the papers quickly and found that they were certificates of our registration as foreigners, signed by the official in front of us.

"Thank you, sir," I said. "May we go now?"

"Go," he answered, "but don't let your conniving Jewish minds fill you with false hopes. You can tell all your friends that we shall rid the earth of all you pestilence-carrying Jewish vermin." We turned to go, but just as we were about to reach the door, a thought occurred to me. It was too impulsive to reflect on. "Sir," I said meekly, barely above a whisper, "may we be exempted from wearing the armbands?"

He stared at me stonily and then, choking with fury, shouted with heavy sarcasm, "I thought you'd never ask. This is yet another Jewish trick that won't help you a bit. Yes, you may, but not because of that damned Geneva Convention, which doesn't apply to the likes of you, but because of the generosity of the Third Reich. Incidentally, if we ever catch you without your documents, you'll be shot."

Stretching my luck to the breaking point, I blurted out my final plea: "Sir, may we have this exemption in writing, so that we can carry it with our papers?" For a moment I thought he was going to pounce on me, for he got up, kicked over his chair so that it fell clattering to the floor, and started moving toward us. As he came close, he stopped in his tracks and slowly pulled his gun out of his pocket. Just as I stood frozen to the floor, certain that we were done for, he turned around, retraced his steps, picked up his chair, and, with the gun now on the desk at his right hand, started banging on his typewriter again. Yanking the piece of paper from the machine, he threw it toward us and laughed gloatingly. "Here is your exemption. See how much good it will do you. You'll have to have two more copies made. I have tolerated you long enough. Raus!" I quickly picked up the paper and, without looking at it, ushered Mother and Hela out the door.

In the brilliant early winter sunshine, we stopped outside and took some deep breaths, our eyes filling with tears of both humiliation and relief. We flexed our legs, stiff with tension, and slowly made our way home. I tossed in bed all that night torn between feelings of temporary triumph and an agonizing sense of futility. So far, my invisible father's hand had snatched us from the Gestapo's clutches. But had it been worth it? I wondered. Was it a pyrrhic victory after all?

Danger and Disappointment

Throughout that winter and spring of 1941, I worked feverishly to get the elusive exit visas. Our friends and neighbours looked upon our Nicaraguan passports as a fresh impetus to our cause and to the removal of our armbands as a positive sign and encouraged me to take advantage of our improved legal status to redouble my efforts. While we three, too, felt relieved for a while about our diminished visibility and the possession of what we liked to feel was a trump card, we continued to be wary, for we knew that our ostensible rights would be disregarded by the first German policeman who might stop us. If he asked about our armbands, he was not likely to bother looking at our passports or listening to our explanations.

How well founded my worries were was brought home to me some time during that period when Hela, after an afternoon outing, failed to show up at curfew. As the relentless minutes ticked away, Mother and I craned our necks out the windows trying to spot her, but as the darkness of the winter night failed to yield any sight of her, we retreated to a room where we sat fidgeting in our growing nervousness, powerless to take any action. Horrifying images of which we were loath to speak kept filling our minds and, after about an hour, we despaired of seeing her alive again. Just as the first cries of panic escaped from us, there was a loud rapping on our door. I opened it, clenching my hands into tight fists to prevent them from trembling, and saw

Israel Schmuckler. His face was contorted with anxiety, which I first took to be a confirmation of my worst fears. He said that a friend of his had seen Hela being picked up by a Gestapo man and taken to the headquarters minutes after the curfew. If I ran quickly, he suggested, stammering, maybe there was something I could still do.

On an impulse, I grabbed Hela's winter coat, which she had left behind when she had gone out, and made a quick search of its pockets. My hunch was correct: in one of them, I found her passport and the Gestapo certificate. She had forgotten to take the papers with her when she had changed coats. Hurriedly, I ran out of the house and bounded all the way to the Gestapo headquarters. Without hesitation, I swung the door wide open and burst into the familiar antechamber. Darting a quick glance around, I spotted Hela in one corner, standing with her body folded almost double and with her eyes fixed on the floor. At the desk, two Gestapo men were having a conversation, seemingly disregarding her altogether. Without thinking, I interrupted them. Holding Hela's documents out to them, I launched into a jumbled account of how she had inadvertently forgotten her papers, pleading with them to let her go as this was her first offence, and promising that it would not be repeated. Taken aback by my boldness, the men stopped talking and began looking from me to Hela and back again. "You have a lot of gall, barging in here just like that," one of them said. "Mind you never speak to the Gestapo again unless you are spoken to. As for your sister," he continued, staring at Hela icily, "she ought to be shot for disobeying a cardinal rule."

Before he could say anything else, I started waving the papers inches from his face. "Please, sir," I begged, with a sinking feeling, "let her go this time. It will never happen again. Please make allowances for the fact that she is a Nicaraguan citizen."

"Your citizenship doesn't give you licence to be out in the streets after curfew," he retorted sternly. "Your exemption from wearing an armband is one privilege too many. I don't think you will enjoy it for very long."

He then turned to his colleague and the two of them seemed to deliberate in inaudible voices while I thought that the pounding of my heart could be heard in the silent room. Their talk over, the officer turned to me again. This time he practically roared when he addressed me. "Take her away! We don't feel like bothering with her tonight. But remember, all she has is a reprieve. And that goes for the rest of you. Get out!"

Taking Hela's limp hand into mine, I yanked her toward the door. We ran home without pausing to catch a breath. Once there, I threw myself into a deep armchair and, with my heart still beating wildly in my ribcage, turned to Hela, ready, in my fury, to harm her bodily. Holding back this impulse, I let out a verbal harangue at her. I was almost incoherent as I accused her of endangering her life and ours too and of being unreliable and irresponsible at a time when instant death was the order of the day. Unable to stop, I screamed on and on, but then, looking up at her face and seeing shame and contrition written all over it, I calmed down somewhat.

"I am so sorry," Hela kept stuttering between her sobs and whimpers. Slowly, my anger melted away and was replaced by all-consuming faintness. I got up, inched closer to where she was standing, and held my hand out to her. With a loud cry, she wrapped herself around my body, and we remained locked together until our tremors subsided. Mother came close, too, and comforted both of us. Nothing more was said.

~

With a sense of unreality, I travelled again to Krakow. I kept pushing our growing pile of papers under the noses of the German officials, only to be told again and again that a certain document was missing. Feeling defeated and embittered, I gazed at our passports, sullenly thinking that, while they may have saved our lives a few times, they were as useless as all the other documents for the purpose of emigration. Mercifully, the mail, although slowed down to a trickle, continued coming. After yet another unsuccessful trip to Krakow, we let Father know about our failure, and begged him to explore new ways. We knew that we were clutching at straws as we watched the prized passports lie idly, not bringing us any closer to our escape, for, as far as we could figure it out, there were no other ways left. And yet, full of apprehension and with a sense of loss hovering over us, we doggedly persisted in our inchoate pleas.

All the while, the combatant forces in Europe were locked in a mortal struggle. Hitler was allied with Hungary and some of the Balkan countries, including Romania, from where my uncle Leo and aunt Masza managed to escape with their children at the last minute. This we did not know at the time, but learned about later through a letter from Mr. Marejn. One of our ardent wishes had been to join them, our only family in the German-occupied zone, for we had a transit visa and train tickets to Romania. But this escape route was blocked as well.

Just as summer set in, rumours that Germany was about to break the non-aggression treaty with the Soviet Union and invade the territories it held were becoming persistent. We were not able to estimate or guess the implication of such an event, were it to occur. By common consensus among my friends, it would make very little difference in the Nazis' treatment of the Jews. I, personally, was hoping that, if the Germans occupied Białystok, we might get word from Grandfather and our family there, but I also had grave fears that they may already have been deported to Siberia or killed by the Russians or else that, if they were still alive, the Germans would finish them off.

In answer to our most recent requests for help, we received a letter from Father in which, as in many others, we detected deep worry inadequately concealed under the factual surface. It seemed to me that Father, too, felt that we were running out of time. Even so, he pulled off yet another coup: he wrote that he had been able to contact a branch of a functioning travel agency called MER (Mitteleuropäisches Reisebüro) and had been promised that they would try to get us permission to leave Poland. We dispatched a note to the M E R at their address in Warsaw immediately and, in about a week, got a reply stating that they would act on our behalf, but in order to speed up the proceedings, they would rather not wait for our documents to arrive, preferring that we come in person and bring them ourselves.

With a flicker of new hope rekindled in our hearts, the three of us wasted little time. I held another conference with my friends, who felt that we should take the train and that, since the rail service was badly disrupted, we should not hesitate to sleep over in a Polish hotel in Warsaw as foreigners. During our meeting, Lusia Maschler showed me her false papers, the first batch to be ready, and assured me that if our new efforts failed again, ours could be available immediately. The documents looked genuine enough — especially the ID card, with a different name and different data on it. For the second time, I placed our order, thinking what a bitter irony it was that, cover ourselves as we did on all sides, we continued to be vulnerable and helpless.

We boarded an overnight train for Warsaw within a day of the communication from the Mitteleuropäisches Reisebüro. The train was full of Poles, mainly farmers and civil servants, with a sprinkling of Germans in their military uniforms. Since the lights in the compartment were dimmed because of the blackout that had been imposed a few weeks earlier (simultaneously with the rumours about the imminent German-Soviet war), we could not see the other occupants of the car clearly. We just heard loud snores and the rustling of paper in which food had been wrapped. The place was hot and crowded and smelled of onions and unwashed bodies. People sat on all available seats and on the floor, so that we had to squeeze together on a bench for two that we had found empty upon boarding. Ruefully, I thought of the spanking clean train with its comfortable berths in our own compartment on our way to and from Białystok only two years earlier.

As the pale light of the dawn began to illuminate the shapes of the men and women around us, we stretched our stiff arms and legs and, feeling starved, ate the sandwiches we had brought. We brushed the soot and dirt of the coach from our clothes and prepared to debark. An hour later, the train pulled into the Warsaw station.

I thought I knew the city well, having visited often when Uncle Enoch, while still a bachelor, had lived and worked as a school principal there. I was totally unprepared for the sight that hit us as soon as we reached the first street. Warsaw looked like a ghost town. Some of it was practically in ruins. There were piles of rubble where houses had once stood. Here and there, a single wall, or half a wall, was standing intact with an exposed stove or table balancing precariously between the lone object and the heap of bricks below. The medieval buildings and courtyards on the once beautiful square called The Old Town were badly damaged, and many once splendid parks, their fences broken, were overgrown with weeds. The sight of the devastated city, partially destroyed by German bombs and artillery in the first few weeks of war, depressed and confused us so badly that we could hardly find our destination. Getting directions from a few shabby-looking people hurrying on their way to work, we finally arrived at the office of the MER, a small, dingy room grotesquely intact in an almost completely bombed out building.

With few preliminaries, I handed a clerk our documents, telling him that we would wait until they were notarially copied, as we were not going to return home without our originals. The procedure took almost two hours, and we spent the interval reminiscing how glittering Warsaw had been in peacetime. We wondered sadly how quickly the Warsaw ghetto, about whose starving and decimated Jews we had heard since it had been established so soon after the invasion, was deteriorating. We also speculated when and how to travel back home. Finally, the clerk returned and, with what looked like a forced smile, handed us back our original papers.

"We'll do our best for you," he said. "The documents are in perfect order. Not once during the war have I seen a similar dossier. Don't worry. Go home and wait for news from us." To my question how long it might take, he answered, "One to two months, at the longest."

I wanted to know whether I should continue my trips to Krakow, to which his reply was, "Absolutely not. We'll take care of all this. People on the outside are working for you. They will get better results than you."

Remembering all my abortive trips to the *Passstelle*, I saw the logic of his statement. We thanked him, left the unprepossessing office, and made our way back to the station.

We were never to see Warsaw again. Reluctant to stay overnight in a city of weird shapes and ghosts, we boarded a mid-afternoon train and, after another crowded and long ride, arrived home after midnight. We were so exhausted that we failed to notice it was long past curfew.

The following day, Klara came over and we exchanged our news. She told me that during our brief absence twenty young men, Jews and Poles on leave from the nearby forced labour camp of Pustków, had been rounded up and shot in the square near the Judenrat. I knew it was pointless to ask for the reason; all I wanted to know was whether any of our friends had been among them. Klara did not think so, and then she added excitedly another bit of news: Resia Goldberg and Adam Klimek, a refugee from Silesia who was her boyfriend, had run away on their "Aryan" papers. They intended to get married and live out the war by hiding in some other city. As they both looked gentile, Klara and I felt that their chances were good. We wished them well, although not without a touch of envy at what we considered their good fortune. Klara informed me, too, that she thought that all the false papers that the rest of us had ordered would be ready in a few weeks.

Early in June, we had an unexpected visitor. Somehow, Father had been able to persuade the Portuguese authorities that, since their country remained neutral, they might succeed where we had failed. The tall, distinguished-looking man with greying temples who appeared at our door introduced himself as an emissary from the

Portuguese Ministry of Foreign Affairs; he had been sent by his consulate outside of Portugal to travel to Poland and to request that the *Passstelle* grant us a release. To add weight to his intervention on our behalf, he brought updated transit visas from Portugal and official letters from the few southern Balkan countries not yet invaded by the Germans, granting us permission to travel through them. We were both taken aback and delighted by his mission, and allowed ourselves to hope that, between the double efforts of the MER and our astonishing visitor, we might at last get the long-withdrawn consent to leave from our unbending captors. The man stayed with us overnight and we spent the evening speaking about my father, whom he had never met but for whom he had the highest respect. He seemed to know all that my father had done to get us out of Poland. The following morning, he left for Krakow with a promise to return in a day or two.

Our excitement during the short wait reached fever pitch. I told my friends about Father's latest achievement, and they, too, got caught in my fervour. In their first optimistic responses I had heard in a long time, they beset me with requests and gave me instructions about what to do if (nobody yet dared say when) we got out. We were to contact all possible governments and institutions — including the Polish government-in-exile, the American Jewish Congress, the Jewish Agency, and the FBI — and persuade them to undertake a complex underground rescue. As though in a dream, we tossed around the most convoluted and unrealistic themes. Inspired by the brilliant example of my father, I promised everybody to do all I could do to carry out the multitude of requests and instructions.

It all came to naught barely two days later when, returning from Krakow, the kind and now subdued official gave us the bad news: all exit visas were frozen for an indefinite period. Our last ray of hope was extinguished when, in less than a week after his departure, we received a brief note from the MER confirming the news. Utterly discouraged and convinced that nothing further could be done, I decided not to bother about an official exit anymore.

Three or None

By a bizarre coincidence, our final awareness that we were cut off from Father and might die in Poland coincided with a political event which, though it had worldwide significance, had particular ramifications for Jews under German occupation and inevitably those of Tarnów. It was again Meyer Taub who, on June 22, brought us the news: the Germans had broken the Molotov-Ribbentrop Pact and had begun marching east. The Russians, taken by surprise, were in retreat along the entire demarcation line.

"We thought all of this would make no difference, but I have changed my mind after watching the Gestapo lately," said Meyer, breathless from running and shaking visibly. "If they win, they will celebrate by killing us off. If they lose, we'll be blamed first, with the same results. I am afraid that what we have seen till now has been only a prelude to the atrocities in store for us." I, too, was filled with a sense of foreboding coupled with my despair at seeing all of Father's valiant efforts turn to ashes, and could only nod in mute agreement.

For the next few days, there hung about Tarnów an ominous aura of déjà vu, as on that fateful September 7, 1939, the roar of Nazi tanks and the heavy thud of the infantry's marching boots drowned out all other sounds. Again, it was impossible to cross the streets over which the armoured divisions kept rolling in a never-ending stream. The only difference was that, this time, there were no curious onlookers lining the sidewalks stretching for a glimpse of a smiling young face under a helmet. The sidewalks were deserted. People huddled in their homes and looked for comfort by staying close and keeping outside the events.

Indoors, the mood was that of mourning. Each group tried to deal with the new threat in its own way. In our building, those engaged in "essential labour" clutched their employment cards as a talisman as though coaxing the lifeless paper to be their salvation. The few among our neighbours who were pious turned east and swayed as they chanted prayers and sent up to God their supplications to save them even as He had saved the Children of Israel from perdition in the past. My friends gathered in our apartment where we, too, gave vent to our feelings of impending doom and our sense of defeat by interspersing our talks with the humming of old Zionist songs, as if to draw spiritual sustenance from the memories of a happy past. As the menacing German tanks roared outside on their relentless march eastward, inside the Jewish homes the atmosphere was that of a shiva.

I had neither eaten nor slept for the first forty-eight hours of the new German offensive and that evening succumbed to a dizzy spell and fainted. My friends rallied around me, and when I came to, Mother's and Hela's contorted faces helped to rouse me from my semi-consciousness. With a pang, I realized that I was letting them down, and, putting my arms around them, told them not to worry about me. I chided myself for what I considered an acute case of moral weakness. It was then that I made a firm resolve that, come what may, I would try never to indulge in the luxury of self-pity or self-indulgence. I felt that Father had entrusted me with the lives of all three of us, and I was not going to, at least not willingly, let him down. In that emotionally charged moment, the feeling I had carried with me since the onset of the war became a clear reality in my mind: as far as it was in my power, either all three of us would come to Father intact, or none of us would make it. "Three or none" was to be my unspoken motto from then on.

After all the Panzertruppen (armoured troops) had left Tarnów behind, we kept hearing the announcements on our solitary German radio station about the rapid German conquests and the brilliant military strategies of the Wehrmacht advancing in the Soviet Union. We were witnessing another blitzkrieg. The Germans went from victory to victory.

Our correspondence with Father via Abe Cohn and Herman Marejn continued sporadically. The earlier burning questions about when and how we were going to be rescued had ceased. It was now a matter of self-preservation, unaided, within our shrinking world. Our letters became confined to expressions of love and hopes for Father's well-being but conveyed little about our lot. We had stopped asking for further interventions. In response, Father continued to encourage us by promising new endeavours toward our common goal and even by sending us renewed Nicaraguan passports, valid for two more years, and new transit visas. Though grateful to him for his never-ending work on our behalf, we nevertheless greeted the new documents with indifference as we had had ample occasion to find out that they were going to do us no good.

I reregistered with the Polish authorities and then had to face the Gestapo again. This time I went by myself, as I saw no reason for Mother and Hela to be put through the ordeal, too. The interview went better than I had expected, with fewer histrionics than before. A bored-looking official barely listened to my explanations, took the passports, typed for each what proved to be another *Bescheinigung*, confirmation, and handed me the finished products gingerly, with the tips of his fingers. It was only then that he broke the silence and said, "Ah, so the three foreign Jewesses are still with us. What a pity! We'll have to do something about it soon." He waved me on with the customary, "Raus, Jüdin" (Out, Jewess).

We kept listening to the news, seeking the smallest sign that the Allies had stopped Hitler's troops somewhere or had gained a measure of military supremacy, but the opposite held true. There had been no turning point in the war. The radio offered no solace. The Germans were winning on all fronts. They were pushing deep into the Soviet Union, breaking all resistance on the way. Daily, the announcements kept boasting that since their Luftwaffe had completely crippled Great Britain from the air, the invasion was imminent, and success assured. We heard something about the British evacuation at Dunkirk the year before, but it did not seem significant enough to change the military situation or ours and so we had to lay to rest our lingering myth that the Allies would come to our rescue before it was too late.

Throughout the rest of that summer, a new pattern in the killings of Jews began to emerge. Nightly, long after curfew, a Nazi officer carrying two guns, one in each hand, would break down the doors to as many as a dozen Jewish apartments. Aided by his guards, he would demand to be told where the hidden money and goods were. As he usually got no answer, he would slap the Jew's face and kick him with his boots. He would order the man to dress, while the others beat the rest of the family and filled their pockets and specially prepared bags with anything that was portable. The victim would then be pushed outside and made to wait, under guard, while the officer rounded up, in similar fashion, the others selected for the nightly quota. The group would then be taken either to one of the larger stores, the big town square near the Judenrat or a conveniently located yard. The spectacle would invariably end, after a brief interrogation, with successive shots from both revolvers. A single night might yield Malottki forty to fifty dead Jews whose bodies were carted away and thrown into a common grave that other Jews had been forced to dig. The common grave, making its first appearance late that summer, was there to stay and proliferate. And yet, blindly and stubbornly, those of us who had so far escaped getting caught clung tenaciously to the "not me" attitude.

Soon, the Nazis organized a Jewish police force (Ordnungsdienst) from among able-bodied Jewish men. From what I could see, those chosen enjoyed no special privileges. They were just a handy tool for the Nazis to speed up their now almost daily raids, as they, along with the Jewish Council members, were ordered to lead the way to Jewish dwellings and to round up certain Jews at the Nazis' bidding.

One member of our small group, Jurek Bayer, had been selected to be a member of the Ordnungsdienst, as had Israel Schmuckler, Hela's boyfriend. We had long ceased poking fun at Jurek's gauche behaviour and naïveté. The Nazi regime was a great leveller. By making us focus only on our mortality, it made us oblivious to and almost obliterated our individual traits, good and bad, thus undermining our essential humanity. Jurek, like the rest of us, was a mere digit in the Nazis' scrupulously accurate accounting system.

On hearing the news, he came to our apartment and began bewailing his fate, saying that he should have gone east with the others rather than become a stooge for the enemy. "How can I go around collecting my own people and delivering them into the hands of the murderers? Why, it amounts to fratricide," he moaned. I tried to console him, quoting from our much-neglected moral philosophers that what he did under the pain of death was neither collaboration nor betrayal. Meyer joined me, adding with a touch of bitterness that Jurek's new position would at best prolong his life by a bit, rather than spare it. Not much comforted by our reactions, Jurek went off, deeply depressed, to report for his hateful duties.

~

Ever since Germany had captured all of Poland previously held by the Soviet Union, we were expecting either to see or hear about our friends who had escaped east at the onset of the war. It took some time to get the news. And it was not what we had hoped for.

In one group that came back were Zyga and many others; they told us that a large number of Jewish refugees had been deported by the Russians to Siberia, and that their lot remained unknown. We barely had a week in which to welcome them and discuss what had happened to us under the two different regimes.

For the few days following Zyga's return, he and I were constantly together. Our time was filled with a gamut of emotions — from
deep depression about our now common and precarious situation to
exultation at having discovered that we still felt strongly about each
other. In the preceding months and years, I had put Milek completely
out of my mind. It was Father who, thinking Milek was still my boyfriend, had been periodically mentioning his whereabouts. It seemed
that Milek had left Glasgow and was fighting with the British Army.
I later learned that he became part of the army's Palestine Regiment
in North Africa and then eventually settled in Palestine. He had been
keeping up a regular correspondence with my father. He hoped to
be reunited with me after the war, Father wrote repeatedly. Since, to
me, the phrase "after the war" had become unmentionable, I recoiled
from it in anger and frustration. At the same time, I was conflicted, as
I continued to feel vaguely guilty about Milek, especially because his
parents, still alive in Tarnów, had been treating me as though I were
to be their future daughter-in-law, showering me with kindness and
gifts of beautiful fabrics they had hidden from their dry goods store.
Even so, I defiantly convinced myself that Milek was no longer a part
of my world while Zyga was.

My interlude with Zyga was one of great intimacy. We desperately
clung together in any place that afforded privacy. Throwing our parents' strict sexual taboos aside, we made love, unrestrained and fierce
almost to the point of violence, drowning our fears and forgetting,
for a few glorious moments, what had become of us and what was
still to come. I found myself physically as fulfilled by Zyga as I had
always been dazzled by his erudite and brilliant mind. For us, the
lovemaking was our supreme carpe diem and we had no thought of
tomorrow.

Abruptly, the ecstatic episode came to an end. One night, the Gestapo, aided by all police branches including the reluctant Ordnungsdienst, snatched every person they could find from the group that
had returned from Lwów and had them brought to the large inner

courtyard of the building at 4 Lwowska Street where Zyga lived. Amid mothers' shouts for mercy and the wails of the children, they were all arranged, through shoving and pushing, into neat rows facing the firing squad at the yard entrance. They were all gunned down, except for the last row. This one was made to march behind several carts, already filled with corpses by the Ordnungsdienst and pulled by other Jews, to the Jewish cemetery nearby. There, the people in the last row, mainly young men, performed the final task of their lives. Hurried on by rifle butts, lashes and blows, they dug a deep and large grave. They were then ordered to throw the bodies, grotesquely piled atop the carts, into the gaping hole. Their job done, they were told to kneel at the edge of the grave, facing it, where they, in turn, were shot down by the firing squad. The Ordnungsdienst men and the other Jews who had been assigned to the job went to work with spades and shovels, covering the grave with the freshly dug up earth. The dead included some of my parents' acquaintances and my friends. Zyga was among them.

There was no time for grief and mourning. Those of us who were still alive began to realize that the murderous process we had been witnessing — encompassing increasingly large numbers of people and occurring at more frequent intervals — was not a part of some small war of attrition but an element in a premeditated, carefully calculated plan to annihilate us all. What we could not imagine was how that plan, however meticulously designed and followed, could possibly be accomplished.

All we could do was pray for time. There were too many of us left, we speculated, to be decimated with great speed. We consoled ourselves that we would somehow circumvent the Nazis' design on us either by escaping on "Aryan" papers or by keeping out of their way as much as possible and by waiting for a possible turn in the vagaries of the war to the advantage of the Allies. If they were only to begin scoring some victories, we felt, they might do something about our plight, of which we were sure they undoubtedly had knowledge.

We could not waste our time dwelling on our questions and doubts; we proceeded with all speed to prepare what we saw as our only avenue of escape — our specialists in forgery had completed their task, and on a bleak afternoon, Meyer smuggled our "Aryan" papers into our home. I looked them over carefully and duly admired a job well done: ironically, the papers looked as official as our Nicaraguan passports. We hid them in a false bottom of a chest of drawers, but not before we had memorized and rehearsed all our new information so that we were able to recite it without the slightest hesitation at a moment's notice. With great bitterness I marvelled how Mother, Hela and I, possessors of three documented identities, had actually no identity at all in the eyes of the Nazis, who were hunting us down like animals to be trapped.

At home, we began to discuss one escape scheme after another, but found each flawed and pitifully inadequate. We were now on much more dangerous ground than we had been while working, side by side with Father, on the legal and official ways of leaving. Nevertheless, we decided that, if we could arrange it with our milkmaid, Zosia, we would slip out of the house under the cover of darkness and seek refuge in her farmhouse only a few kilometres outside Tarnów. During her most recent visit, we had divulged our alternate plan to escape with her aid and had asked her for help, which she had promptly promised. She thought there might be a number of hiding places on her farm where, if lucky, we could stay till the war was over. We now had to wait for Zosia's next visit to arrange the details with her.

The trouble was that Zosia had been coming infrequently, both because the risk of smuggling food to Jews had increased and because supplies of farm products had run very low. Acute shortage of most staples had set in, caused by the Germans' plunder of the outlying farms and their order to the farmers to submit a large percentage of their produce for the consumption of the occupational forces. There was little left for the civilian population. However, a black market in food had been quickly organized and operating for a while now, and as we still had our tobacco and cigarettes, a small supply of the much sought-after American dollars and some pieces of jewellery, we managed to exchange those for food, mostly with Poles who became the intermediaries.

This last method of exchange came to an abrupt end when eventually a proclamation was issued that all Jews were to bring their valuables — including fur coats, jewellery, gold, silver, any Polish money above five hundred złoty and all foreign currency — to the swastika-adorned *Kreishauptmannschaft* (the district headquarters) on the penalty of death. For days, the Jews were hauling all the requisitioned goods to the designated place, relinquishing their personal possessions to the authorities in charge and returning home empty-handed. Here and there an attempt was made to hide some designated items. As it turned out, subsequent events severely curtailed any search for them, and many a valuable cache remained under Tarnów's soil, never to be retrieved. The three of us, along with Klara and her parents, stole out one early morning to a neighbour's former lumberyard where we dug a hole into which we put some silver and pieces of jewellery. We never had the opportunity to go near it again and in the end forgot the exact location, and even the existence, of our hiding place.

Meanwhile, a small number of Jews, some of my friends among them, disappeared without a trace. My first thought after each disappearance had been that the missing person had been killed by the Nazis; the chaos was such that it was often impossible to know for days who was dead and who was alive. However, part of the puzzle was soon cleared up when Meyer, through his secret connection with his so far reliable pipeline, told us that our missing friends had fled to various destinations, purporting to be Poles. I found out much later that a few survived by joining the Polish underground or being hidden by friendly gentiles. Most of them, however, were eventually caught, submitted to more than the usual dose of brutal torture, and gunned down. The stories did little to encourage me in my wish to escape with the help of Zosia. I thought that if it were difficult for a single person to remain hidden, it would be nearly impossible for three. Even as I was thrashing about between my decisions and indecisions, I held fast to the vow I had made to myself earlier of "three or none."

A Last Letter

In early December 1941, we heard the first of the many announcements to be repeated on the radio throughout the day that the treacherous United States, in conspiracy with the despicable international Jewry, had entered the war. There were some gleeful comments about the mighty United States navy having been almost completely destroyed by the brave Japanese in a place called Pearl Harbor, and about the French and English now having an ineffectual clay-footed giant as their new ally.

Whatever political or military mileage was to be made from the latest twist of the already tangled events, and however beneficial the act may have been, or potentially was to be for the Allied cause, it nonetheless spelled further disaster to us. We remembered only too clearly what had happened just a few months earlier when the Soviet-German war had broken out.

Personally, we received our hardest blow yet now that the letter route to Abe Cohn was cut off. All we could do was to write sporadically to the Marejns in Stockholm, who, we hoped, would relay news of us to Father; the return mail was dispatched in a similar manner. It was a roundabout and agonizingly slow process, but we had no other choice, at least not until the time when even this thin thread of communication was abruptly cut off. At the same time, the food parcels stopped coming and, to Mr. Marejn's persistent inquiries whether we were getting them, we had to answer in the negative. For the first time since September 1939, there were days when we went hungry. This, however, we considered a minor inconvenience. Together with all the other Jews in Tarnów, we knew, without having any hard facts to support our knowledge, that we were entering our most devastating period of brutalization and degradation at the hands of the Nazis.

Our intuition was correct. The Gestapo now had a new *cause célèbre*. We received a hint of what was in store for us barely forty-eight hours after the radio announcement on the United States entering the war. All the Gestapo brass, accompanied by dozens of SS men and police, spread out fan-like through the city. Each column broke down the doors of tens of Jewish homes, and the officer in charge shot, without a word, the first two people who staggered toward him and pushed the rest of the family out into the street. Converging from all directions, hundreds of men, women and children were made to march to the Jewish cemetery where they were ordered to dig huge graves for themselves and were then speedily shot. As their bodies were being thrown into a hole by the newly established workforce of Jewish gravediggers, and as the corpses of those shot on their doorsteps, brought to the cemetery in death carts, were being added to the pile, obscenities were shouted about the Jews' responsibility for the move by the United States. From our apartment, we saw the death carts loaded with bodies and kept averting our eyes from the sight, fearing that our turn might come at any moment. By another quirk of fortune, no one came to our door, and we were spared this time again.

By this time, our group had dwindled to virtually three: Meyer, Klara and myself; our other classmates, Regina Feigenbaum, Lusia Maschler and Jurek Bayer were somewhat on the periphery of our group. Meyer, especially, had stepped in to fill the void, and unexpectedly, I found out that he did it as more than a friend.

One day, he came to our apartment to discuss possible dates of our respective escapes on "Aryan" papers. Selflessly, and against my protests, he was going to wait till we made our move before he arranged his own. He and I were alone at the time, and for once, he was not offering and discarding plans, but seemed subdued and strangely ill at ease. When I noticed his uncharacteristic mood and inquired about it, he blurted out quickly, as though afraid that he might not say it all if he stopped, that he had been in love with me ever since he had first become my classmate at the Safah Berurah. He had kept his feelings to himself because he had been too inhibited and shy to voice them; and anyway, I had been involved first with Milek and then with Zyga, and he knew that he had no chance. Now, in his opinion, the situation was drastically changed. There were only the two of us left, and we might die any minute. "Why don't we become lovers," he stuttered with a mixture of hope and anguish, "when there is no time to lose?"

I was completely unprepared for this turn of events, for I felt no physical attraction to Meyer and had never thought of him as more than a dear and devoted friend. I tried to tell him so gently, adding that our relationship was unique: it had more depth and significance than any other I had known before for we were as one in sharing insights and facing our common danger. It took me a long time to persuade Meyer to leave things between us as they were. Feeling rejected, he burst into tears, cursed our lot, and confessed to me that, were it not for the moments he hoped he would snatch with me once in a while, he would readily kill himself. As I soothed him by saying that we would be close and together at every available opportunity, I realized that the sudden mention of suicide had aroused my interest. I asked him how he would do it.

"You know my older sister, Rosa, who is a nurse in what remains of the Jewish hospital? I can get pills from her. In fact, I have started collecting them," he added, drying his tears. "Do you think you can get some for us?" I asked with a tremor in my voice, startled at my own question. "I'll find out and let you know," he answered. "I have heard that other people are collecting pills from friendly pharmacists and doctors, too. But remember, they have to be thought of only as the last resort. There may still be a chance for your family. I am sure your father is continuing his efforts to get you out." "It's too late for that," I said firmly, as I could not tolerate the thought of yet another futile attempt and a certain failure, "and you may as well know it. I have vowed that the three of us must stick together. We may get killed one by one, as I have no control over the Nazi minds and their triggers. However, if, by some miracle, we survive, it won't be one or two of us that will get out of this hell. It'll be all or none. Is it a deal about the pills?" "It's a deal," Meyer answered dejectedly, "but let's forget about them for now."

When he left, I burst into a sardonic laughter. What a revelation it had been! I had made an amorous conquest, was the owner of Jewish, "Aryan" and Nicaraguan papers, and maybe, before long, I would have enough barbiturates to lay to rest all our assorted nationalities. On reflection, however, the idea of the pills seemed appealing because it was novel. I knew that under no circumstances would I seek, or suggest to Mother and Hela, self-inflicted death.

~

By the spring of 1942, Malottki and Nowak had been transferred; now the new command were men by the names of Josef Palten and Wilhelm Rommelmann, who, with lightning swiftness, earned the reputation as the chief henchman and executioner of Tarnów.

Rommelmann was joined in his command by Karl Oppermann, who was already in Tarnów, and along with Palten, the triumvirate was ruthless. Meyer had quickly figured out that these men had committed atrocities in other towns and Jewish ghettos. It soon became evident that massacres on a much larger scale than those executed earlier were being readied to be put into effect.

The principal task of the Judenrat and the Ordnungsdienst soon became burying the bodies of Jews daily gunned down by Rommelmann. The rattling of death carts became commonplace as Rommelmann, with a style and flourish all his own, elevated the shootings into slow-motion art and went about them like a choreographer arranging an orchestrated dance. His method was to saunter down a street at a leisurely pace, stop Jewish men and women, often with small children in their arms, and say something to them softly. Acting on the mellifluous instructions, the people thus approached would kneel down on the sidewalk. Then, on another word from Rommelmann, they would turn around with their backs to him. After savouring the spectacle long enough to satisfy his sense of drama, Rommelmann would shoot them, one by one, directly behind their ears. He would then defile each corpse by slowly rolling it face up with his boots and digging into the dead faces with his spurs. He was often joined by his large entourage, which at that time included German women. Laughing diabolically at the top of his voice and swinging a whip that he would bring down on anyone who happened by, he would gather his company, hop into a waiting Jeep or horse cart, and leave amid crude jokes to seek out victims in another neighbourhood.

Our correspondence with the Marejns in Sweden had been more difficult of late, but I decided to write to them anyway. I let them know about the enormity of the change in our situation. I told them in veiled German that we were going through a particularly difficult early summer. The heat was more intense and the humidity more oppressive than at any time since the war began. We felt constantly as though we were on fire, and our bodies were drenched with perspiration, making sleep impossible. All three of us had developed chronic bronchitis, which made it hard for us to breathe, and I was suffering from frequent and profuse nosebleeds that refused to stop. Our doctor had told us that there was no known treatment for our assorted ailments. We hoped that the Marejns and Izak were well, and thought that perhaps our family in Nicaragua might consult a physician there and send us some medication from Managua, as there were few available in Tarnów.

To our surprise, we received an answer within a week. We sensed that this unexpected letter might be the last one from Sweden (it was). We read it carefully, examining it for possible clues about Father's further plans. Mr. Marejn reassured us that Izak and the family were all well. The news about our ill health had caused everybody grave concern, and Izak was doing everything in his power to send us effective medication. He also wanted to know whether the clothes that had been sent to us earlier were still fitting or whether we had to resort to wearing our old things dating back to 1939. If so, perhaps new, Nicaraguan-made winter coats could be mailed to us to protect us against the cold of the coming winter.

"What do you think Mr. Marejn means by the Nicaraguan coats?" I asked Mother and Hela. "Our passports are valid, so he can't possibly mean more of the same."

Mother thought for a while and then shook her head from side to side. "I don't understand it at all," she moaned. "I don't understand anything. Nobody can help us anymore. I wish that the end would come quickly. It would be better than to be separated and be sent to different camps. I am so tired…" She let her voice trail and turned to stare at the window. After a few moments of silence, Hela exclaimed with sudden excitement, "I have an idea! Mr. Marejn means that Father will ask the Nicaraguan government to get in touch with some German officials in Berlin and request our exchange for Germans. Remember what the Gestapo man mumbled about repatriation when we brought in our passport the first time?"

I thought that Hela's interpretation was brilliant and, for a moment, got swept up in her excitement. However, it did not take us long to regain our sense of reality and separate it from fantasy.

"No, Hela," I said sadly. "We are not heading for any exchange. The Germans have enough non-Jewish foreigners to exchange for Germans without looking for them among Polish Jews who might not even be alive. Let's not entertain any more illusions. It's bad for us to raise our hopes at this point."

And so, Mr. Marejn's last letter remained unexplained, and we soon forgot all about it as we had to give our undivided attention to a new and unexpected event.

In Seven Days

It was June 10, 1942, that marked the climax of the decimation of Jews and spelled the beginning of what was to be the end of the Tarnów Jewry. We were awakened early that morning by a loud ringing of our front doorbell. "The Gestapo!" we motioned to one another, struggling into some clothes. Opening it, we were relieved to find a young Ordnungsdienst man standing outside with a list in his hand. He began to speak in a carefully measured monotone: "All Jews between the ages of fourteen to fifty are to report today to their respective Arbeitskommandos (work details) where they are classified by the work they do. Let's see now," he added, trying to sound neutral as his eyes were scanning the list, "I don't see your names. You'd better be there at 3:00 p.m. with your work permits." "What is it for?" I wanted to know. He hesitated for a minute or so. "I can't really say," he replied, not looking at us. "It has something to do with a mass action that all the police units are planning to put into effect tomorrow." "No!" I screamed, aroused from my immobility into an uncontrollable fury. "We are not going anywhere. We are Nicaraguans. Do you hear? Nicaraguan subjects. Neutral foreigners. We are exempt. See?"

We pulled out our passports and the Gestapo registration certificates with the big stamp on them. The policeman was visibly upset by my outburst. "I am merely carrying out my orders. And you'd better save your talking for where it counts," he said in a hollow voice. "Do as you please. But remember that Jews are forbidden to leave their homes right after their return from their work commandos until further notice on the penalty of immediate death." With a shrug of his shoulders, he turned back and descended the stairs.

Within an hour, the town was electrified by a sense, vague at first but gaining momentum as the day advanced, that something unprecedented was afoot. The streets were swarming with new faces and a variety of uniforms that had not been seen in the town before. Meyer had ferreted out somewhere that dozens of specially assigned SS and police units had arrived from Krakow to swell the already increased local contingents, and that the entire Schutzpolizei was out in force. Many neighbourhoods, according to the latest reports, had been cordoned off. Down in the streets, Jews were scurrying in all directions to reach their *Arbeitskommandos*, go through the as yet unknown formalities, and return home as ordered.

After curfew we were able to find out what had happened at the various offices. The young, the able-bodied, and those working at high-priority jobs had had their work cards stamped with a large Gestapo seal bearing the *Hoheitsstempel*, that is, the high stamp of sovereignty. All the others, women, children, the old and the sick, had their ID cards stamped with a small Gestapo seal marked simply K. Everyone had been told to go directly home, stay indoors and await further instructions.

It was clear that, for the first time, an organized "selection" (a dreaded word that was to make all Jewish hearts freeze with terror in the months to come), not of a segment, but of all Jews had taken place. Sitting with our neighbours the Holoszytzes and Kleinhandlers well into the night, all we could surmise after lengthy debates was that we were now facing the implementation of a carefully devised master plan to annihilate us all wholesale. What we still could not or were loath to conceptualize was by what means, other than group shootings on the spot or in concentration camps, and to what extent, it could be carried out. The elimination of Jews might become more systematic than it had been before, as we were now clearly classified in certain categories, but there were still at least thirty thousand of us and we could not imagine a way of disposing of such a large number quickly. Of course, we had no other clues than those we had already witnessed.

That night Hela, Mother and I went to bed with the passports inside our night clothes. After checking that our "Aryan" papers were safely out of sight, we tried to get some sleep. Instead, we spent many hours anticipating what the next day might bring while nervously holding our papers.

Early in the morning on June 11, we saw from our windows members of the combined police and SS squads enter house after house and re-emerge within minutes preceded by large numbers of Jews whom they kicked and prodded with rifle butts. Before I could figure out whether there was any pattern to the selection, I recoiled from the window as I saw a small, fully armed detachment enter our building. We huddled together for a few seconds of comforting physical contact but, abruptly, our door was forced open by a heave of strong shoulders and we saw, framed in the doorway, three helmeted SS men pointing their rifles at us. I froze for a few split seconds, then quickly recovered from my state of numbness and touched Hela and Mother lightly on either side of me. Responding to the signal we had rehearsed untold times, we whipped our papers out of our pockets and held them with outstretched arms as close to the men as we dared. One of them detached himself from the group, grabbed the papers, and, with the rifle still pointing in our direction, stepped back to rejoin his comrades, so that they could read our documents together. Our tension mounted so that we thought we could not bear it any longer, and Mother's legs were beginning to give out. Hela and I quickly placed her between us and supported her so that she would remain upright, for we were afraid of what the consequences of her fall might be.

Still holding our papers, the stocky leader of the group screamed at us at the top of his powerful voice, "I see you are exempt from wearing armbands! This will do for today, but I don't guarantee that your exemptions will be honoured tomorrow or the day after or the day after that. Friends of ours may come to get you any time this week. There," he added contemptuously, "keep your precious papers." With these words, he flung them toward the ceiling from where they fluttered down to the floor, scattering all over the foyer. Still in a state of shock, we gathered them wherever they fell while the three SS men quickly ripped through the apartment, except for the room of the German whose name was on the door, opening cupboards and drawers, and finally getting away with some of our clothes and cans of imported food from our few remaining parcels.

Rousing ourselves from our stupor, we rushed to the windows overlooking the street. The sight was not very different from similar ones we had seen, except that the numbers of Jews were larger than any before. An unruly procession of Jewish women, children and the elderly, with a sprinkling of young and middle-aged, was moving up the street. On either side of it, policemen kept watch over the prisoners. We heard sporadic gunshots, but the crowd was so thick that we could not make out who and how many had been felled. It was only when the group had rounded the corner and was out of sight that we could see the bodies sprawled on the pavement. They were mainly those of women and little children. They did not stay there long. Within minutes, two Jews pulling a wagon picked them up, flung them on top, and carted them away. After the mingled noises subsided, dead silence descended on the street.

We were alone in the apartment and did not have the courage to make rounds of the building to find out how many of our neighbours were still there. All through the afternoon and during the entire week, we remained confined to our rooms. The SS and the other officers did not return to our street, but, day in and day out, we kept hearing in the distance continuous pistol and rifle shots and what sounded like rapid machine-gun fire.

When, after a few days, unable to cope with our isolation and un-certainty any longer, we stole down to the Kleinhandlers' apartment, we found them as ignorant about what was happening as we were. The only bit of heartrending news we learned was that the younger of the Holoszytz boys, four-year-old Marek, had come out of a cupboard where Mrs. Holoszytz had hidden both her sons, and had been taken away by the SS. Sick with grief for our neighbours, we wondered how we were going to face them.

On the fourth evening, Mr. Kleinhandler, who was a member of the Judenrat and had a special permit to go out when summoned by the Gestapo, was able to enlighten us a little more. All he was able to tell us, though, with his face deathly white and his voice a hoarse whisper, was that a mass action was taking place every day in the large Platz (square) adjacent to the Judenrat offices. Thousands of Jews were kneeling there daily. There were guards posted at all four corners of the Platz, and many Jews were sprayed with machine-gun fire while others were taken in groups to the railway station. Beyond that, he had no information other than that two apartments in our building had been completely emptied of their residents, and that the so-called action, now also alternately being called *Aussiedlung*, re-settlement, would be called off on June 18. It seemed, too, that every-body whose identity card was marked with a K had been taken to the square and that, as I had guessed while looking at the street earlier, some who had the *Hoheitsstempel* had not been spared either.

Meyer, who was among those allowed to remain for the time being, came running up our steps on the day after the "action" had come to a stop. He was almost unrecognizable. His clothes were tat-tered and his cheeks sunken, covered with the stubble of a week-long beard. His eyes were red-rimmed and burning as though on fire. He was trembling all over and was unsteady on his feet. Wiping the beads of sweat on his forehead, he sat down, resting his head between his two hands, then using the table for support. When he began to speak his voice was halting and there were long pauses between his phrases and sentences.

We learned that his parents had been taken away on the second day. So were, at one time or another, Klara, Regina and Lusia, and almost all of our remaining friends. He himself had stolen out of his apartment and had found a dark nook in the shadow of one of the houses surrounding the square where, perched on a rung of an abandoned ladder, he had an unobstructed view of the proceedings. It had been very difficult to identify his parents in the undulating tide of the kneeling human bodies, but he had finally spotted them. He had fixed his gaze on them until they were ordered to march with their contingent to the railway station. By a gruesome coincidence, Milek's parents had been part of that group. Filled with anguish, he had remained in his place, and, returning to his watch every morning, had seen the entire selection from first to last. And so, he was able to fill in the details we had been unable to get from Mr. Kleinhandler.

With the aid of the Ordnungsdienst, the SS and other Nazi officers had brought the victims to the square in groups of two hundred and fifty to five hundred. There, literally looked down on by the Gestapo who stood on a stage-like platform, with Rommelmann in command, they had been ordered by a series of policemen to kneel and put their hands over their heads. The Gestapo were on the alert for those not obeying the orders fast enough. In each such case the people, especially mothers who could not or would not put their infants down, were shot by rifles or sprayed by machine-gun fire. Thousands were perishing in this manner, with Rommelmann adding a Mephistophelian touch to the proceedings.

Each day, the dead had been driven away at regular intervals in new and larger carts specially built to speed up the action. The staggering schedule was precision-timed: the square would be emptied and ready to receive a new contingent as soon as it had been cleared of the preceding one. The marches to the station, too, had been made to coincide with the changeovers in the square. Each time the square would be cleared of the dead, a group would simultaneously be taken to the station. There, people were made to stand sideways in overcrowded, sealed cattle cars. The trains headed east. For an entire week, Jewish blood ran like a red river in the gutters all around the square, forcing its way into adjacent streets. In seven days, approximately twelve thousand of Tarnów's Jews were eliminated through death or deportation.

Meyer had more horrors to divulge, although they were as yet unconfirmed. He had heard through his grapevine that similar "actions" had taken place in other towns where Jews had lived either in ghettos or still scattered among the gentiles. The procedure was the same. The survivors of the selection — those not shot on the spot — had also been sent east where, according to rumours, they were being systematically murdered. There was some vague talk about the majority of the inmates heading for a camp with newly erected gas chambers, about black, thick and stinking smoke from their chimneys visible for many kilometres. The name of a new camp, Belzec, joined the names of camps already familiar to us: Auschwitz, Buchenwald and Dachau.

We held our breath during Meyer's long recitation. The story was too mind-boggling to believe. Even Meyer, bearer of the bad news and a hardened pessimist, while conceding that it would be a diabolically clever method of getting rid of the Jews en masse, thought that the reports about death camps had been exaggerated. Our neighbours, shaken to their very core by the events of the week, were of the same opinion.

With tragic irony, when we received the answer to our interminable "how?" we, the Jews of Tarnów, put our powerful denial mechanism to work for self-preservation. If we had given credence to what we heard, if we had believed that we, too, were slated for the gas chambers, we probably could not have coped with the relentless demands of everyday survival.

Hour to Hour

On the morning after the June action, a proclamation appeared simultaneously in all prominent and highly visible places. It stated that within the next forty-eight hours all Jews were to leave their homes, taking whatever they could carry in their hands or with the help of pushcarts, and move into a ghetto. A map of the ghetto followed. It was a small, squarish area corresponding roughly to the old Jewish district. No living quarters were being allotted. The Jews were to settle that problem among themselves. The ghetto would be surrounded by barbed wire and guarded by Polish police on the outside and the Ordnungsdienst on the inside. No one would be allowed to leave, except to go to work under guard in the morning and return in the same manner in the evening through the only four available gates. An attempt to leave was punishable by death, as was any attempt to enter by unauthorized gentiles.

The reaction among the Jews was swift and mixed. While some felt that, once settled in the ghetto, they would be left alone provided they did essential work, others were convinced that it was a further step toward faster and easier annihilation: to have Jews concentrated in one area would make them readily accessible; besides, it would make escape on "Aryan" papers virtually impossible. To add weight to their arguments, the pessimists cited examples of other ghettos, already in existence, where Jews had certainly not been allowed to live out their days peacefully. While the issue was hotly debated, time was running out. And so, all discussions were put aside while we all began to prepare to go.

As soon as we read the proclamation, I knew that my last chance to clarify our status with the Gestapo had come and that I must not waste any time. I collected Mother's and Hela's documents, added them to mine and, my pulse racing wildly, ran to the Gestapo headquarters. Although I was fully aware that I might not come out of there alive, I rose above my fear, for I was compelled by the need to know, once and for all, where we stood. The establishment of the ghetto, gruesome as I thought it to be in its implications, was, for my purposes, the last straw.

I remember that it was a balmy, sun-drenched day and that, just before turning the knob of the dreaded door, I stopped for a moment, struck by the profusion of colourful, blooming flowers in front of the building. My mind darted back to our pre-war hikes in the country, when the boys had picked flowers and the girls had woven them for garlands around their hair, but I forced myself to shut out the memories and think of my mission.

I entered the now familiar room and felt the gaze of the bureaucrat seated behind the desk fix on me with intensity. He cleared his throat and said, "You are a Jewess, yes?" I did not know whether it was a statement or a question but decided to treat it as a question. "Yes," I began to answer, "But...." He interrupted me and wanted to know why I was not wearing an armband. His hand was touching the gun lying at the edge of the desk. Without stopping to pause for breath, I blurted out my usual litany about being Nicaraguans, exempt from wearing the armband and eligible for an exchange transport, and then, stunned, as on earlier occasions, by my verbal calisthenics, I stopped without a further word. He wanted to know where the others were. I told him that they were at home, awaiting a ruling.

"What do you want?" he asked finally, his hand still on the gun.

"I have come to ask that we may be exempted from moving into the ghetto," I said, practically under my breath.

On hearing this, he threw his head back and shook with laughter, which ended in a coughing spell. Red-faced from the exertion, he returned to stare at me and retorted with heavy sarcasm, the mirth still lingering in his voice, "The masquerade is over for you, pig. Get out of here and head straight for the ghetto with all the other scum. And let me not catch you without an armband. The exemption is hereby rescinded. Out!" At this point, he let go of the gun and made a gesture with his hand as though slitting his throat.

I gathered the papers and, before hurrying home, had another look at the flowers, certain that I would never see the hues of nature again. Mother and Hela, who had been nervously pacing our apartment during my absence, greeted me at the door, asking me the question with their eyes before putting it into words.

"We've got to go. Let's hurry. It is late already," I said. We pulled the armbands out of the drawer into which we had flung them after getting our exemption so long ago, put them on and began packing haphazardly. Like everybody else, we were having trouble with the logistics of the enterprise. We filled a few empty food cartons with some clothes and the remaining food. We could make a few trips back and forth with these, but how were we to transport our precious fuel?

Suddenly, I had an idea. Our lodger at the time was an Austrian civilian from Linz, Herr Rudi, who was doing some clerical work. He had shown us some kindness in the past. When he had been in an expansive mood, he had brought us Dutch chocolate, French cheeses or a bottle of Rhine wine. I had sensed that he was disgusted with the Nazi death machinery, even though he had never discussed the subject with us. When Herr Rudi came home at noon and saw the apartment littered with boxes, he wanted to know, "Was ist los?" (What is going on?) I quickly explained and asked him whether he knew of a cart or another conveyance to take our small stock of wood and coal into the ghetto. He raised his eyebrows on finding out that we, too, had to go, for he had come to regard us as Jews with special privileges. When he heard my request, he turned around and left, assuring us that he would send us help in no time.

About twenty minutes later, a wagon pulled by two Poles arrived at the side entrance of our building, and, following my directions, the men loaded it with our portion of the wood and coal from the cellar. We added a few boxes to lighten our load, and then, weighed down by the heavy suitcases we were carrying, we slowly made our trek to the ghetto, the wagon behind us. In our haste, we did not look back even once at the place where, long ago, we had been a happy family.

As we approached the ghetto through the gate marking its principal street, we could see the barbed wire fence stretching on both sides until it was out of our sphere of vision. Inside, we met two Ordnungsdienst men, members of the contingent assigned to keep order and to report any attempts of escape. When I asked them where we could get living quarters, they pointed at some vague destination, and, in well-practised phrases, told us what they must have been telling everybody who came before us. "Anywhere you will find room. Keep asking until you can make arrangements."

The two Poles pulling the wagon were beginning to fret and curse under their breath. They were anxious to unload and be gone. We had to hurry up and pick whatever was still available. The narrow, cobbled streets were littered with people, carts and cartons of all kinds, and there was hardly enough space for us to move.

We finally caught up with the Kleinhandlers and the Holoszytzes, who were still homeless as well, and decided to look for lodgings with them. Since her little boy had been taken, Mrs. Holoszytz was in deep mourning, hardly eating or talking to anybody. Even so, I felt that it would be best for her and for the rest of us to throw in our lot with people whom we knew and liked. Joining forces, we fought our way through a few dingy apartments, finally deciding to occupy one that was somewhat larger than the others we had seen. The two Poles quickly carried our boxes upstairs to our new home and unloaded our wood and coal in the cellar. They were gone with their cart before we could thank them.

Our new quarters were at 8 Folwarczna Street which, together with several adjoining streets and alleys, formed the entire ghetto — an abode for close to sixteen thousand Jews. The small building with a big courtyard that housed the Jewish Council was diagonally across from us. On all sides, there were old wooden shacks, some black with soot, others rotting with age. There was not a speck of green or any other colour to relieve the overall drabness.

We found ourselves in a tiny three-bedroom apartment. Each family occupied one room, and we all shared the windowless kitchen and the closet-size bathroom. In all, there were eleven of us, sleeping on improvised beds, old mattresses, cots or whatever else we could find. We were severely cramped in the small space; and yet, at the end of our first week together, we had adapted to the daily routine. All adults except Mrs. Holoszytz, who could not bear to be separated even for a minute from her surviving son, went to work in the morning and returned at dusk. Food and water were scarce. We were continually hungry and less than clean. We divided our dwindling supplies equally among us and carried on from hour to hour.

For the three of us, the move to the ghetto meant a final break in our contact with Father, even through Sweden, as most international mail delivery had ceased. Our only hope now was Zosia, but the possibility of her coming into the ghetto was so remote that we had stopped seriously considering our rescue with her help. From time to time, I would take out all our documents — the Nicaraguan passports, the lapsed visas, the "Aryan" papers and the receipts from the Polish officials and the Gestapo — wondering whether I had been dreaming for close to three years. The temptation to throw them all out as rubbish was strong as my depression turned into hostility. The self-lacerating question why? had become a shout of anger, of hate even, directed at all real and imaginary forces that were letting us perish. "They have all forgotten us. They are all having a good time while we are condemned to death," I kept repeating to myself. "They" represented anyone who was not incarcerated in a ghetto or a concentration camp. It stood for our chief oppressors, the weak Allies, my fellow Jews who had managed to flee, the Marejns, my uncles with their families and, yes, even Father.

For days after our move into the ghetto, I waged an inner war, racked by my ambivalent feelings of wrath and guilt. When I finally realized that my state of mind had bordered on madness, I took myself in hand, and, pulling Father's creased and yellowed photo from inside my slip, silently begged his forgiveness for my monstrous thoughts. I was sure that in his magnanimity, he would have understood. Knowing that, and strengthened by my love for him, I calmed down and got ready, once again, to face the real villain.

Within days of our move, we were assigned to various jobs. Many were put to work to sort and help transport the loot from the homes now emptied of Jews. Loads upon loads of personal belongings were collected in a few school buildings, unused since the beginning of the war, from where they were either shipped to Germany as property of the Third Reich, or requisitioned for the use of the local Gestapo, SS, Schutzpolizei, and the German civilians employed in administration.

The Gestapo had handed lists of places of "essential" labour to the Ordnungsdienst and had ordered them to see to it that every healthy Jew spent ten hours a day at work. Mother and I were to go to a factory where German military uniforms were sewn, and Hela would be going to a factory that manufactured horse brushes. For the first time since the outbreak of the war, we were to be formally separated during the day. The news unhinged me, but all I could do was repeat to myself the vow I had made earlier: however the Nazis dealt with us, either we were going to join Father together or not at all. How I was going to put my oath into practice, I did not know; but then, many of my ideas and perceptions were tinged with the irrational. Paradoxically, this dictum held true for everybody I observed, all the bereaved parents, orphans, siblings, relatives and friends. It was some such touch of insanity that helped us all keep a degree of sanity necessary for survival.

Every morning, all of us in our apartment who worked would rise at 6:00 a.m., take quick turns at the cold-water faucet of our only sink, and have a hasty breakfast consisting of a piece of stale bread and a mug of ersatz coffee. Mr. Holoszytz would embrace his son and wife, admonishing Mrs. Holoszytz not to venture out under any circumstances and let the boy be seen, although he knew only too well that she needed no such instructions. Mother and I would shower Hela with kisses and entreat her to be careful. We would then emerge from the dark entrance of our building and move like shadows toward the closest gate. We were joined by many similar shadowy figures. Sometimes, we formed grey shapes under the rosy brilliance of the rising sun; at other times, we merged imperceptibly into the fog and rain. At the gate, under the watchful eyes of German or Polish police, we were arranged into lines and then escorted to our different workshops outside the ghetto. The procedure was repeated in reverse at 6:00 p.m. when, after letting us in, the police locked the gates while we ran hurriedly to our apartments to make ourselves invisible before the 7:00 p.m. curfew.

My work would have been absurd if I had not been playing a deadly game. The fact was that I had never sewn a stitch on a sewing machine. I had no idea how to use the thing, nor did I know how to handle the large pile of khaki cloth on the floor beside me. Mother could not help me, even though she knew how to use the machine, as her place was across the large room from mine. A teenage girl sitting on my right must have seen my predicament and quickly came to my aid. Whenever the supervisor, a rotund, middle-aged German woman, was busy elsewhere or out of the room, my neighbour grabbed a piece of material, already cut, and, stealing over to my seat, showed me the merest rudiments of machine sewing. I was glad to discover that each of us had only one part of a uniform to sew and that my task was childishly simple: that of stitching together pre-cut sleeves. All I had to do was to sew a straight seam and put my finished products into a large carton marked "sleeves." In a few days, I was as proficient and productive as all the other women. Hela's work, as she told us when we got together at home, was more exacting. She had to cut hard bristles and insert them into wooden slabs, often bruising and pricking her fingers in the process.

As we lived from hour to hour so, in a way, did the Gestapo. Every day, a few of their officers, now always accompanied by women, would arrive in the ghetto in a horse-drawn carriage. On their way to the large courtyard framed by the small building of the Judenrat, they would shoot everybody who happened to be on the mostly deserted streets: young people presumably absent from work, older men and women painfully shuffling their feet from one house to another, probably on the prowl for some food, and children who had strayed away from their watchful mothers. Rommelmann, who hardly missed a day, often used a bullhorn and, in a loud voice, audible through the windows and thin walls of the ghetto dwellings, shouted that the sick, the old and the children were unfit for labour, were a burden to the German state, and therefore had no right to live. He and the others would then proceed to the courtyard, which had become known as the supplementary Platz. He would order the Ordnungsdienst to choose a number of people from two or three randomly selected houses and bring them to the yard. There, he assembled the entire Judenrat to listen to him and, after a brief lecture about increasing the purity of the "Aryan" world in direct proportion to the elimination of the Jews, would command his victims to form his favourite neat rows and shoot one after another. Members of the Judenrat who witnessed the rampages reported that it had never taken Rommelmann more than one shot per person. A month to six weeks after the establishment of the ghetto, our unofficial estimate was that about five to eight hundred had died as a result of those shootings.

We learned that the Germans were still advancing in the Soviet Union and that all was quiet on the Western front where Hitler's troops and occupation forces were in full control. Many Jews in ghettos scattered throughout Poland were trying to get forged Central American passports or "Aryan" papers. Some had chosen to hide in monasteries, on farms or in the elusive hideouts of the Polish underground. Meyer was now convinced that, with his stereotypical nose and the giveaway singsong of his Polish pronunciation he should not venture an escape; besides, he knew that every male suspected to be Jewish was ordered, under any interrogation, to undress and was doomed when he was found circumcised. On the surface, he seemed resigned to continue working in the stables to which he had been assigned and kept trying to dodge the Nazis as well as he could.

Although despairing of his own rescue, selfless Meyer often urged me not to give up the thought of ours. During those August evenings, when we were too filled with a sense of gloom even to discuss the absence of sex between us — an idea that Meyer had not yet completely given up in spite of my repeated protests — he encouraged me to try to contact Zosia, perhaps when I was at work outside the ghetto, hoping he might still smuggle us out to her. "Don't forget," he told me over and over again, "your father is waiting for you. Your life still has a meaning. Besides," he would add occasionally with muted anger and sorrow, "you still have your Milek if you want him." "No," I answered curtly on one occasion, to end any further discussion on that subject, "I have not got Milek."

From my vantage point now, our relationship was infantile. Anyway, it had ended when he boarded the train that took him out of this hell hole. I told Meyer, too, that I was sure I had missed our opportunity with Zosia and that I, together with Mother and Hela, was in the same exact position as he was. We were in it together. After each talk, our silences became longer as there was little left to discuss.

Silence in the Cellar

One balmy morning in September, we woke up at our usual time and proceeded to the gate. In shocked surprise, we found it locked. Instead, we saw what looked like new SS reinforcements milling around inside the ghetto enclosure. From the commands issued in loud German, we gathered that they were to fan out three abreast, to tighten the seal around the ghetto and to be particularly watchful at street corners, which could serve as openings for escape. All of us were told through a bullhorn to go back home and to await further instructions. "Another displacement will take place tomorrow," the voice roared. "You will be told what to do."

At the sound of the dreaded word, we all convulsed with panic. We were as if paralyzed and totally immobile. This did not last long, however, as the helmeted police started to push back the dense crowd and reach for their guns. We all then began to run as if in a stampede, elbowing our way home, stumbling over the cobblestones, and keeping our balance by holding on to the walls of the houses and to any strong shoulder that happened by.

The three of us were breathless when we reached our apartment and lunged for every available chair to slump into. We had not expected another "action," at least not yet. Nor did we have any idea how this one would be carried out. Would the large Gestapo stamps held over from the June massacre count? Would they be giving out new ones? What about all those who had a K stamped on their ID cards? In the end, defeated by our lack of information, we had to stop our agonizing speculations.

By mid-morning there were new developments. An Ordnungs-dienst man came to our apartment with an order from the Gestapo that those holding K cards were to line up in the square where Rom-melmann, accompanied by Palten and other Gestapo officials, would change their K to the large Gestapo stamp. Since the *Hoheitsstempel* had accorded a small measure of immunity earlier, Mrs. Holoszytz, the only resident in our apartment holding a K, felt her hope rise and began to feel some relief. We watched out of our window and saw her with her son join a long procession of other mothers with their young children heading for the square. By mid-afternoon, everybody in our apartment had the much-coveted large stamp except the three of us.

I did not know what to do. We had been issued work cards after being forced into the ghetto, but our cards had no stamps at all. How could I explain to Rommelmann and Palten that we did not have them because we had been exempt from the earlier action as foreign-ers? How would I dare to approach them at all, as a mere Jewish indi-vidual, when they were setting up their massive machinery aimed at wholesale butchery the following day? Trembling with agitation and anxiety, I finally realized that there were just three possibilities for us: one was to get permission from the Gestapo, by some miracle, to be exempt again; the other to be shot; and the third to be deported.

Late in the afternoon I watched the line of returning women slow down to a trickle and knew that I had to act quickly, before the two Gestapo chieftains called a halt to their preparatory work and or-dered the proceedings to begin the next morning. It was going to be another of my direct confrontations with the Gestapo, although it would be the first time that I would face their superior officers.

With the documents in an envelope held in my trembling hand, I ran to the square and was at first blinded by the blazing afternoon sunshine suffusing the large and now completely empty space in white-gold light. Narrowing my eyelids, I spotted the platform that I had seen in my imagination before and was surprised at how familiar it looked. Those who had been here earlier had described it in minute graphic detail. The platform consisted of wooden planks resting on several cement blocks, and it was shaded from the blinding sunshine by a large tarpaulin stretched over metal poles. The two Gestapo officers were sitting next to each other and seemed engaged in an animated conversation, while about ten other uniformed men were scattered at both ends of the long table, sorting and assembling sheaves of paper.

As I approached, I slowed down, not knowing what to expect. I was so obviously another Jewess with another Jewish armband that, if they wished, Rommelmann and Palten could have fired a few bullets at me. Instead, seeing me hesitate, they motioned to me to come closer. I did, even as I expected that they wanted me at close range so that I would be an easier target. I was allowed to mount the two steps leading to the platform, and I stood across the table from them. In my outstretched, unsteady hand my documents were fluttering in the breeze.

"What do we have here?" Rommelmann wanted to know.

I recognized the round baby face, the steel-blue eyes, and the sonorous voice immediately. In my well-rehearsed statement, I explained that the documents I had were proof that Mother, Hela and I were foreigners and that, even though we had been asked (I did not say "ordered") to live in the ghetto, we understood that, as foreigners, we would be exempt from any deportation. I added that my father, a Nicaraguan citizen living in Managua, was trying to have us included in the earliest possible exchange.

For a few moments, Rommelmann and Palten looked at each other, their mouths opening to emit a derisive sound. It was Palten who answered in his Prussian-accented German, "What do you want to go to Nicaragua for? The climate is very unhealthy in those barbaric, swamp-infested Central American countries. Wouldn't you rather take advantage of our generosity and travel east, where you will lead happy and wholesome lives in the country?"

"Please, Herr Untersturmführer, we've been separated from my father for over three years. We love him and are longing to see him," I begged, vainly trying to fight back my tears. It was Rommelmann who answered me, much more tersely. "It's the contemptible Jews like your father that are responsible for all the spilled German blood. Anyway," he added, his voice softening to the point of sounding seductive, "you'll see your father any day now. In the meantime, go home and make sure that all three of you come to the square tomorrow when you are ordered to do so."

I ventured my last question. "Could you at least stamp our work slips with a Hoheitsstempel?"

"No," Rommelmann hissed through his now tightly closed lips. "You won't need them, be gone if you know what's good for you."

I crumpled the documents in my pocket and turning, started walking away slowly, wondering whether I would be hit by a bullet in the back. When I thought I was a safe distance away, I ran home with all the speed I could muster. Once there, I started crying hysterically; neither Mother nor Hela could stop me for a long time.

When my sobs subsided, I realized that the light in our apartment had turned grey and that the place was strangely quiet. The women had put together some food for the Kleinhandlers' daughters and the Holoszytzes' little boy, but the adults sat in the gathering dusk without eating. Whatever talk there was, it was in whispers. For a moment, I had the eerie feeling that the hovering sense of foreboding was not unlike that at the end of the Yom Kippur service. I suddenly recollected that awesome holiday and how, on the occasions when I had attended the synagogue with Father or Grandfather as a child, I had often wondered, with fear and trembling, whether I would be inscribed in the book of life for the coming year. Now, as then, the very heavens seemed to be closing, with my fate sealed behind their shut gates. *Oh God, in whom I can no longer believe, please, forgive me for abandoning you and let us live another year,* I prayed silently.

How does one prepare oneself for one's last night on earth? It was certainly not by sleeping, as I discovered that my watch showed 1:00 a.m. and that soon September 12, the day designated for the second *Aussiedlung*, would dawn. Mother, Hela and I put our bedding close together and we lay on it, our hands interlaced, a hand freeing itself once in a while to stroke a beloved cheek or hair. Does a bullet hurt much? Try as I did, I recoiled from any attempt to figure it out. From what I had seen, those who had been shot died immediately; even if it hurt, it would be for just a second or two.

The two pairs of hands I was holding in my own were hot and wet with sweat. We kept removing our hands from the tight knot to wipe them on our clothes, and then use our clothes to wipe our wet and burning faces. I must have been losing consciousness or catching some uneasy sleep in snatches, for when I looked at my watch again in the light of a match, it showed 3:15 a.m. At the same time, I heard loud knocking on the door. My first reaction was to freeze in fear, as I thought our hour had come. Rousing myself from the mattress, I took a few unsteady steps toward the door and heard Meyer's urgent whisper, "Open up at once!"

Dishevelled and wild-eyed, Meyer looked as though he had not slept in days. "What are you waiting for?" he asked furiously. "For your death or deportation? I won't let you give up just yet."

He then went on to explain that he knew of an excellent hiding place. If we wanted to try it, we would have to go at once. He, too, would come with us. A hundred questions crowded my mind, but I did not ask any. Rousing Mother and Hela from their light slumber, I packed a few bags of food under Meyer's supervision, and we ran along the dark and silent streets to 4 Lwowska Street. I recognized the place immediately as the building with the large courtyard where Zyga and other returnees from Soviet-occupied Poland had been shot and where similar large-scale killings had been and still were taking place. Meyer motioned us to a storefront door. I recognized the store, too. It had belonged to one of Father's customers and good friends, and I remembered with a start that he and his family had disappeared during the June action.

Expertly, Meyer removed one of the store's many wooden panels, which held shelves now empty of all merchandise, and motioned us toward it. I asked Mother to go first. Sliding through the panel with obvious effort, she disappeared from our view in a minute. Hela was next, and I followed her. When my turn came, I saw, in the shadowy light that had filtered into the store through the open panel, a long, steep ladder that had been hooked up to the improvised opening. As I descended it, the place grew increasingly darker, and, touching the ground, I realized that we were in a large cellar. Mother and Hela were waiting for me at the bottom, and then we waited for Meyer to come down. As soon as he was with us, the cellar was plunged into near-total darkness, the only feeble light coming through the top parts of the small windows along one wall.

As we began to move cautiously forward, we realized that the entire space was already filled with people. Our eyes slowly grew accustomed to the murky light, and we made our way hesitantly, stepping over and around people, toward a corner that seemed least congested. There we put down our bags and stretched out, our legs extended over the clay earth beneath us, and our backs supported by the damp cement wall. Looking around, we could distinguish men, women and children. Most of them were lying on the bare ground. Only a few sat huddled together, talking softly. A steady drone of murmuring voices was the only sound.

After my shock and disbelief had subsided, I asked Meyer to explain what was going on. His story was simple. He had learned from an Ordnungsdienst friend that the action would begin at 7:00 a.m. on that day, September 12. Nobody would be allowed to stay home. Much as during the infamous week of June past, people would be brought in relays to the square where four machine guns had already been installed in the four corners and where the Gestapo would be patrolling on all sides. It was the same friend who had told Meyer about the hiding place and who had promised, if it were not discovered, to open the false door and let everyone out when the action was over. There was room for about three hundred people in the cellar, and it was filled to capacity.

Sitting in a cramped position, we had been there only two to three hours when we began to hear muffled sounds of machine gun and rifle fire. For three days and two nights we remained in the cellar, three out of three hundred, cold, hungry and lice-infested. We slept on the damp ground and ate stale bread, adding some jam and bits of dry cheese left over from our discontinued parcels to still the gnawing hunger pangs. Whenever we heard the sound of heavy boots and barking dogs in the vicinity of our hideout, we held our breaths and were completely silent. Some began to break down under the physical and mental strain and started an incoherent low wail; they were gagged by their immediate neighbours, as we were all aware that the slightest noise would give us away.

Smeared with soot and scratching our scalps until they bled, we would have lost track of the time if it had not been for our tin watches, which we kept winding. Even so, our senses were so dulled that we could hardly tell day from night.

I think it was on the second day that the activity above and around us was stepped up. The shots were louder and more frequent, and so was the barking of the dogs. It was during one of those episodes that an infant, nursing at its mother's breast, began to howl. Crazed with fear, people sitting near the pair closed in on them and, among low hissing of "shh, shh," tried to pacify the crying baby. The howls, however, grew louder just as the soles of the Nazis' boots became visible through the tops of the window. We could hear their crunching sound on the gravel surrounding the cellar. For a minute, there was a furious flailing of arms and the lurching of several bodies toward the mother, who sat like a frozen statue, pressing the baby's head closer to her breast. The infant shrieked loudly two or three times more. Then there was complete silence. With unspeakable horror, we looked in the direction where minutes before there had been frantic activity. All was quiet there now. At the same time, the officers seemed to have moved away.

It was Meyer who ventured forth on all fours to find out what had happened. In seconds, he slithered back and banged his head on the wall, making soundless movements with his lips. Watching him, but not wanting to know, I slid closer to where he was sitting, his bleeding forehead continuing to make rhythmic sounds as it hit the wall over and over again. Concentrating on his moving lips, I could make out what he kept saying: "The baby won't bother us anymore," and again, "God, the baby won't bother us anymore."

I turned my head away, but before I could crawl away, I felt a rising nausea, and, leaning against the wall, started vomiting. I don't know how long the spell lasted. All I remember is that I could not stop; after having thrown up all the crumbs of food I had eaten and the small amounts of the tepid water I had drunk, I continued retching and heaving, my mouth bitter with the taste of my own bile. Panting with exertion, I weakly moved toward Meyer, took him by the hand and laboriously made my way among the moving bodies to bring him back to our corner. I could tell by looking into the haunted eyes of Mother and Hela that they knew, too. Their faces were grey like death masks. We never learned whether the baby was a boy or a girl; nor did we find out the name of the mother.

Every now and again, we heard the panel being removed. Each time our anxiety rose to a fever pitch until we were sure that it was not the Nazis who had found us, but our own Ordnungsdienst man who dropped a few supplies and gave details of what was going on outside: All the houses in the ghetto were being emptied and the square was teeming with Jews, mainly mothers and children. It was on them that the most cruel of tricks had been played: lulled into a false sense of security that their newly acquired *Hoheitsstempel* would afford them immunity, the women had appeared in large numbers. Many had been shot on the spot with their children; others had seen their children shot while they themselves had been ordered to march away. Jewish children, aside from the children of Judenrat members, officially had no right to be alive in the ghetto anymore. Many parents, however, chose to keep their children hidden.

At the end of three days and two nights, close to seven thousand people had either come voluntarily or had been dragged out of their homes and hiding places to be killed or deported.

On what we were told was the third morning of our hiding, we were allowed to venture out. The special police reinforcements had left the ghetto, and it was back in the hands of the regular Nazi contingent. We took turns leaving the cellar, aided by two Ordnungsdienst men who supervised our cautious and stealthy return up the ladder, through the store, into the street, and ultimately into our homes.

Half-blinded by the unaccustomed light and unsteady on our bruised and aching feet, Mother, Hela and I arrived in our apartment on Folwarczna Street and were for an hour or so its sole occupants. Then, first Mr. Kleinhandler and, minutes later, Mr. Holoszytz came in. Both men were alone and silent, locked up in black despair. It did not take long to find out that they were the only survivors of their respective families. Mrs. Kleinhandler had been seen on the way to the station with her two daughters, while Mrs. Holoszytz and her young son had been felled by machine-gun fire in the square. Refusing food, the two men threw themselves on their cots and sobbed uncontrollably. Our hearts filled with grief and compassion for our friends, but we could not console them. We shared their anguish, yet, for the moment at least, thanked our blessings in having Meyer Taub and the few Jewish Ordnungsdienst men who had seen us through the latest ordeal and ensured that we were still alive and together.

Apart from the fact that we were still living, there was little to cheer about. Meyer continued his frequent visits and was at times joined by Israel Schmuckler, Hela's Ordnungsdienst boyfriend. They confirmed the chilling news that about seven thousand Jews had fallen victim to the second *Aussiedlung*. They learned more about the fable the Germans had been spinning about the "healthy east": there were definitely more death camps there, Treblinka, Sobibor, Majdanek. The few eyewitnesses who had managed to jump off the trains or had hidden behind embankments near the platforms where the trains had stopped had put the details together, and the information had already circulated. During the trips, Jews had been made to stand in the cattle cars, body leaning against body, for the Germans to crowd in the largest possible number. The cars had reeked of human excrement and the smell of vomit. Many had fainted and some had died but had remained upright propped up by the thick wall of intertwined arms and shoulders.

We heard much later that upon arrival in many of the camps, people were ordered out to face SS or other Nazi officials who made their preliminary selection, first throwing those who had lost consciousness or were dead onto a heap to one side. In some camps, able-bodied men and women formed one line, while the old, the sick and the children separated from their parents were whipped into another.

There was more news. With terror in their voices, they added that they had heard that German doctors and scientists were conducting heinous experiments on both live and dead specimens; there were rumours that Jewish fat was being used to manufacture soap; even hair, shaved off Jewish heads, was apparently being used to make soft brushes; and they reported that young Jewish women were being raped.

On another one of their secret visits, Meyer and Israel told us that they had heard more rumours of camps equipped with gas chambers, that the Nazis were killing a number of inmates every day and every night. In other concentration camps, apparently people were temporarily spared, assigned to back-breaking toil amid hunger and torture, kept in filthy, largely unheated and foul-smelling barracks where rampant diseases, such as typhus and dysentery, often accomplished the same task as the steady gassing in the death camps. There would be no survivors, they said. The gas would billow down on us all.

The ominous belief that we were heading for a "final solution" was now beyond dispute. The Nazis were engaging in perhaps the most massive genocide in human history. Their system was meticulously efficient, and we realized, with a finality which no longer permitted any false hopes, that every single Jew was heading for death. We wondered, too, whether with merely nine thousand Jews remaining in Tarnów, after the next action the ghetto would become *judenrein*, free of Jews. The "how" having been answered in a way that precluded any further speculations on the subject, it was now simply a matter of "when." Until then, we had no choice but to live with the knowledge that our case was terminal. Even though we went listlessly about our work and whatever else we had to do to live from day to day, in our hearts Mother, Hela and I had said our final goodbyes to Father.

Barely Alive

A week or so after the September massacre, Mother and I came back from our uniform factory, where the group of seamstresses had dwindled to about half, to find a young woman waiting in our room. I recognized her as Rosa, Meyer's sister, and saw by her hollow-cheeked, tight-lipped face that something was desperately wrong. She must have noticed the anxiety in my eyes, for she spoke immediately. Meyer was alive, she told me, but very weak. It had not been a German bullet, but his attempt to kill himself. Rosa felt guilty, as it was she who had been supplying him with barbiturates. Whenever he had complained of insomnia, which had been often since his parents' deportation, she had been giving him the pills generously, eager to relieve his anguish and wishing him to get more rest. An elderly woman who had been hiding in the apartment in which he lived had heard Meyer's laboured breathing shortly after noon and had gone to fetch his sister. Rosa had pumped his stomach and had administered all necessary first aid until he had regained consciousness. He was now suffering from fatigue but was fully conscious and kept asking for me. "Will you come right away?" she pleaded urgently. "I am afraid he may do it again."

I did not tell her that he probably had no more pills left, as he had been sharing them with us for the past few months. Ours were hidden in a vial under a layer of tea leaves in a small can. I had thought about them and counted them from time to time, but had known that there had not been enough for a lethal dose for all three of us. And, although I had completely abandoned hope that we would see Father again, I had grown certain, as the weeks went by, that my vow of "three or none" did not include the idea of suicide. In fact, remembering Grandfather's teachings that life is sacrosanct under any conditions, I had felt a moral revulsion at the idea of taking our own. Now, having found out about Meyer's serious attempt, I thought of myself as somewhat sullied for having begged for them in the first place.

I told Mother not to worry and to explain my absence to Hela when she came back from work. Then, heedless of the late hour, Rosa and I ran the short distance to where Meyer shared his cubbyhole of a room with another man whose family had been wiped out. I found him lying on a dirty cot, covered with a worn-out blanket as grey as his face, the muscles of his body twitching, his eyes closed, and his unruly black hair matted on his folded coat that served as a pillow. He was fully dressed in the same tatters that I had come to know well, and, except for the spasms, was motionless. I approached and kissed him on his damp forehead. "It is me, Sonia," I said, fighting back my agitation. "You have done a stupid thing. All is not lost yet," I continued without conviction. "Besides, who is going to find a hiding place for us next time? I am counting on you, and you mustn't let me down."

Meyer opened his eyes, propped himself up on his elbows and said weakly but distinctly, "You are a fool. After next time, the ghetto will be declared judenrein and there will be no one on the outside to let us out of hiding, nor will there be anywhere to go. Next time, all in their right mind will hurry to the Platz and will disobey some silly command in order to be shot right away rather than be sent to one or another of their death camps."

I tried to find a response but could not think of anything convincing to say. I had no right to impose my moral scruples on him.

Why, then, was I insistent on depriving him of the only free choice he had and was determined to take? I guess that, although I did not love him, my feelings for him were deeper and more complex than for any other man I had known. I wanted him around for he was a unique friend and was now my only symbol of our carefree pre-war past when he, our other friends and I had lived in blissful ignorance of our real future and had dreamed about making our romantic ideals come true. All I had left were my memories, and without Meyer, they would die. I needed them as much as I needed my love for Father in order to live until the Germans came to get me.

And so, I kept arguing with Meyer illogically and, covering his face with kisses and stroking his tangled black mane, exacted a promise from him that he would not do it again. "Actually, you don't need my promises," he said in parting, some colour returning to his face, "there are no more pills available, and Rosa is out of her job. I guess she was too worried about me to tell you. Yesterday, a small police detachment entered the Jewish hospital and shot some of the patients in their beds. Rosa told me about it last night. I expect the Ordnungs-dienst have just about finished the digging of another mass grave. I understand there is no more room in the cemetery and the new graves are now being dug in the swamp field outside its walls."

Fully conscious now, Meyer must have noticed the growing pallor on my face as he was telling me the news, for he managed a whimsical smile and added with an attempt at humour, "Who is closer to suicide now, you or I? If you are so intent on living, the murder of a few more people shouldn't bother you so much. You have seen worse. You'd better go now. It is after curfew, and you wouldn't want to get caught just yet, would you?" Ignoring the sarcasm, I kissed him once more, ran out of his room and hurried home. The conversation with Meyer had a shocking effect on me. As soon as I got home, I took out the vial full of pills, opened it and without hesitation flushed the contents down the toilet.

Mother, Hela and I spent the rest of the evening finishing our delousing process. Immediately after our return from hiding, we had launched an all-out attack on our hair, which was crawling with lice. It had taken many hours of washing it with scalding water from our communal kettle and picking them dead and alive from one another's scalps. After I had come back from Meyer's room, we waged our final battle with the lice and were reassured that we were rid of them. *When they come to get us*, I thought grimly, *they will shave three lice-free Jewesses before disposing of them.*

As we were readying ourselves psychologically for a virtually certain death, our lives were not without the occasional diversion or relief. As we had done when we had lived on Sowińskiego Street, we became friendly with the few remaining neighbours in our building, seeking the warmth and comfort of others. After curfew we led a busy social life. During our get-togethers, some played cards, some engaged in games left by a child who was no longer alive and others talked. Unconsciously perhaps, our conversations had little to do with the present and the future; they centred on reminiscences about the time before the war. We told stories and anecdotes, at times jocular, about the homes we had had, people we had known or schools we had gone to. If ever our topic strayed to some of our friends who were either dead or perhaps lingering in a concentration camp, we avoided referring to their state; rather, we singled out events in their lives that had touched ours when we had all been free, and kept the tone of any tale light, ever frivolous. Only after a neighbour failed to return from work did we permit ourselves to face reality. At such times, we grimly debated the advantages and disadvantages of a few hiding places, or bunkers, as they had come to be called by then, which had been prepared for another anticipated *Aussiedlung*, and wondered whether it would be worth the effort to use them. We now fully expected that, next time, the ghetto would be dissolved and no Jew would remain alive.

～

In the evening of November 14, Israel Schmuckler came to our apartment with a list in his hands. By conditioned reflex we knew what it meant, so that his appearance did little to rouse us from our somnolent state. The orders were that on the following day, the action would begin at 7:00 a.m. All Jews were to stay in the ghetto and come to the square early next morning, except those engaged in essential labour, who were to proceed, as usual, to their places of work. Just as I suspected foul play in the gracious distribution by the Gestapo of the coveted big seals and marvelled at how inexhaustible the bag of Nazi tricks was, I saw Israel take out another list from which he read the names of the factories considered "essential." Mother's and mine were not on it but Hela's was. When I realized that we were going to be separated in the next onslaught of murder, terror shattered the inert limbo of my mind. This separation, I feared, would be permanent.

My thinking became feverish and disjointed. On the surface, the announcement sounded as though all Jews who remained in the ghetto would be wiped out, and those at work saved for another while. In this case, I speculated wildly, trying to outwit the killers, the ghetto was not yet fated to become completely *judenrein*. As we had prepared a bunker, Mother and I could hide there. If we were not uncovered, we could perhaps sneak out after it was all over and join Hela, who presumably would be unharmed and allowed to return home from work.

I felt that, so far, my reasoning had not been completely off the mark, but it had left many loopholes unplugged. I had no guarantee that Jews at work would survive; the Nazis were ingenious enough to have thought of some other way of disposing of them. Then, too, if Mother and I went undetected in our bunker, how would we account for being still around when all Jews not employed in essential services were supposed to have been eliminated? With a start, I realized that I was engaged in the kind of Talmudic argument and counterargument that would have pleased Grandfather David Roskes in the years gone by. Only now my self-debate was not an academic exercise: our very lives depended on its proper resolution. Every time I tried to reason beyond the obstacle of being alive while presumed dead, I reached an impasse. There was no choice but to let events take their course in the hope that once again, somehow, we would land a tiny step ahead of the Gestapo.

Shortly before dawn, after another sleepless night, Mother and I tiptoed over to Hela's bunk where she was sleeping soundly. Her regular breathing and the softness of her youthful face in repose filled me with pain and compassion. "God," I heard myself saying, oblivious to the futility of my prayer, "please, try to save her. She is too young and innocent to perish without a trace. Please, please, save us all and keep us together."

Reluctantly, I woke Hela, for it was time for her to go to work and for us to evacuate the apartment. After an agonizing send-off, my eyes followed her flaming hair till she disappeared around the corner. Mother and I took the few bags of food we had prepared for our next hiding episode and went down to the ground floor where we knocked on the door of a neighbour's apartment according to an agreed signal. It was opened by one of our group who then led us and others to the bathroom. Moving the bathtub away, he disclosed a narrow opening in the tile floor. Another ladder, another cellar: the very sight of another bunker made my stomach turn, and I had to grip the bathroom window ledge to keep my balance.

Our neighbour proceeded to explain, amid the complete silence that had fallen on the group intent on his every word, that we were to go down one by one, find a spot and stay there noiselessly until he himself joined us. He would then try to space us as comfortably as the small area would allow. An Ordnungsdienst man who had been briefed in advance would replace the tiles and move the bathtub back into its proper place. We were not to utter a single word while the action was going on, for this time the Nazis had been alerted to the existence of hiding places, and they would be much more watchful than before. After it was all over, the same Ordnungsdienst man would give us an all-clear sign by removing the tiles and helping us to get out. The neighbour then added that all the arrangements had been made on the assumption that there would be some Jews left in the ghetto at the end of the *Aussiedlung*. He did not mince words: if there were none, he said grimly, the cellar would become our grave. He finished his speech, his voice breaking, by wishing us all good luck.

Growing accustomed to the darkness, I realized that our cellar was considerably smaller than that at 4 Lwowska Street. It held about seventy people, most of whom were mothers with small children. Some moved about, their silhouettes assuming distorted shapes in the gloomy light, while others lay or sat like so many motionless statues. Mother and I found a relatively free spot and were glad to discover that this hiding place had a hard wooden floor; at least we would not have to lie in the mud as we had done earlier.

Shortly after dawn, we heard the first shots coming both from the general direction of the square and from somewhere much closer — possibly the building we were in. While we could not see the Nazis' boots, as the place was windowless, we heard their thuds, accompanied by the barking of the dogs. At one point, we literally tried not to breathe, for the Nazis were obviously conducting a search in the very apartment our bunker was in.

We heard the scraping sound on the floor of the apartment of furniture being moved, and the crash of metal utensils. The searchers were directly above us for about fifteen minutes. When we were sure that they had left because the noises had subsided, we let out our collective breath, feeling close to suffocating. I looked at Mother; beads of perspiration covered her face and she had a vacant look in her eyes, staring, without blinking, straight ahead. I shook her shoulders and whispered to her that we were, for the time being, safe, begging her to lie down on the floor and rest. Without acknowledging that she had understood my request, she obeyed, probably unable to sit up any longer. The main action seemed to have moved further away from us, but the roar of the rifle shots and the rattle of the now familiar machine-gun fire intensified as the day wore on.

Will they come back and find us this time? I kept asking myself over and over again. If they do, I thought, while my heart felt as though it were being stabbed by knives, what will happen to Hela? Will she survive on her own? Or will she, too, die when they are ready for her, separated from her mother and sister, the feeling of being abandoned and alone adding to her agony? I sat cross-legged on the floor, while my body was swaying to the voiceless tunes of my queries and incantations, my consciousness ebbing with every passing minute. No doubt I was hallucinating. Mother in her reclining position was like a figure cut in stone. I kept confusing her with Niobe and the Mater Dolorosa. Father seemed to lurk somewhere in the shadows, too. Although my lips did not move, I carried on a conversation with him. Finally, before my fears about Hela and our cellar being discovered could hurtle me into the abyss of madness, I fell into a dreamless sleep.

Without any warning, I was awakened by a noise directly above us and felt Mother's fingers closing on mine. "They have found us," she kept whimpering, "our turn has come." There was the sound of tiles being removed, and a sudden light from the bathroom blinded us, revealing to our squinting eyes the forms and shapes of our cellmates. We all sank to our knees and began to pray for mercy, expecting a brutal grip on our shoulders to drag us upwards and out.

A minute passed. Looking up, I saw, not leather boots, but a pair of female legs coming down the ladder. When the rest of the body, its back to us, became visible, Mother and I started to cry hysterically and ran toward the ladder. Tripping over bodies to be with her as soon as she touched the ground, we called, "It's Hela, our Hela!" Hela turned around, and my first reaction was that of relief that she had no visible marks of violence on her. Only her face, where her tears must have flown for hours, was puffed and smudged. After we had given her a bite of food and had settled her as comfortably as the cramped space permitted, she told us her story.

Hela had started work as usual, wondering what would happen to us and whether we would be together in the evening or whether she would return to an empty apartment. Suddenly, at about 11:00 a.m., the factory door flew wide open and a handful of armed SS men came in, barking the order: "All Jews out. Right away. Proceed with all speed to the square." Panic-stricken, all the workers dropped whatever they had been doing and were led away to the Platz. Once there, they were told to kneel, and deafening shots began to pierce the air.

Hela saw that the square was packed with Jews. This time, the young and able-bodied, like herself, shared the place with the old, the disabled, mothers with babies and some children alone and unattended. Unclear as her thoughts were, she nevertheless surmised that the Nazis had made a significant stride toward making the ghetto *judenrein*: obviously, they had felt that they could dispense with those Jews who were still able to work, and they had certainly found many hiding places, as witnessed by the category of people who, in terms of the "master plan," had no right to have stayed alive.

As Hela was wondering whether she would be shot by a rifle, machine-gunned or ordered to march to the station, she felt a hand touching her arm. Looking up through a mist of tears, she discovered that it was Israel who was leaning over her. "Get up," he said, "and come with me." Mechanically, she first crouched and then slowly straightened out, gingerly stepping between the kneeling bodies all around her, avoiding the open spaces in the middle and headed for the walls of the buildings surrounding the square. She and Israel continued walking on the periphery of the crowd until they came close to the raised platform. The last few steps brought them face to face with Rommelmann. He had been enjoying himself and did not like being interrupted.

"Sir," Israel addressed him, "I have brought a girl who is my fiancée. We are going to be married next week. Can you exempt her this time?"

Rommelmann lowered his gun for a moment and looked at Hela. "What's the difference?" he wanted to know. "You'll both go within weeks at the latest." Israel then pleaded that she should be spared anyway, at least until next time.

Rommelmann seemed to hesitate, but still withheld his verdict. Resorting to his final try, Israel took out of Hela's hands the Nicaraguan passport and the Gestapo *Bescheinigung*. "Please, Herr Sturmscharführer," he continued pleading, "look here, she is a Nicaraguan citizen."

Rommelmann's curiosity was pricked for a second. He stretched out his gloved hand and read the documents. Handing them back to Hela, he said in his booming voice, "All right, for now. Take her away." With these words, he turned back to face the crowd and started shooting.

As Hela hurried to reach our bunker, the crowd of which she had been a part was being moved to the station, and, darting a quick look sideways, she saw many bodies sprawled on the ground, some bleeding profusely and writhing, others completely still. There was a rattling of death carts, followed by a fast clean-up of the square. When she was just about to reach our building, she spotted another large group being escorted by the Nazis and their dogs in the direction of the now almost deserted Platz. Then, aided by Israel, who had known where Mother and I were hiding, she returned to us.

In relief and amazement, I looked at my sister, pulled her toward me and held her in a tight embrace, reluctant to let her go. Our shoulders shook with our muffled sobs and our tears mingled, and it was a long time before our bodies separated. All three of us huddled close together in our corner, trying to make sense out of what had happened and to map out strategy for the immediate future.

In my mind, the episode assumed a vast symbolic dimension. It was a scaled-down replica of the larger odyssey that had been our entire existence under the Germans; it was a close parallel to the incredible course our lives had taken since the beginning of the war. All three of us had been repeatedly saved, just as Hela had been saved barely an hour earlier, by the inexplicable combination of Father's help on the one side and providence, on the other. Our chief weapon in the form of the Nicaraguan passports would have been worthless if we had died with the thousands of others; however, since we had succeeded so far to stay alive — by sheer coincidence, a helping hand, manipulation, being a short step ahead of the Germans — the documents were accomplishing at least a part of the task they had been designed for. And yet, for all the good they had done, they could not be relied upon to keep rescuing us. The situation was explosive and tomorrow, of necessity, remained a question mark.

The November "action" lasted only twenty-four hours and netted the Germans over two thousand Jews. With about six thousand left alive, it was beyond question that between the daily shootings and a final *Aussiedlung*, the ghetto would be liquidated. It was incongruous that it still existed. Our assumption was that either the gas chambers could not accommodate the swelling numbers quickly enough or that the Germans were savouring their ever more refined methods too much to finish the jobs. That they were going to finish it, there was no doubt.

All was quiet in the rooms of our apartment, which the drawn shades had plunged into semi-darkness. There was ample evidence it had been thoroughly searched. Dresser drawers were open, cots and mattresses were strewn all over the floor, our meagre supply of clothes was scattered everywhere, and contents of cans and jars were spilled in the kitchen. I ran immediately to our bedroom to find out whether our "Aryan" papers were still in their original drawer. They were. The false bottom had not been tampered with. Swinging them back and forth, I laughed hysterically when the thought struck me that they would make softer toilet paper than the newspaper we had been using. Mother and Hela, too, joined me in my uncontrollable giggles, and it was a while before our fit of nervous tension subsided and we sobered up.

In the afternoon, a grim-faced Israel Schmuckler came in. We were reluctant to listen to any more news, but I sensed that what he had to divulge this time was of a personal nature and gave him my attention. He told us that our earlier hiding place in the cellar of 4 Lwowska Street had been discovered. Screaming for mercy, three hundred people were either clubbed to death, shot on the spot or marched to the Platz where Jews found in many other bunkers had already been kneeling. Most of the hiding places had been disclosed, and those discovered in them had been treated with a brutality more vicious than the Nazis had resorted to before.

Israel seemed to have come to the end of his report, and yet I felt that he had left something unsaid. Darting his eyes at me specifically, he opened his lips once or twice as if to add something, but each time no words came. I suddenly had a moment of revelation, such as I had seldom experienced.

"It is Meyer, isn't it? Isn't it?" I kept shouting, my voice rising to a crescendo and finally becoming too rasping for utterance. Israel recoiled a step or two and, averting his face from mine, uttered the one monosyllabic word I feared: "Yes." I stared at him unseeingly as the enormity of that confirmation slowly sank in. Unable to stand on my feet, I lowered myself onto one of the mattresses covering the floor. Fighting to regain my speech, I asked in a voice that sounded alien to me, "How?" I wanted, had, to know.

Israel said that Meyer had been in hiding at 4 Lwowska Street with his sister. The false shelf the group had been hiding behind was found and removed, and the Nazis hit with a rifle butt each emerging head. Meyer had been in line right behind his sister, heard her scream when she received her blow. Emerging from the opening, he was clubbed, too, but seeing his sister's face covered with blood, he lunged for the first helmeted man he found and hit him on the mouth until the man, too, began to bleed. Within seconds, two bullets coming from two different guns made Meyer sink to the cement floor of the store, and he died instantly. The cause of the commotion, Rosa, was shot, too, and fell right beside him.

I listened in silence, my thoughts taut and clear. When I finally spoke, I addressed myself to Meyer. "Meyer," I said, aware of my minuscule audience, "now you know that your suicide attempt was all wrong. You never claimed to be a hero, but in my eyes you were always one. And you did get a chance for your last act of heroism. No one except the handful of us here will ever know it, and we may take this knowledge to our graves with us, but you did it just the same. That's all that counts. You kept your human dignity till the end." I kept my eulogy simple and brief, afraid that I might break down physically and emotionally if I tried to embellish it and make it wordy.

Hela and Mother drew close and sat down beside me, concern and pity written all over their faces. "Don't worry about me," I told them evenly. "I have lost the best friend I have had or will ever have, but I'll never forget him. Now that we have almost no friends left, except Israel, we shall have to love one another all the more." I propped myself on my elbows and brought their faces near mine. Our sense of grief kept our arms interlocked for a while, but we were aroused from our momentary oblivion of the world around us when Israel spoke again.

"Unfortunately," he said, "I have more bad news. I would delay it if I could, but there is no time." He stopped before going on, giving us a moment to refocus our attention, as we had learned to do almost mechanically.

The ghetto would be divided into two: ghetto A and ghetto B. Ghetto A, of which our building on Folwarczna Street, the quarters of the Jewish Council and the big square formed a part, would house all Jews who worked. Ghetto B, which included the notorious 4 Lwowska Street, would be inhabited by the unemployed, that is all those who were there on sufferance. There would be no communication between the two ghettos. Those found where they did not belong would be disposed of immediately.

There was more. Jews in Ghetto B would be allowed to go out for only four hours a day, between noon and 4:00 p.m. The area itself would be made smaller. A number of streets close to the fence, now completely emptied of Jews, would revert back to the city. Any child under age fourteen found either at home or in the street would be killed instantly: German generosity did not extend to children, who had officially ceased to exist after the second *Aussiedlung*.

The order was to go into effect the following morning. Since Hela was supposed to stay on Folwarczna Street while Mother and I were to go into Ghetto B, this was to be our last night together. I was not going to let it happen. I was going to stop it even if it meant that I, or all three of us, would die in the process.

My resolve made me sound bolder than I felt and had been even on the occasions when I had confronted the Gestapo. Turning to Israel, who was just about to leave, I detained him by saying that I had an important request to make. He looked at his watch, said that he had a few other apartments to cover with the same announcement, but decided to give me a few minutes. I asked him whether his list contained individual names. He answered that the Gestapo had stopped bothering about names before the second action. However, everyone in Ghetto A would be issued a new work permit to replace the earlier one with the *Hoheitsstempel*; those in Ghetto B would have no new identification of any kind. I told him that, in that case, I did not think Hela should go to work, as the Gestapo would not know the difference between those present and absent. "Remember," I said, "what happened yesterday? Jews are not safe at work either." I knew, I said, that there would be raids on Ghetto B, but we simply had to take our chances. What I did not divulge to him was my private "three or none" philosophy. I thought he might find it ridiculous that I had adopted Mother and Hela as my unofficial charges and that I felt responsible for them, if to no one else, then at least to Father and maybe even to myself.

I knew my argument would not make any sense to him under the circumstances, with the dissolution of the ghetto imminent, when all efforts were doomed to failure and we had lost the last shred of control over our lives. I was afraid he would think it absurd that my sense of responsibility had grown in direct proportion to the mounting hopelessness of our survival. I wanted to keep my obsession to myself.

We argued for a while. I knew that Israel was deeply concerned about Hela. There was no doubt that he, the rest of the Ordnungsdienst and the handful of Jewish councillors would be eliminated as soon as the two ghettos ceased to exist. Israel did not agree with my reasoning and refused to grant my request. Crestfallen, I begged him to agree to a compromise. Hela would go to work, but he himself should smuggle her into our ghetto every night. It was a lot to ask. I realized that by consenting to my proposal he would jeopardize whatever life he still had left. I was therefore surprised and grateful when I heard him say, with just a slight hesitation, "All right, it doesn't make any difference to me. Nothing does anymore. But I see that you are very adamant about it. I'll do it." With these words, he turned to Hela, and the two of them were soon lost in a brief but passionate embrace. After he left, I looked at my doomed family and felt strangely comforted by my love for them.

Waiting for Hela

All three of us left the apartment immediately after having made the decision and went looking for new quarters for Mother and me. We did not have far to go, as most of the dwellings had been abandoned and most doors had been left ajar. When we arrived at the large building at 4 Lwowska Street, which had been designated as one of the few streets in Ghetto B, we found that we had a wide choice. We could either move into a place by ourselves or share our quarters with some other survivors. We decided not to be alone, as we felt that we could not endure the tension in isolation, and thus chose a second-storey apartment where we found two women, about Mother's age, trying to coax some heat out of the kitchen stove with a few sticks of wood. When Mother asked whether we could move in with them, they shrugged their shoulders with indifference, and, with their backs to us, murmured something incomprehensible, which we took for consent.

It was going to be our last night together at Folwarczna Street. The apartment was empty. Mr. Holoszytz had not come back after the last action, and Mr. Kleinhandler, who, as a member of the Judenrat was still at large, had decided to move out. He could not bear to stay in the apartment where the memories of his family haunted him. Images of my own dead friends and relatives kept appearing and disappearing in my mind's eye. I conjured up Zyga, Meyer, Klara and Lusia, but saw my grandparents and all my Białystok relatives as well. In my vision, some were dressed in rags, others stood naked, their bones protruding, in a line heading for an iron door of a squat building from which the chimney was spewing into the air billowing black smoke, and a few others were sitting in the grass amid green trees and multicoloured flowers, their rucksacks beside them, engaged in an animated discussion. I had to drive both fists into my eyes to wipe out the mirages. Time was relentless and did not leave room for daydreaming and flights of fancy.

We stayed up late that night, glad to have a few practical details to attend to. Having found two battered suitcases, we packed the few clothes we possessed. We put most of Hela's with ours, loath to separate even the inanimate objects we owned jointly; besides, if she were going to sleep in our apartment, she would need them to get dressed in the morning to go to work. Hela left one or two dresses in the cupboard, so that she might be prepared for any sudden shift in plans or any contingency that might arise. Having nothing further to do, we lay down on our cots and mattresses, but sleep would not come. The night was almost an exact counterpart to that which we had spent in the same apartment before the September action. This time, however, there would be no Meyer to force us into hiding, nor was there any place to hide.

Early in the morning, Hela gulped down her weak coffee in which she soaked a few pieces of hard bread and started toward the door. "Stop," I cried out, overcome by despair. "Promise that you'll come back to us right after work. Swear on all that is holy to you. Swear on Daddy's life." She turned around, Mother and I touched her face, whispering endearments. She answered weakly, "Don't worry I'll come, I promise on Daddy's life." Then, unable to say goodbye to us, she ran off and was gone.

In total silence, Mother and I picked up the two small suitcases that contained all our worldly goods and started walking through the newly fallen snow to our new home. All around us, emaciated people, grey except for the sparkling white snow that had settled on their hats, scarves, mufflers and coats, shuffled their feet on their last pilgrimage — destination Ghetto B. When Mother and I arrived at the apartment on Lwowska Street, the two women, in ragged black dresses almost purple with age, were again engaged in their battle with the stove.

As they did not acknowledge our greeting and altogether gave no sign that they had seen us, we quickly examined the apartment and found a small bedroom that looked as though it had been abandoned in a hurry. The two beds with their narrow mattresses were heaped with dirty sheets and torn blankets. We straightened out the mess as well as we could, unpacked our belongings, put them into a rickety dresser with drawers that would not close, and cleared a pile of dirty dishes from the table in the middle of the room. We tried to talk to our two new roommates, but all we could get out of them was that we would be allowed to put a kettle or maybe a pot of soup to boil on the uncooperative stove, and that the bathroom, serving six apartments, was down the hall. To our question about the amount of available coal, they replied in monosyllables that the supply would not last the winter.

I did not blame the two women for their unwillingness to chat. They were probably the only survivors of what once must have been two whole families, and it was obvious that they, too, lived from one minute to the next, in expectation of inescapable death. It would have been cruel and pointless to try to draw them out. Besides, since our lot was as inexorable as theirs, I did not feel exactly talkative myself.

Just as we were about to settle down to wait for Hela's return from work, counting every slow minute, we became dimly aware that some activity was going on in the yard, which was enclosed by three parts of our three-angled apartment building. Reluctantly, we moved toward the window to find out what was happening. The two black-clad women did the same. Nazi officers were whipping a group of young men and women into two lines. Some of them had festering wounds visible through the holes in their clothes, others were limping. All were barefoot on that frigid November afternoon. Obeying orders, they started moving through the opening of the yard into a narrow corridor that led into the street, but they did not reach it. We heard several salvos of gunshots, and about fifteen minutes later, the rattle of death carts rolling down Lwowska Street and stopping at the entrance of our yard. After some moments, there was no sound other than the muffled voices of the corpse bearers and the clatter of the death carts growing fainter as they moved away from our building in the direction of the Jewish cemetery. Judging from the age of the victims, I was sure that they had either been taken out of the factories where they had worked or discovered in clandestine places where they had been hiding illegally with their relatives in one of the ghettos. The spectacle did not portend well for Hela, and I was seized by a spasm of panic.

We waited for her, unable to busy ourselves with any task, however trivial, all day. Finally, she came, well after the darkness of evening had descended on the ghetto. By the light of our only candle, I saw that she was flushed from running and looking healthy. Her freckled cheeks were rosy and on her red hair the snowflakes, now slowly melting, had formed a sparkling coronet. After supper, we decided that Mother would take the smaller of the two beds while I took the larger, so that Hela would sleep with me and would have more room to hide if the Nazis came to search our apartment. Feeling the warmth of her young body curled up next to mine all that night filled me with such relief that I fell into a sounder, more peaceful sleep than I had known since the past June.

This routine continued for a few more days and nights. I don't remember what Mother and I did, ate or spoke about while waiting for Hela. Only when she came were we able to have some conversation over our soup at supper. On the fourth night, Hela told us that the Gestapo had been raiding several workplaces and taking people out at random, leaving some behind. They had not paid a visit to her factory yet. Also, systematic searches had begun in Ghetto A, which the Gestapo were combing house by house, killing everyone who was supposed to be in Ghetto B. This last piece of information came from Israel, but I had already surmised as much on witnessing the episode in our yard a few days earlier.

Naked terror, which had lain in wait since the first cozy night when Hela was with us and slept with me, returned to haunt us and dealt us another staggering blow. Hela would probably be safer, and there would be fewer risks, if she slept in Ghetto A. On the other hand, I agonized, what was the difference? They were going to get her and everybody else in the end anyway. Defiantly, and blocking all our self-created objections, we were going to continue.

On the fifth night, at about midnight, we were roused from our sleep by the sounds of screams and shots coming from the floor directly below us. Darting a quick look at the pitch-black yard, I was able to distinguish, by the waving arches of light coming from the flashlights, a group of people in their nightclothes standing in the far corner. It was clear that all the apartments were being searched. Every few minutes, more people were pushed to join the group already assembled. I barely had time to whisper to Hela, "Hide," when two gunmen came through the unlocked door of our apartment. They snapped on their flashlights and began to look everywhere, wreaking havoc with the furniture, rifling through the bedding and kitchen utensils.

I heard a voice in the room next to ours where the two women slept. "Papiere!" While there was a rustle of papers next door, I pushed Hela, who had already hidden under the blanket, further into the corner, and felt her breath on my feet. I then arranged myself into the most natural-looking position, pretending to be asleep. The two men entered our room, shone their lights right at us and, pointing their guns, commanded us to produce our papers. Pretending that we had just been awakened by the sudden light, Mother and I reached under our pillows and took out the battered documents. The men took their time looking at them, and then held a conversation in whispers. I could not make out what they were saying. Handing us back the papers, they asked the expected question: "Anybody from Ghetto A hiding here?" Our eyes lowered, we moved our heads in a motion of denial. "Okay," one said, while they were both backing toward the door, the guns still in their hands, "but you'd better not hide anybody from Ghetto A here. You know what the punishment is."

Our bodies tense, we waited a long time while they dealt with the group downstairs in their usual manner. Only after the last shots had been fired and the sounds of boots crunching in the snow had subsided did I tap Hela with my foot and told her that she could come out. There was panic in her eyes when she emerged from under the blanket and put her convulsed face on my chest. In her hand, she was clutching her Nicaraguan passport and the Gestapo *Bescheinigung*, and her fingers, which had closed around the documents, were rigid. She was crying noiselessly. I gently kissed her hair. As so many times on similar occasions in the past, Mother made her way to our bed, too, and we held on tightly to one another in a silent vigil that lasted all night.

The next morning, Hela did not go back to work, nor did she return to Folwarczna Street to fetch the rest of her belongings. Whether or not she showed up at her factory did not matter anymore. Nobody was counting the remaining Jews either in or out of the two ghettos. The Nazis, having applied their final solution, were now engaged in mere mopping-up operations. We made no new plans, for we knew that another night like the one just past would spell our end.

In the mid-morning, while we busied ourselves with innocuous household chores, debating whether to open our last can of sardines for our uncertain lunch or keep it for just as uncertain a supper, there was a knock on our door. We at first froze in our tracks, convinced that another raid was on, but I realized almost instantaneously that we were mistaken, as it was not the custom of the Gestapo to knock on ghetto doors. A young Ordnungsdienst man entered and with a paper in his hand, asked whether we were Ida, Sonia and Rachela (Hela's full name) Roskes. We nodded in assent, amazed that someone was asking for us by name. The man then explained that Rommelmann himself had come to the courtyard of the Jewish Council to ask whether anybody knew our whereabouts, as he wished to see us.

There was no choice but to go. Although we would have preferred to stay rooted to the floor, we joined the young emissary and had to run to keep pace with him. Breathless, we arrived at the substitute Platz and came to a halt, trembling, in front of Rommelmann, who was flanked by Oppermann and Palten. All their hands were gloved but none held guns. Rommelmann was the first to speak. As he was scrutinizing us from top to bottom, he said, "I see that the Nicaraguans are still with us. I wouldn't have thought so. Anyway, since you are here in the flesh, it is my duty to inform you that you will take part in an exchange between Americans and Germans. Go home and pack your belongings. And make sure you are back here in twenty minutes." With a wave of his hand, he dismissed us and turned to speak to his cohorts.

We backed away slowly, and only when we realized that they were not paying any attention to us — we heard them order the Ordnungsdienst man to bring to the yard an assortment of twenty Jews from Ghetto B — we turned and ran as quickly back to our apartment as we had rushed out of it on hearing the summons. While we were throwing some clothes into one suitcase — for that was all we had decided to take — we racked our brains as to what Rommelmann might possibly want with us. We could have easily been among the other twenty he had asked for, and yet he had sent for us specifically. It was the first time since the wholesale action in June that the Gestapo had singled out individuals by name, as far as we knew. This was going to be the ultimate trick, I thought, a sick joke on us for acting as foreigners.

There was very little in the suitcase we carried out on our way back. We would not need even that little, I thought cynically. But why were they playing games when the easiest thing to do was to kill us without any preamble? I searched my mind and strained my imagination for an answer, but none came. We were so sure that we were going to our deaths that terror had intensified and held us in its icy grip by the time we reached the yard.

We found the trio of the Gestapo brass gone and heard a death cart rounding the corner. Fresh blood was splattered over the stones of the large enclosure. A tremor went through us when a lone Gestapo man, who had been pacing back and forth, stopped in front of us and said, "Come with me." To our utter disbelief and mounting anxiety, he led us out of the ghetto, through the gate, into the city proper. When he saw that we had difficulties carrying the suitcase, he turned to us. "Leave it right here," he commanded. "You won't need it." We dropped the suitcase in the middle of Wałowa Street, now certain beyond any doubt that he was taking us to our deaths. I saw the furtive glances of a few passersby and thought that I detected signs of compassion in them. But why? Why? The question darted back and forth in my mind. Why all these special, elaborate arrangements to get rid of three insignificant Jews?

It was going to be some time before the question was answered. In the meantime, our guard deposited us at the Gestapo headquarters where we were asked once again to produce our documents, this time to men who seemed of a higher rank than Rommelmann. There followed something resembling a mock trial. We fielded a volley of questions about Father, our Nicaraguan citizenship, our inability to get exit visas, and all the many related issues with a feeble "yes" or "no." As the faces and voices of our interrogators became increasingly hostile, I was on the verge of asking them to put us out of our misery. What stopped me was a nagging doubt I had started to entertain on the way out of the ghetto, and some rapid reasoning: if they wanted to do away with us, there was no need for the theatrics. None had been used for the past six months. Could it be, I asked myself tentatively, that there was some truth to what they were saying?

Uneasy Journeys

The interrogation at the Gestapo headquarters lasted about a half an hour, and at the end of it we were still alive. We were marched under guard to the railway station. We shivered in our worn-out coats because of the biting frost and because of our mounting apprehension of what was awaiting us at the station. When we arrived there, we were motioned to a sealed and windowless car of a long train and were surprised to find that we and our guard were its sole occupants. We sat down and started massaging our frostbitten fingers and toes. Our guard sat down, too, on the seat across from us and let his rifle rest between his knees. As the train started moving, we hoped that he would volunteer some information about our destination, but he remained silent throughout the trip.

My watch told me that we had been riding for an hour and a quarter but since we could not look out, I was unable to determine the direction of the train. Finally, the brakes screeched to a stop, and our guard acknowledged our arrival with the familiar "Raus" (Out). It was still light outside and the sign on the station building read Krakow. It was only five hours since we had stumbled out of our ghetto apartment to answer Rommelmann's summons, but the uncertainty of its purpose made it feel like eternity. Hatless and gloveless, with our coats pulled tight around us, we followed our escort through a number of darkening, unfamiliar streets. On one street, the guard stopped and said contemptuously, pointing to a barbed wire fence which, intent on what was happening to us, we had not noticed, "This is what remains of the big Krakow ghetto. It will be liquidated any day now, just like yours." He sounded like a tour guide giving information to ignorant tourists. We showed no reaction. He quickened his pace and continued on. Soon we found ourselves in front of a large, foreboding looking building, surrounded by a high cement wall. We were on a street called Montelupich, and I recognized the building as one of Poland's largest prisons before the war. We had heard that the Germans had turned it into a jail for political prisoners. Anybody who committed either real or imaginary crimes against the Third Reich, including runaways from labour camps, was imprisoned there.

Upon arrival we were ordered to stand in a garishly lit corridor, full of Gestapo guards. We had been joined, to our surprise, by a score of other women and children, all wearing Jewish armbands or yellow stars on their chests. A young Gestapo officer, obviously in charge, looked at the hue intensely and said something coarse to the other men, who burst into laughter. When the merriment had subsided, the commander faced us directly once again, raised his gun, pointed it at us and shouted, "Alle Juden mit der Nase an der Wand!" (All Jews with their nose to the wall!) We obeyed. My throat had gone rigid and I prayed that death should be mercifully quick. I glanced at Mother and Hela on either side of me and saw that they were faltering when a surge of panic shot through them.

After what must have been seconds but seemed like hours, the commander ordered us to face him again. "I should have really killed you, all of you, filthy Jews," he said, "but you have some pretensions to a special status. We'll see." He then sent us off, marching single file, with one guard leading and another closing the rear of the procession, through long prison corridors, along which we noticed cell after cell, each occupied by a single prisoner.

We finally reached the room where we were to stay. It was considerably larger than the cells we had seen, had three small, barred windows looking out on the gaping darkness outside, and mattresses strewn all over the floor. A smell of urine and vomit assailed our nostrils as we were about to enter, and I was close to fainting from inhaling the foul odours. I must have hesitated and held back at the door, for the guard in front poked my ribs with his rifle butt and pushed me in. I fell and sprawled on the floor but was not otherwise hurt. When he was satisfied that we were all in, he shut and bolted the door.

Somebody helped me up and I rose to my feet. In the falling dusk of that late November evening, we could barely distinguish our cell-mates. All we knew from our brief encounter downstairs in the corridor was that they were women and young children. We had no idea why they were there and why, for that matter, the Germans had seen fit to send us to Montelupich. We were not aware that there had been any stops or side trips on the way to the death camps. I could not rid myself of the feeling that we had been picked to amuse the Gestapo, and that, after the black comedy with its ironic twists had been played out, we would be added to some human compost.

Suddenly, a light came on in the two low-hanging bulbs obviously switched on outside. As the illumination made us see distinctly, we looked over our new neighbours carefully and with great curiosity. They were indeed women in their thirties and forties, and young children up to about ten or eleven years of age. The women looked unkempt and dirty, and the children were hopping among the mattresses with running noses and unwashed faces, scratching their heads continuously. I asked one of the women whether there were any spare mattresses. She was very friendly, showed us three unoccupied lairs, and even helped arrange them side by side. From a pile in the corner, she brought three blankets and told us to use our coats for pillows. Everyone did the same.

Her name was Mrs. Pilicz, and she had a ten-year-old daughter with her. She and the child had survived three actions by hiding in the city of Rzeszów, eighty or so kilometres east of Tarnów, and had been collected in much the same way as we had. Her citizenship was

Bolivian and legitimate; it had been sent to her by her husband, who had run away from the retreating Polish army and had made his way to Bolivia. As far as she could make out, there was only one other family that she suspected had legitimate papers — Mrs. Schmelkes, who said she was the wife of an American citizen, with her son and daughter. She told us that her husband, a concert pianist, had been on a North American tour since the summer of 1939 and that he had tried to get his family out before the United States entered the war, but could barely establish any contact with them.[1] The others, Mrs. Pilicz said, had foreign, mainly Central American passports — all forged. So far, the Germans had not detected the forgeries. One family had come from Warsaw where, at the time of their departure, the remaining Jews had started to prepare seriously for an armed uprising.

Mrs. Pilicz relayed that most of them had been in Montelupich for about ten days. They had not been assaulted in their cells. The only times they had been sent for and brought downstairs for a command performance like the one we had just taken part in had been when two new groups had arrived; ours had been the second of the two. She, too, was afraid that the Germans were playing some diabolical trick on us but, like the three of us, could not guess either the reason or the outcome of the game.

As we were exhausted from the events of the entire day, we lay down on our mattresses, fully clothed, and tried to sleep. We even disregarded the lice that crawled all over our makeshift beds and were embedded in the seams and crevices of the filthy mattress covers. As long as we remained in those surroundings, we knew that it

---

1   Editor's note: Rita B. Ross (née Schmelkes), the daughter of Mrs. Schmelkes, wrote a memoir titled *Running from Home* (2008), in which she describes their actual circumstances. Mr. Schmelkes was not yet an American citizen, nor was he a pianist. It is possible that Sonia misheard the story — the Schmelkes family did have a close relative, Artur Schnabel, who was a renowned pianist — or that Mrs. Schmelkes did not want to disclose their true circumstances.

was pointless to battle them: soon, we would be crawling with them even as our cellmates were.

"What do you think it is all about?" Mother asked between yawns, raising her head a little. "Let's not think tonight at all," I answered. "We'll think tomorrow. Try to sleep, Mother. You'll need your rest." I walked over to the edge of her mattress and hugged her. She seemed to have calmed down and fell asleep almost instantly. Looking over my shoulder in Hela's direction, I saw by her even breathing that she was sleeping soundly. Despite my fatigue, I remained awake, wondering how long the jail would remain our new home and whether our death was truly imminent and inescapable. It was clear that we were in the midst of a new exercise. In some respects, the situation appeared to be in our favour: it could not have been by chance that we all had American or Central American citizenship. If the Nazis had wished to get rid of us, they would not have had to go to all the trouble of snatching us from different ghettos. Each of us could have been killed or marked for deportation more easily where we had lived. And yet, the idea that we were all headed for a puzzling but cruel hoax persisted. Disturbed by my inability to outguess the Germans, I tossed and turned on my lice-infested mattress and could not fall asleep.

Life in the cell was much like that in the bunkers, but with one significant difference. Here, the Germans were aware of our existence. Their kitchen help brought us slop, which passed for food, three times a day. Otherwise, the guards remained unseen for days. I got to know our other cellmates, who confided in me that their passports had indeed been manufactured in Poland. When one woman showed me hers and her children's (it was Venezuelan, I believe), I found it a fairly accurate imitation but felt that it would not stand up to scrutiny. She was obviously of the same opinion for she said, with fear and timidity in her voice, that she hoped that neither she nor her husband, who was incarcerated in a different cell in Montelupich, would ever have to present them for inspection again. I wished her luck, but without letting her know, brooded over her documents and similar ones held by the others.

The three of us were covered with lice within two days of our arrival. Like everyone else, we scratched our scalps until they bled, but there was no way to get rid of them. Since we had no books to read and no work to do, picking the lice off one another's hair and shoulders was our chief pastime. Unable to wash, we began to exude the same odour that had overpowered us when we first entered the cell.

After about a week, we were treated to an unexpected outing. A prison guard came in and told us to get ready for an hour's excursion. We were going to the remnants of the Krakow ghetto, he said, to see whether we could find a store left to buy some food and cigarettes. We did not believe him but, since we could not refuse without incurring severe punishment and possibly death, we reluctantly trooped out of our cell and made our way in the direction of the ghetto. Apparently, he had not lied to us. The ghetto looked exactly like its Tarnów counterpart, with many ruined houses boarded up and few human shapes wearing yellow stars on their chests walking stiffly but hurriedly, their heads bent. We finally came upon a store, which was no more than a gaping dark hole in the ground. The owner was about to cry out in alarm on seeing the group of us and our fierce-looking, helmeted and armed guard, but quieted down on realizing that we were fellow Jews. He was able to give us some cigarettes and a few bars of soap, but his place was completely denuded of food. We emptied our pockets of all the coins we still had and handed them to him, but he took them reluctantly, obviously conveying to us the unspoken message that he had no use for them anymore. He seemed relieved to see us go, failing to understand, just as we did, the meaning of the strange episode. On the way back, our guard offered an unsolicited statement: "You'll be leaving in a few days, let it not be said that we treated you badly." The idea of a Nazi guard trying to create a good impression on Jews was so novel and surprising to us that we stared at him in amazement.

After the guard's disclosure, I became almost convinced that our experience in Montelupich was related, in some positive way, to our foreign citizenship. True, while we were jailed and watched over by the Gestapo still hungry for our blood, any of their men could easily account to his superiors for a few deaths among us. Yet, even as they starved us and denied us means to maintain basic personal hygiene, it became clear from their insinuations and oblique allusions that they were going to deliver us somewhere. But where? To Treblinka, Auschwitz or Belzec? And could they kill us on the way on the pretext that we had disobeyed orders? Afraid to ask and at a loss for answers, we all met each coming day with uneasiness, finding a little comfort in the fact that we were together.

Two weeks later, the door of the cell flew wide open, and we heard a yell. "Alle heraus!" (Everyone out!) We scrambled into our coats, stuffed our tattered shoes with rags to protect our feet from the December frost. A few of us carried paper bags with the remnants of our supplies. We gingerly walked along the snow-covered streets until, shivering with cold, we arrived at the train station. The locomotive of a short, sealed train ready to depart puffed clouds of smoke into the cold, pale blue sky. We were hoisted up by the guards into different compartments at a considerable distance from the ground, and before we found our seats, we were moving. I had judged by the position of the engine that we were heading west.

Night had fallen. In the compartment where Mother, Hela and I were sitting with Mrs. Pilicz and her daughter, our guard started snoring loudly. Yet, despite his relaxed vigilance and the lateness of the hour, we could not sleep. The car had become so steaming hot that we had to take off our shoes and loosen our clothes. We sat for hours in silence, unable to look out the barred and blacked-out windows, while the train continued its mysterious journey at a steady speed, the trip stretching interminably before us. I had smoked most of my cigarettes and forced myself to keep a package intact. Then, Mrs. Pilicz distributed a slice of several-days-old bread, hoarded and hidden from our daily prison ration, to each of us to assuage our growing hunger pangs for a while.

After we had travelled for several more hours, we realized that the train was slowing down to a stop. Our guard, now fully awake, ordered us to stand up and get ready to disembark. The train came to a halt and, once on the platform, we made out indistinctly that we were in Munich. As we were being herded toward the exit, joined by our cellmates emerging from other compartments, we became aware of a droning noise coming from above. It sounded like something I had heard a few years earlier. It did not take us long to recognize the sounds and realize that Munich was in the throes of an air raid. In the distance, we heard a few loud crashes and saw flames of fire shooting into the black night, accompanied by the roar from German anti-aircraft guns. Despite our apprehension and fatigue, we rejoiced in our hearts at the sight of the Allied air force penetrating deep into Germany. However, we could not savour our gladness, for we had problems closer to home; I, for one, having taken off my shoes in the infernal heat of the compartment, could not put them on again, as my feet had swollen badly. And so, I and a few others hobbled in our bare feet over the snowy gangway leading to the station house. Once there, we lay down, by order of the guards who had emerged from all the train compartments, on the metal slabs of huge tables and were to stay there until further instructions.

The resounding noises of the bombardment seemed to subside as we tried to make ourselves comfortable on our Procrustean beds, but the unyielding surfaces made it hard to sleep. Some of us asked to be granted permission to sit in a few scattered chairs or lie down on the floor. The guards did not care as long as we remained silent. And so we did, including the children, who, heedless of where they were finally bedded down, were sound asleep instantly. In the meantime, the noise grew fainter, the all-clear had sounded, and all was still again.

My watch showed 5:00 a.m. when we were rounded up again. Bleary-eyed, our muscles stiff and throbbing from the broken sleep of the night just passed, we finally got into our shoes and followed the guards to another, smaller train. *Is this the one heading for a death camp?* must have been the question on everyone's mind. As we received no enlightenment from our Nazi companions, we boarded it without a word of protest. The locomotive of the new train, too, pointed west. Searching my memory and knowledge of German geography, I realized that I didn't know of any concentration camps in the southwestern part of the country. Although by now pretty sure that the Gestapo had not transported our small group of thirty all the way across Germany in order to kill us, I could not rid myself of the suspicion that we were the actors in some play they had devised, perhaps because they were bored by now with gassing Jews. The thought that persisted was that we were being taken to some sort of a tribunal to verify our passports. But where was it located? And what was its ultimate purpose?

New Year, New Refuge

The new train had some redeeming features about it. The windows were not barred, the compartments afforded more leg room, and altogether it looked bright and almost cheerful on the crisp December morning. As far as our eyes could see, there was clean white snow covering the fields and undulating meadows, and at the edge of the horizon we detected some farmhouses, adding a splash of colour to the white-blue landscape. We travelled for a few hours during which a kitchen attendant brought us cups of steaming coffee and slabs of fresh black bread with jam. Hungrily, we threw ourselves on the first tasty meal we had had in a long time and consumed it within minutes.

The train began to slow down at the station of a small Württemberg town called Meckenbeuren. It then switched tracks and came to a full stop on a siding, just a kilometre or two beyond the city limits. We craned our necks through all the windows of our compartments and jammed the tiny platform in anxious anticipation of what was going to happen next. In a short while, we saw a group of women heading in our direction. They were quite indistinct at first, but even at a distance we marvelled at their erect postures and light steps. When they came closer, we could not stifle a cry of disbelief and rubbed our eyes to make sure that we had not conjured up in our imagination otherworldly apparitions. Those women were not concentration camp inmates. They were, for the most part, young, attractive and stylishly dressed. They wore makeup, and altogether looked better groomed than all the women we had known and seen at home since the Nazi occupation.

Their leader was an elderly lady with stone-grey, short-cropped hair and a weather-beaten face who introduced herself in broken Polish as Mrs. Froom. Sensing our disquiet, she spoke to us gently. She informed us that she and the others in her group would accompany us to camp Liebenau, within walking distance, of which she was captain. She herself was a British subject and had been captured by the Germans as an enemy alien, and the women in her company were all British and American. Reading the agonizing question at the mention of the word "camp" in our eyes and responding to our dazed look, she added quickly that camp Liebenau was not a concentration camp. It was an internment camp for civilian women, equivalent to a prisoner-of-war camp, under the protection of Swiss authorities and the International Committee of the Red Cross. Although it was guarded by aging German soldiers unfit for combat, it enjoyed a fair level of self-government. We were in good hands, she continued with friendliness and warmth, soothing to our despairing hearts. No one would kill us there. We would stay either until the end of the war, or, if we were fortunate, until our names were listed for one of the repatriation transports that were taking place from time to time. As most of the women with her spoke English only, we found it hard to communicate. And so, it was only Mrs. Froom, having taught English at the University of Warsaw, who answered questions we could no longer contain and which came rushing out from our throats until we were hoarse.

We walked together quite a ways toward the camp gate, leaving the train and our guards behind. When we reached the entrance, there was a small building inside that Mrs. Froom told us was the guardhouse. The half a dozen men in Wehrmacht uniforms actually smiled at us benevolently and waved us on, saying that Mrs. Froom and her "girls" would take care of us. Beyond the guardhouse, the camp looked clean and serene swathed in sparkling white snow. The circular area in the centre was surrounded by three large buildings named, as Mrs. Froom explained, Josefshaus (Joseph's House), Clarahaus (Clara House) and the Schloss (the castle). In our bewilderment, we wanted to bombard Mrs. Froom with more questions, but she told us patiently that we would learn all about our new home in time and that there were certain preparations we had to submit to.

We were first taken into a spacious "cleansing" room where, after having our hair rubbed with a special delousing salve and tightly wrapped in towels, we were invited to luxuriate in bathtubs where we used fragrant soap. We were then given new skirts and blouses, and each of us received a supply of underwear, a box of toiletries and some bed linen. We learned that the handsome buildings we had seen were all part of an institution for Germans with intellectual disabilities, run by nuns, which explained the tall steeple of a white-walled Catholic church in the middle of the grounds. In both Joseph's House and Clara House, the internees had to share the corridors and bathroom facilities with the patients, but Mrs. Froom assured us there had not been any incidents, as they were quite harmless. Their job was to pick apples in the summer and make cider in the winter, as Liebenau was situated in one of the richest apple-growing regions in Germany.

According to the German nuns who had run the institution — the *Anstalt*, as we all came to call it — before the arrival of the first internees, the establishment had been doomed to extinction as the Nazi system would not tolerate the existence of psychiatric patients. In fact, hundreds had been murdered after the nuns had heard that the place was going to be converted into an internment camp. Yet, they were reassured when they realized that the rest of their charges would be safe, and they were greatly relieved about their own safety as well. A Dutch-English girl, Lizzy McIntyre, with whom I formed a friendship and who had been among the first to arrive, told me that the nuns had practically kissed the hands of the British women who had formed the first contingent. They cheerfully looked after everybody's food and, in time, joined the ranks of those internees who chose to become teachers of Liebenau's polyglotic children.

It took me at least a month to grasp the enormous implications of being in an internment camp. Up until our arrival, I had had no inkling that such places existed. Suddenly I found myself in one and learned that there was another, also for civilians, in Vittel, occupied France. Scattered throughout Germany, there were also prisoner-of-war camps for British and American army personnel captured in battle. However, as I soon discovered on one of our escorted walks, the same privileges did not extend to Russian and Yugoslav prisoners of war, held in a camp nearby. Through the barbed wire surrounding their compound, we saw emaciated figures in prison clothes digging the earth with picks and shovels while a guard kept his whip busy lashing them mercilessly. During our brief and infrequent talks with them, exchanging a few words when the guards were not looking, we found out that they were dying like flies. Often, we would toss them cigarettes and, in season, apples we had picked off the trees lining the road. To me, they were a vivid reminder that, despite our new and superior accommodations, despite the reassurances often repeated by Mrs. Froom and her senior officers, we were still on German territory and the long arm of the Gestapo might snatch us, the Jews, any time from our recently granted and perhaps deceptive refuge.

At first, Mother, Hela and I were assigned a room in Joseph's House. Although our stay there was not altogether pleasant, we found it a haven compared to what we had left behind. All but two rooms on our floor were occupied by the German patients, and we were startled many a time when we encountered one of them at night on our way to the bathroom. Although I was reluctant to complain, I went to see Mrs. Froom to ask whether a change of quarters would be possible. As she had learned about the atrocities we had suffered and realized that our final destination was Canada rather than Nicaragua, she invited us to move to the second floor of the Schloss where we were to share a room with four British women until she found one suitable for a family of three.

In her wisdom, she realized even before we did that it was impor-tant for us to learn English, something that would be much harder to do in either of the other houses where people were multilingual, us-ing mainly one or another Slavic language. Delighted with her deci-sion, we moved into the Schloss and were immersed in a totally Eng-lish environment as English was the only language our roommates, and most women on the floor, spoke. Many of them were unmarried women of varying ages who had been seized while teaching English at schools and universities in countries now under the Nazis. They had been interned in Liebenau, the population of which had grown from two hundred or so women and children brought there origi-nally to about six hundred at the time of our arrival.

The brightest and most encouraging feature of our internment was the official permission to write letters to Canada directly and to receive mail in return. The maximum allowed was a twenty-four-line form letter per person per week, but we found it a veritable embar-rassment of riches. The first letter I wrote to Father with a trembling hand was so blurred by my tears that I had to rewrite it. Mother and Hela wrote, too, and those initial messages after many months during which Father must have presumed us dead, separated from one an-other or slowly expiring in a death camp were filled with reassurances that we were alive and well and with anxious requests for him to get in touch with us immediately and let us know about his state of health and anything he wished to share with us. We spoke of Liebenau with enthusiasm, describing to him the charm and beauty of the country-side and the uncommon kindness of our new friends. Awaiting his reply, we settled down to learn more about the camp and to become active participants in its life.

The camp was a model of self-organization. Although the German Foreign Office made all the formal decisions, the guards accompanied the internees on their daily walks and, after a nightly roll call, locked the door on every floor of the three houses, the internal life of the campmates was regulated with remarkable efficiency by Mrs. Froom and her committee of floor captains and chiefs of various services.

From what we learned of the camp's early history, it had not always been so. At first, the situation in camp was chaotic, and any viable community life threatened to fall apart. The outbreak of the war and the subsequent occupation of many European countries by the German armies had brought forth the internment of British subjects residing on the continent. The process of civilian internment, conducted by the Gestapo and other security forces, had been characterized by atypical disorder and discrepancies. Some British women were seized late in 1939 and early 1940, while others were left in their residences, only to be interned two years later.

And so, after Anstalt Liebenau had been declared a civilian internment camp for women subjects of enemy countries in 1940, there came to it from various cities and jails of Europe a motley collection of women and minors, children, representing different and mixed nationalities, religious creeds, occupational strata, social positions and ethnic and cultural backgrounds.

As soon as the preliminary question of accommodations for the steady stream of newcomers had been settled, the camp slowly began to take on the shape of a near-normal community. The rapid increases in the number of internees, the many changes in the structure and function of the German Foreign Office, which had jurisdiction over the internees, and the occasional exchange transports that took place between the camp's foundation and its final liberation impeded orderly administration. Even so, under the flexible but firm leadership of Mrs. Froom, the administration had become a fact and, despite chronic difficulties and setbacks, facilitated a communal life that otherwise would have been utterly unstable or, worse, taken over by the Germans.

Although all official matters were dealt with by the German Foreign Office and Switzerland as a Protecting Power aided by the International Red Cross, the captain and her body of assistants acted as the campus executive and took care of all aspects of the internees' daily lives. Often thwarted and impeded by the German authorities, this democratically elected body maintained order and a high sanitary level in all houses, looked after the distribution of mail and parcels, prepared duty rosters for jobs that the internees were to perform, and even settled personal disputes.

An important step toward that unique if limited self-government was the creation of a few social service agencies. The Educational Committee managed the school for camp children, two libraries and classes for adults. The sanitary and health personnel — of unparalleled value in a crowded setting to which people had come from many sordid jails in Europe — provided voluntary nurses, paramedics and dieticians. In co-operation with the camp's ancient camp doctor, it helped distribute such medications as were available and to quarantine people with infectious diseases to prevent epidemics. A special committee dealing with the inmates' variety of religious affiliations, consisting chiefly of interned British nuns, ensured an adequate number and quality of inter-denominational services. Under the supervision of the six floor captains, the food committee had a list of rotating duties — supervising the bringing of meals from the *Anstalt* kitchens, taking care of the boilers for the afternoon tea and arranging special food for the occasional festivities. The recreational committee organized, from time to time, shows and plays put on by the internees by special permission in the canteen, and programs for the various holidays.

The problem of food, at first difficult to handle, had found its satisfactory solution a year or so before our arrival. Three meals daily were provided by the large *Anstalt* kitchen supervised by the German nuns and staffed by the psychiatric patients. If the internees had had to depend on their subsistence on these alone, they would certainly have been undernourished from the inadequate, vitamin-deficient diet. The daily ration consisted of two slices of stale bread, one piece of waterlogged meat, saccharine sweetened coffee substitute and a ladleful of half-rotten vegetables. However, Mrs. Froom, with the consent of the Swiss Legation in Berlin, had contacted the International Red Cross in Geneva. For the past couple of years, each internee had been receiving her biweekly British, and later American, Red Cross parcel, which contained food items ensuring a balanced diet and staved off hunger. The absolute equality of the distribution process was further manifestation of the scrupulously democratic principles underlying Liebenau's internal organization.

As I found out shortly after arrival, the Educational Committee was the nerve centre of camp life. It was headed by Mrs. Vidakovic, an Englishwoman and former Oxford graduate in her forties who had taught English at the University of Belgrade. She was by far the person I most admired throughout the entire war period; having adopted me as her favourite charge, she had become, in a sense, my surrogate mother. Unobtrusively, steadily and with quiet efficiency, she contributed more to the welfare of the internees than anybody else in camp, with the exception of Mrs. Froom. Owing to her ceaseless requests for the necessary supplies from the Red Cross and her untiring energy, an educational system had been introduced, progressively encompassing all internees, including those with American passports who joined the earlier group after Pearl Harbor. Although every minute of her working day was filled with her exacting duties, Mrs. Vidakovic found time to listen to me and to comfort me whenever I felt sad or still exhibited signs of my former fears and worries. I basked in her warmth as much as I had in that of my now extinct Białystok family, and I equated her brilliance, keen intelligence and humble wisdom with the qualities I had adored in my grandfather.

The school for the children was divided into two departments, upper and lower, the former meeting in the little library room, and the other wherever it was convenient at the moment — in one of the dining rooms, corridors or attics of the three buildings. The headmistress, an English nun of the teaching orders, and a staff of voluntary assistant teachers (mainly young women between nineteen and twenty-five years of age) were giving six to eight lessons a day to a crowd of sixty-odd pupils, among whom it was difficult to find two having the same level of knowledge, the same degree of intelligence or even a common mother tongue. Consequently, the classes — each divided from the next by a wooden bench or table — had to be numerous and highly flexible. The curricula depended on the group as well: while some had to be taught the English alphabet and given the first, simplest phrases in the unknown language, the more advanced enjoyed mastering arithmetic, geography, history, popular science, French or German.

The little school, although without official recognition by any formal authority outside camp, was nevertheless serving an invaluable purpose. It gave the children an education; it induced them to greater mental effort by offering possibilities for quick advancement, and, above all, it helped transform an unruly, mainly fatherless group of youngsters who had suffered many traumas and had tasted much wild, unchecked freedom, into responsible, prejudice-free individuals whose self-respect had grown in direct proportion to their respect for authority and for others.

Haunted by the memories of all the dead and death-bound ghetto children, I greeted with a mixture of joy and sorrow the sight of happy-go-lucky young ones running eagerly to "school," engaging in gym and limited sports, and shouting cheerfully "Sister Laetitia" (the headmistress) in the yard. It was touching and amusing to behold this multicultural group, for besides those of European origin, some were of Black descent and had come from Benghazi in North Africa, arguing with one another in twenty different languages and what was gratifying to observe — understanding one another with great ease. Toward the end of our stay in camp, each child had, besides speaking several broken languages, a perfect command of English and a sound foundation for his or her future studies.

The classes for adults were as well run as those for the children. Mother, Hela and I must have been thirsting for them through the fog of all our war years in Poland, for we joined them immediately on our arrival. Mrs. Vidakovic and her assistants, many of them teachers and university graduates captured in Europe, conducted courses in beginner, intermediate and advanced English, English literature and history, French and Spanish. The conditions under which the teachers were working were primitive and difficult. Despite Mrs. Vidakovic's persistent efforts, the supply of texts and writing materials was too small to meet the requirements; the classrooms were cubbyholes, not always available; the hours arranged for lessons often interfered with duties the internees had to perform in order to keep the community functioning; and last but not least, the atmosphere was not always conducive to concentration on studies, for the crowded rooms offered no privacy, repatriation transports stirred disappointment and impatience, lack of news from families outside disrupted self-control, and political events were, at least at first, a source of chronic depression. And yet, the will to learn and ingenuity had prevailed and by writing on pieces of cardboard from the Red Cross parcels, substituting chips of coal, if necessary, for pen and pencil, and sharing in quick rotation the few well-thumbed textbooks, the internees attended their classes enthusiastically and studied with uncommon diligence.

Another, no less important, aspect of the Committee's activities was the establishment of two libraries. The supply of books was irregular and subject to Nazi censorship, but adequate enough to satisfy the inmates' need for reading matter, denied to them during the long years under the Nazis. The fiction library was under the supervision of a trained librarian and two assistants, and it comprised some two thousand well-catalogued and widely circulated volumes. The other section, consisting mainly of non-fiction and such textbooks as the Red Cross had made available for teaching purposes, was managed by Mrs. Vidakovic herself. As soon as she had discovered my fondness for books, she appointed me her assistant. I found my new position a source of great joy; not only was I able to observe Mrs. Vidakovic's remarkable efficiency first-hand, but I was in her physical presence much of the time, and, as an added attraction, for the first time in over three years was able to throw myself upon book after book, eager to devour them all.

A Fragile Peace

For the first year of our stay at Liebenau, Mother, Hela and I found it hard to believe that we were actually there. Not only did we eventually get our own room, but we were able to go for walks, watched over by indifferent and unarmed guards, in the surrounding countryside amid a sea of rosy apple blossoms and green farms, made good friends with women of all kinds of nationalities and professions, and were receiving our biweekly Red Cross parcel. But most of all, to our profound relief, we were in steady correspondence with Father and seemed far away from the watchful eyes of the Gestapo. Hesitantly at first, we began to look on ourselves as full-fledged human beings again and to rekindle a hope that we would survive the war after all.

With the memories of the horrors we had been through indelibly imprinted on our minds, and never forgetting that we had been singled out from millions to enjoy relative peace and security in the very stronghold of Nazism, we turned into exemplary campers. We studied English zealously, Hela and I taught the children, we shared the extra parcels of food and clothing we were receiving regularly from Father with our new friends, and we volunteered for every job whenever a need arose. Personally, I had developed a reputation of my own as a letter and petition writer. As soon as I had mastered English and when word got out that I spoke and wrote German and fluent Polish as well, I was besieged by requests from some of our less literate co-internees to compose love letters to their boyfriends, send messages to their families in America, write official petitions to the German authorities and fill out reams of forms. My new occupation kept me busy and gained me wide respect, but I kept enough free time to write to Father, study and read. It was a blessing, I felt, to be transformed from a useless parasite and a caged animal into a purposeful, constructive person.

Together with our English and American friends, we poked fun at the camp's ineffectual paymaster, who pushed around useless papers on his desk for lack of any money, ridiculed the old, tottering camp doctor, who could not distinguish between a sore foot and a sprained ankle, climbed to the roof of our tallest building, the Schloss, to watch "our boys" — the British and American pilots — fly overhead on their missions, and actively took part in any internee-sponsored festivities and all national holidays. We learned to knit using the string from the Red Cross parcels and to make costumes for our shows out of scraps of old fabrics provided by the German nuns amid whatever else was handy. Although liberation was nowhere near, I abandoned myself totally to the feeling that the three of us were free from danger and closer to a reunion with Father.

Our state of euphoria lasted for some nine or so months. In September 1943, an event took place that brought about drastic changes in the atmosphere and running of the camp. For some time before, ever since the German defeat in Stalingrad, news had got out that the mighty Reich had begun crumbling — at least at the edges. We knew that the German army had retreated in North Africa and that the German soil itself had become — as witnessed by our own eyes — almost a daily target for the British and American bombs, which began to level the industry and war installations to the ground and knocked much of the legendary Flak (anti-aircraft defence) out of commission. Even as we rejoiced over all these greatly desired setbacks, the Prisoner of War division of the German Foreign Office, with a group of Gestapo ostensibly acting as their bodyguards, moved into Liebenau for an indefinite stay. The high Nazi officials, up until that time living in Berlin under the constant threat of Allied bombs, had found the internment camp, a virtually ex-territorial zone, a safer residence.

The consequences of the move were felt immediately. All internees, with the exception of those who were known Nazi sympathizers, were removed from the most spacious of the three buildings — Clara House — which was from then on to house the arrivals from Berlin. The two other houses became severely overcrowded, more so because new transports of internees kept arriving frequently. The classes were curtailed and sanitary conditions deteriorated. The government officials took over all authority previously exercised by the guards, nuns and the paymaster. Unlike their paternalistically benevolent predecessors, they meted out punishment for all activities previously considered harmless: looking out of windows during air raids, picking apples in the countryside and offering cigarettes to the Yugoslav prisoners. The punishment ranged from withholding the Red Cross parcels and mail and restricting the walks, to transporting some of the worse offenders to forced labour camps. Deliberately, the higher-ups in the Foreign Office began to meddle in the composition of the exchange transports, giving preference to people who were not on any official list and who were notorious Nazi collaborators.

While our British and American friends lamented the curtailment of their privileges and the intrusion of an obviously vengeful enemy on what they considered their territory, and while they were furious about the abuses of the fundamental principles of the Geneva Convention, Mother, Hela and I, and the handful of our former Montelupich cellmates, began to feel the old dread all over again. The sight of the Gestapo threw us into panic, reminding us dramatically that our lives still hung in the balance. Ironically, we had lived to see Germany edging closer to defeat than we had dared imagine, but we were no longer sure that we would actually live to see it accomplished.

I tried to explain to my good friend Lizzy, who complained about missing her walks, how enormous our concerns were compared to her few minor inconveniences, but she did not seem to understand. Only after I had sat up with her many nights in the dimly lit corridor of the Schloss, telling her my tale, did she begin to grasp the precariousness of our situation. From then on, she hardly ever left me out of her sight, as though trying to protect me from harm. I had similar heartrending conversations with compassionate Mrs. Vidakovic, and she, too, contrived to be somewhere close to me more often than before. However, nothing our well-meaning friends did for us helped dispel our despondency at having rediscovered our vulnerability.

Our fragile peace was shattered to bits in early 1944 when Herr Schneider, the head of the Foreign Office, summoned to Mrs. Froom's office two mothers and the five children they had between them, and announced to them that they would be taken out of Liebenau and reunited with their husbands who had been interned in a similar camp, in Vittel. Those women had been with us in Montelupich, and I knew that their passports were forgeries. They, however, greeted the announcement with glee and were off, amid warm goodbyes, the next day. Casting my forebodings aside for the occasion, and again lulled into a false sense of security by the plausible-sounding explanation, I joined their well-wishers and entreated them to write to us, as we were all eager to know how Vittel compared to Liebenau. Perhaps I envied them a little, too, for I thought that they would be safer away from the Foreign Office and the Gestapo, and would see their families reunited long before we would be with Father again.

In less than a week, news leaked to Liebenau that the two families, husbands included, had been taken out of Vittel and deported to Auschwitz. At first, I was too stunned to believe it but in the end, the news was confirmed in carefully guarded words by Mrs. Froom. It was obvious that the Germans had become alert to forged papers. It seemed, too, that beginning to lose the war and having liquidated the ghettos, they were still looking for any Jews they could find outside the death camps to get rid of them in a rush to complete their final solution.

Since I had no idea whether the Germans were going to stop at forged papers or scrutinize all unusual or dubious documents, however legitimate, my fears for our lives redoubled. I chided myself for my credulity; again, I thought bitterly, I had been fooled by the Nazis. I should never have dropped my guard, and I should have been mindful of the Gestapo's repeated statements to me that "once a Jew, always a Jew."

To add to my growing tension, we found out through the few pro-Nazi internees in our midst, who broke the news to us gloatingly, that the Germans had uncovered the sources of the forgeries through informers, and that Jews with false passports were being systematically removed from various jails from where they had expected to be taken to one or another internment camp. It seemed that when the ghetto survivors had found out about the existence of such camps, there had been a great rush to obtain forged papers. Some of the new passport holders were shot and others were sent to Bergen-Belsen concentration camp where, according to our informants, there were still some Jews alive with genuine foreign citizenship. Nobody knew why the latter group was there and what lay in store for them.

How safe were we now? I kept asking myself. So far, we had no evidence that they were going to touch all of us, including the Piliczes and the Schmelkes family, who had bona fide papers. Yet the presence of the Gestapo on the camp's grounds cast a long shadow, and I knew no peace anymore. I reduced my involvement in camp activities, of which I had been one of the most enthusiastic supporters, and I performed my daily tasks mechanically, my mind on thoughts of mere survival. I still studied, taught and assisted Mrs. Vidakovic but after a year of inner tranquility and frequent merrymaking, I again forgot how to laugh.

Weeks passed, and there was no sign that the Vittel incident would be repeated. Life in camp went on as usual. My fellow internees began to disregard Mr. Schneider and his assistants with impunity, their mood once again that of elation and exuberance. There were now unmistakable signs that Hitler was losing the war. The British and American aircraft were flying overhead unimpeded, their bomber planes so low that we could make out the insignia on them, their target being the heavy industry in Friedrichshafen, on Lake Constance, from where we heard frequent heavy detonations by day and saw blazing flames by night. The women, heedless of all warnings, climbed to the roof of the Schloss during every air raid to wave to the flying pilots and their crews, sending up to them shouts of encouragement and cheer. The German authorities, obviously in great disarray, and, from what we had heard from one of our older guards, now convinced that defeat was at hand, gradually relaxed and then stopped altogether enforcing their earlier prohibitions. The general feeling was that they wished to ingratiate themselves to the internees so that perhaps they might escape punishment or prosecution by the Allies at the camp's liberation.

Personally, I was not yet able to share the general euphoria that swept the camp. Instead, brooding over the risks we were still facing, paradoxically so close to the end of the reign of evil of which we had been victims, I took interminable walks around the camp's grounds, sat around with Lizzy and Mrs. Vidakovic pouring my heart out into their receptive ears. From their more objective point of view, they argued that we had nothing to fear: the Germans were clever and experienced enough to distinguish between manufactured and legitimate documents.

Yet I continued to have no peace. Optimistic letters and a steady stream of food and clothes packages kept arriving from Father but did little to cheer us up. One day, not having used our allotted quota of mail during that month, I decided that the three of us should write to Father simultaneously, two letters each, fall back on our old symbol about worn-out clothes, and impress on him, by the sheer volume of our verbiage, that our situation had worsened and that there was an urgent need to have our names put on the first repatriation transport that was leaving for Central America. We complained to him that our Nicaraguan clothes were wearing thin, and that we could hardly wear them any longer. It would be best if he could get us to Managua where we would get fitted for a new wardrobe. Some of our friends, we continued, who had a similarly worn-out wardrobe, had contracted pneumonia and were gravely ill. If it was impossible to bring us to Managua, we beseeched him to send us solid and wearable coats made of real Canadian wool. Otherwise, we were in danger of becoming as ill as our friends were, which would put our reunion with him in jeopardy. Having communicated to Father some of the apprehension we felt, we tried to settle down to await his reply.

While we waited, the war news, to which we listened on a radio clandestinely rigged up by one of our British floormates in the Schloss, was growing more encouraging every day. Hitler was being slowly but systematically brought to his knees. His army was in hasty retreat before the Soviets who kept advancing ever further west, and there was talk of the Allied invasion on the French coast. What later became known as D-Day was approaching and, if successful, it would mean that the German army would be trapped on both fronts. Even the news on the German loudspeaker in our dining room began to transmit a feeling, albeit couched in phraseology full of circumlocutions, that the myth of the invincible Wehrmacht was being eroded. There were announcements of a small German retreat here and there for strategic purposes and vitriolic speeches berating the merciless bombing of the Allied air force which, meeting with almost no resistance from the Flak, was flying unimpeded over the entire country.

About a month after our combined S.O.S. call to Father, we received a letter from him indicating, as always, that he had well understood the new threat to our existence. Our news had propelled him into intensive action. The letter was brimming with significant and hopeful information. Father had seen himself, and had a copy of, an official document sent by the Nicaraguan government to the Swiss authorities, requesting them to intervene on behalf of some Nicaraguan nationals living under German occupation. Heading the list was a highly placed diplomatic attaché by the name of Portocarrero and his family, a few other people with Spanish-sounding names, and the three of us. The list was to be forwarded by the Swiss to the German Foreign Office with a request for the inclusion of the people on it in the first exchange headed for Central America. According to Father's information, such a repatriation was being planned for very soon. As for our solid Canadian clothes, Father continued, casting aside our private language code, he himself would be eligible for Canadian citizenship in about a month and would send us our Canadian passports, as, by the laws of Canada, we were eligible for naturalization as his dependents. He closed his letter with reassurances and promises that he would not rest until we were on our way to him.

The letter did wonders to build up our sagging hopes and to bolster our spirits. Once again, Father had engineered a masterful and stunning coup. We threw ourselves with renewed vigour into various camp activities. Mrs. Vidakovic was moved to tears on seeing me, her assistant librarian, take up my duties again with great zest. We plunged back into our studies of English, Hela and I poking good-natured fun at Mother, who used to do her homework in bed after the nightly roll call surrounded by textbooks and scribblers, peering at us with her glasses at the tip of her nose, asking us to explain a word or phrase she could not find in the dictionary. She was doing so well that she began trusting herself to write to Father in English. Hela and I felt rewarded by the success of our teaching; our young charges spoke fluent English by then and, ironically, had lost their foreign accents completely, something that we two, being older, could not quite achieve.

With the awareness that war was drawing to a close, the friendships we had formed became more profound and more meaningful. Soon we would be scattered all over the globe, but we vowed that our mutual affection would not cease and that we would continue to keep in touch our entire lifetime. My thoughts turned to all my childhood friends whom I had lost in Poland, the members of my father's and mother's families wiped out in Białystok, and all of Poland now finally as *judenrein* as the Germans were able to make it before buckling under the might of the victorious Allies. The friends I had made in camp were dear and close to me, but I felt that they would never replace those with whom I had shared the ecstasies of early youth and the agonies of the Holocaust.

Would I ever learn to live with my nightmarish memories? It was Lizzy who intuitively felt my sorrow under my facade of thin optimism. "Listen," she told me during one of our strolls, "I know you are grieving over some irretrievable losses. So am I, even though I am not Jewish. If you want to go on with life, you must learn to transcend the violence done to your soul and lay yourself bare to new relationships and good experiences that may help heal the wounds."

"Yes," I answered, "but all my feelings have been brutally wrenched and twisted, so that I am not whole anymore. I consist of fragments, each fragment someone I have lost or some indignity I have suffered. Frankly, I fear that so-called normal people will look at me as though I am a freak of nature."

"No," Lizzy assured me emphatically, putting her arm around my shoulder. "Nobody will find you strange. On the contrary, I think that the hell you have lived through will make you more sensitive to the suffering of others."

"We'll see," I said with a ghost of a smile on seeing my friend eager to rehabilitate me. "Let's be practical. Let's get out first. There will be plenty of time for psychological repairs to my personality after I have achieved physical freedom."

Another summer passed. The foliage around Liebenau was ablaze with the reds, yellows and magentas of the changing season, reminding me poignantly of that other autumn, in 1939, when the Nazis had begun to trample on our humanity. Now the Germans were on the brink of collapse: the Soviets had advanced to the city limits of

Warsaw, and the Western Allies, having successfully launched their offensive on D-Day, were cutting deeply into France, wiping out pockets of dwindling Nazi resistance.

Although encouraged by Father's latest news, I continued to be buffeted by fears and doubts praying that our documents would arrive or armistice be signed before the Gestapo were successful in blocking our rescue.

Freedom Beckons

One day in September 1944, a small package was delivered to us. It had been mailed by the Government of Canada, Department of External Affairs, Ottawa. With unsteady hands, we tore away the string, removed the paper, and took out three brand-new Canadian passports, one for each of us, and an accompanying letter. Jubilation swept through us as we hugged the passports to our chests and then opened the letter.

In it, the Department of External Affairs informed us that as soon as Father had received his Canadian citizenship, his wife and minor daughter (Rachela) had automatically become citizens. Since I was over nineteen years old and legally not entitled to the same privilege, the Canadian government, mindful of the hardships undergone by Mr. Roskes in Canada and his family under German occupation, had conferred citizenship on me by a special Order in Council. Looking at the iron-clad evidence of my new identity and filled with overwhelming gratitude to the Canadian government for its humane act, I choked on my tears and could not find my speech for a while. After I had swallowed a few times, I went racing around the camp, telling everybody that we were now Canadians and joined the general hilarity on our behalf. Mother, Hela and I felt like heroines of a fairy tale, basking in all the attention and in unaccustomed serenity.

I broke away from the group to the privacy of my room to indulge

in one of my personal conversations with Father. When I was sure
no one was around, I whispered, "Daddy, there is nobody like you in
the world, I'm sure you haven't slept one night since our separation,
stretching your brilliant mind beyond its limits, thinking of ways to
save us, clutching at every straw. You must have suffered terribly. I
promise I'll make it up to you when we are together." I was a little
ashamed of myself for my many secret talks with Father and my
wordless supplications to him, as I was already twenty-two years old,
and felt that my interior monologues were a symptom of unresolved
infantilism. By then, however, through the sheer force of repetition
and because they must have filled a desperate need, my inner reveries
had become habit. I clung to them in times of emotional peaks — of
both the blackest despair and the shiniest hope — and found them
cathartic. My shame then gave way to a rare sense of self-respect as
I was gratified by our holding out against every threat of death that
would have annulled all of Father's superhuman efforts to save us.
The complexity of our lot struck me so forcefully that I was staggered
again and heard myself exclaiming, "If I live to tell the story, nobody
will believe it."

That night we could not fall asleep. We talked about the seder at
Grandfather's in 1939, the pain that Father's departure had caused us,
the atrocities perpetrated by the Nazis, friends who had disappeared
in the genocide, and then, the mist of bleak memories lifting gradually, we ventured to visualize ourselves as metamorphosed, reborn
beings, enjoying a life of peace and beauty by Father's side.

After the roll call, we stole out of our blacked-out rooms and sat
on the floor of the long corridor, our backs propped up against the
wall; our floormates joined us, bringing delectable morsels from their
Red Cross parcels, and we donated a whole can of Spam and a jar of
Nescafé for our nocturnal banquet. Against regulations, we put on
the big boiler in the middle of the night, consumed cup upon cup
of coffee, ate our fill of hastily arranged canapés and desserts, and
chattered like magpies until the wee hours in the morning. It was a

true celebration such as we had not participated in since the war, a party of which we were the honoured guests. The constant drone of planes flying overhead and the sporadic loud explosions from what we guessed were the bombed factories of Friedrichshafen added gaiety to our festive mood, sending us into peals of laughter. It was with reluctance that we finally dispersed into our rooms to snatch an hour or two of sleep.

After my breakfast chores I ran to find Mrs. Vidakovic, as I longed to be alone with her. I found her in the deserted library, cataloguing a batch of books that had arrived from the Red Cross. "Oh, it's you!" she said when she saw me. "I wondered whether I'd get a chance to tell you how happy I am for you. I have a feeling you will leave before I do. Where will I get another assistant?"

I tried to match her light tone, but all I could do was rush over to her and break into unrestrained sobs. We both sat down on a bench, and Mrs. Vidakovic held me close until my spell subsided. "I can't explain how I feel," I stammered when I could speak again. "I am infinitely happy and infinitely sad. And I don't know how to thank you for restoring my self-confidence and making me realize that my soul had not been corrupted by those sadists."

"Don't thank me," she replied, smiling, "I had faith in you and knew all along that you would survive all obstacles to your release. I'll miss you when you go, but I will be glad to hear that you have resumed your studies and are enjoying life in Canada with all your family."

Since I was not sure when, or even if, we would leave, I told her that I would carry on my duties as before, and added, embarrassed at my own show of affection, that she had been, and would continue to be, one of the most inspiring influences in my life.

～

In December, we were summoned to Mrs. Froom's office. We found her sitting primly on one of the half a dozen chairs arranged in the room for her committee meetings, while Mr. Schneider sat in her own chair behind her desk. He was a swarthy man, with a shock of black hair, his dark-rimmed, heavy glasses hiding the expression in his eyes. There were all sorts of papers in front of him. On seeing us, he pulled out a long, densely typed sheet. When he first started to speak, his voice was cool and formal. "Our office has received a request from the Nicaraguan government, forwarded to us by the Swiss Legation in Berlin, to release you for an exchange to Nicaragua. We have granted this request. You will leave here on the next repatriation transport."

He then let the papers rest on the desk and raised his glasses to have a better look at us. Before I could interpret his attitude, he turned to Mother and asked her sarcastically, "How did your husband do it? He is either an Übermensch (superman) or else he must have very important connections. Do you think," he went on, his sarcasm merging with something that sounded like a plea, "that he could use his connections or influence to help me?" We gaped at him incomprehensibly, so taken aback by the unaccustomed tone and the serious-sounding request that we forgot all about the exchange for a minute. Too stunned to offer a coherent answer and at a loss what to say, Mother started mumbling, "I have no idea, sir..." She did not finish her sentence.

Herr Schneider, now obviously hot in pursuit of his own thoughts on the extraordinary subject, did not bother about her answer. Instead, he quickly continued, "Not only do you have Nicaraguan passports, but now you are Canadian citizens as well. If this is some kind of a game, I wish you'd explain it to me. Never, in all my years at the Foreign Office, have I come across such abundance of documents owned by a single family."

I recovered quickly when I realized that the tables had indeed been turned and that the Nazi in front of us was actually pleading for his life. Speaking with a boldness I could no longer contain, I took over where Mother had left off. Without removing my belligerent stare from his face while I poured out my current of lies, I told him that Father had lived in Nicaragua for a few years before the war but had then immigrated to Canada where business opportunities were more favourable. I did not know all the details, I added, hearing the venom in my own voice, because the Gestapo had forced us into a ghetto where there was no communication with the outside world. I ended by announcing icily that, if they had had their way with us, we would not have been sitting in Mrs. Froom's office learning about our eligibility for repatriation.

My hostility was not lost on Mr. Schneider as he answered almost apologetically, "Your ghetto in Tarnów was liquidated in September last year. Frankly, I don't know how you managed to survive and retain your papers." His voice still kind, he added, "Anyway you are here now, very much alive, and you should feel privileged that the formal request for your exchange was on a special list containing the names of important Nicaraguan officials. But remember" (here his voice turned formal and official for a moment) "that you are leaving as Nicaraguans, not Canadians. There is no exchange with Canada for the time being. Nor," he finished with a trace of ill-concealed bitterness, "will there be many more exchanges in the future as the war can't last much longer. You are lucky. You may go now."

Out in the corridor, we pondered Mr. Schneider's meek, almost polite, dismissal of us and, comparing it to all the earlier, sinister orders by the Gestapo of "Raus, verfluchte Jüdinnen" (Out, damned Jewesses), savoured the sweet taste of victory. After close to five and a half years of terror and misery, buffeted and battered, our dream had triumphed over the forces of evil bent on obliterating it. Desolate with grief over the annihilation of the Tarnów ghetto with all our remaining friends, and particularly Israel Schmuckler, in it, we nevertheless had a sense of having been liberated. Our fear of the Nazis had fallen away, and we were ready for our beckoning freedom.

The emotional goodbyes began. We exchanged addresses and swore to maintain contact. I left my post as the assistant librarian, and Mrs. Vidakovic was in the process of getting a replacement. The classes Hela and I had taught were absorbed in other groups. Then, as a grand finale, we gave several unopened food and clothing parcels to our floor captain to distribute the contents as she saw fit.

On the day of our departure in January, we went down to see Mrs. Froom. Even though her penetrating blue eyes and erect posture gave the impression that she was a younger woman, her skin was wrinkled and fell away in folds. She must be very old, I thought as I scrutinized her face carefully. There was an unmistakable aura of leadership about her, commanding respect. As we were aware that she did not look favourably on any display of emotion, we sat in our chairs facing her, trying to compose our feelings and sound calm. Besides Mrs. Vidakovic and Lizzy, she was the only person in camp who understood fully, and had deep empathy for, our harrowing odyssey.

She said, with controlled warmth in her voice, that she was glad to have known us personally. We had been an asset to the camp. We had shown responsibility in carrying out both our assigned tasks and those we had undertaken voluntarily. "I wish you luck," she said after the somewhat unusual accolade. "You have fought hard for your lives, and you deserve it." My statement to her, on behalf of all three of us, was terse but fraught with feelings, which I managed to keep in check. I thanked her for her intuitive understanding and strong support. I said I appreciated how busy she was, acting not only as camp captain but also in the demanding role as liaison between the campmates and the Germans; I was therefore exceedingly gratified that she had always made time for us whenever we needed her. Venturing into a wider sphere, I assured her that she was the best administrator I had ever known. It was owing to the rare combination she possessed of competence and compassion that six hundred women and children, imprisoned, away from their homes and with the hope of liberation often dim in their hearts, were organized into an exemplary community. She was the soul of the camp and we had been privileged to be under her personal guidance and protection. The example of her eminent humanity, I finished quickly, fearing that I had embarrassed her, would remain with us wherever we went.

After firm handshakes all around, we retired to our room and started packing. At the bottom of the suitcase donated to us by our floor captain on our arrival, we found the three Jewish armbands we had removed as soon as we were rid of our guard and had reached the camp's grounds. Our initial impulse was to keep them, to show them to Father and others in Canada as the symbol of our slavery under the Nazis. However, on reflection, we realized that we would probably undergo a search before crossing the German border. The armbands would be confiscated, and we might experience some last-minute harassment, which we were anxious to avoid. And so, we cut the armbands into shreds and threw the pieces into a trash can.

We were packed and ready to go a few hours before our official departure time. I spent the whole afternoon exclusively with Lizzy, while Mother and Hela sought out their best friends. "I don't know," I said to Lizzy, "where we will be tomorrow. All I know is that, happy as I am to go before the end of the war, there is also much I shall miss here."

"I can understand that," Lizzy replied. "This camp has been a refuge and a resting place for you for the two years you have spent here. I bet you, though, that as soon as you are on the train, you will be too excited to think of anything and anybody in your past. All your thoughts will be focused on the future."

"Probably," I replied, "but it will be so only initially. My past and my future are inextricably interwoven in my mind, it cannot be otherwise."

In the evening, two guards led us to the gate, where we climbed into a Jeep that was to take us to Meckenbeuren, the small city where we had disembarked two years earlier, and from there to Fried-richshafen on the Swiss border. To our surprise, Herr Schneider climbed aboard too. During the minutes that we were on our way to the train, nobody spoke. When the Jeep arrived at the blacked-out station, Schneider climbed out first, stretched out his hand to help us all down, and took our suitcase personally, guiding us through the pitch-black night into the compartment of a train that stood waiting, its locomotive puffing clouds of white smoke into the dark sky. When he was asked by the astonished guard why he was treating us with such great civility and submissiveness, we were close enough behind him to hear his answer: "Der letzte Eindruck ist der beste." (The last impression is the best.)

We savoured momentarily this second exhibition of a Nazi official virtually grovelling in the dust before us, but we were too full of novel and strange impressions to pay him much attention. Someone propped up the steps and preceded us to our compartment. Vaguely, we realized that other people were sprawling all over the seats and even the floor, but we could not really see or recognize anyone. There was no sound except for some low moans emanating from two corners. The train remained stationary at Meckenbeuren for a long time — so long, in fact, that some of my nagging doubts about whether we were indeed going to leave returned. However, as we learned, the departure was delayed because every passenger was being searched thoroughly. Two men came into our car, focused their blinding flashlights on us and asked us to open our suitcase. They hesitated somewhat on discovering the *Oxford Book of English Verse*, Mrs. Vidakovic's favourite poetry anthology, which she had given me as a going-away present during our last conversation but, after leafing through it and shaking out the pages, were evidently satisfied that it did not contain contraband or anything that might be construed as having political significance. Handing it back to me, slightly the worse by the rough handling, they snapped shut their flashlights, and the compartment was plunged into palpable darkness once again.

Slowly, the train began to move, lurching wildly from side to side as it gained uncertain momentum. In an hour, it slowed down again, and I guessed that we had reached the border and were in Friedrichs-hafen. In the distance, we could hear the lapping of the waves on

Lake Constance, but try as we might, we could not see even the barest outline of the city as the blackout all around us was complete. We must have arrived at the end of an air raid, as we recognized the wailing sound of the all-clear siren and saw the reflection of red flames tracing fiery patterns on our tightly closed window shades. The two men who had searched us earlier came in to explain that there would be another indefinite delay because the British planes had bombed places all around the station, and the bombs had ripped up some of the tracks, which had to be repaired before we could move on. This was yet another time that we heard a Nazi sounding crestfallen and almost apologetic. Savouring the heartwarming spectacle, we did not mind the delay, even though we were eager to leave German soil.

We were then allowed to light the single kerosene lamp in our compartment, but not before the men satisfied themselves that our windows were thoroughly blacked out. By the feeble light of the lamp, I looked around and found that there were twelve of us in the compartment. Mrs. Pilicz and Mrs. Schmelkes were there with their children, but the other three men and one woman were unfamiliar to me. While our small group spoke in whispers, we reached for some food we had carried in our suitcase, as our hunger was intense.

I had the opportunity to have a good look at the strangers. Their bones stuck out through their ill-fitting clothes, their faces were immobile, their gaze was fixed on a point in the ceiling, and their lips had white foam around them. I edged closer to them, offering some food from the paper bag we had brought in with us. "Water, please, some water," the woman, who looked slightly more robust than her companions, whispered into my ear. The others did not utter a single word. After a painful effort to ease themselves out of their half-crouching, half-sitting position, they managed to spread out on the floor and shut their eyes, looking indistinguishable from corpses.

When the guard came back, I asked him to bring some water. Looking keenly at the three lifeless figures on the floor, he handed me a water flask, which I quickly passed on to the woman. She snatched it from my hands and took the liquid in one big gulp. She then bent down over her companions and held the flask to the lips of one of them. His mouth did not respond, and the water just dribbled out. She repeated the same procedure with the other two, getting the same results. The guard came closer, poked the three men with his boots, and then crouched down to determine whether they were alive or dead. Without speaking to us, he quickly left, and, in a few minutes, was back with some uniformed men carrying stretchers. The stretcher bearers took out the motionless figures, resting them side by side on the platform of the station. As we had occasion to peek through the open doorway, I threw a hasty look and saw, by the dim light of the cloth-wrapped station lamp, similar, stretcher-like cots lying in rows all over the platform. Then our door was sealed again, and as we got back to our seats, we questioned the middle-aged woman about the meaning of the occurrences we had just witnessed.

She told us that all four of them had come from Bergen-Belsen, where they had been incarcerated with thousands of others. As the camp had been full to overcrowding, disease and hunger were rampant. Some inmates had had to toil day and night, exposed to constant brutality and violence. In the meantime, many had died of starvation and diseases. Her husband had perished in Auschwitz and her two children had died in Bergen-Belsen. By her own admission, her heart had turned to stone; she was so devoid of any feeling that she could not even mourn her family.

She then went on to describe in a hollow monotone how, a few weeks earlier, a group of SS and Gestapo had entered the camp and their superior officer had produced a list of names, asking whether anybody whose name was called was still there. They had combed Bergen-Belsen for survivors with foreign passports. She herself was an American, and so had been her husband, since both of them had been born in the United States. Most of the names had to be crossed out, as the people no longer existed. She did not know the other three presumably foreign citizens like herself but guessed by their scarecrow looks that they had been in camp longer than she had.

"I suppose," she continued, as she started to bite into the sandwich we had given her, "that the Nazis must provide a specific number of people for the exchange in order to get an equal quota of German repatriates. Having rounded up all those still alive with legitimate papers in the ghettos, jails and internment camps, they are rifling through the concentration camps as a last resort. Incidentally, I don't know what is happening in the war zone, but there were some unusual activities in camp for the past several weeks. The entire administration was changed."

After she had given us the sketchy information, she lapsed into silence again and quietly finished her sandwich. Sensing her reluctance to be drawn out any further, we left her alone. The brief, garbled report revealed more than we wished to know. What bitter, tragic irony, I thought with vehemence, it was for the three unconscious or dead men I had just seen, and for others like them, to have survived Bergen-Belsen, to have been given a last-minute chance for freedom, and then to collapse and die within a hair's breadth of reaching it. I shuddered with fury and disgust, and all night long could not get the martyred figures out of my mind. The three bodies we had seen crumbling might have been ours. Had it not been for the spectacular rescue operations engineered by Father, aided by amazing circumstances, we, too, might have not reached the Swiss border, where our train was now standing, poised to cross it.

End of an Odyssey

It was nearly morning when the train began to move again, but it did not get very far. After some thirty minutes, it halted. Raising our window blinds, we saw that the sign on the station read St. Gallen. We were in Switzerland. Our German guards seemed to have vanished. As we all rushed to the exits, practically falling over one another in our haste to get out, shouts of joy pierced the frosty morning air. Amid crying and laughing, strangers tumbling out from all six of the train's compartments embraced one another. Some were dancing wildly, others were singing. A few knelt down and kissed the frozen ground. The noise was deafening. Mother, Hela and I clasped our hands together and sobbed with abandon, our tears those of pure ecstasy.

After some fifteen minutes, a few men in unfamiliar uniforms came upon the scene and allowed our spontaneous celebration of thanksgiving to go on for a while longer. Then, one of them took out a whistle to indicate that he wanted silence. He told us that we were in Switzerland and that we would have to stay in St. Gallen for close to a week because the formal exchange, which was going to take place in Geneva, had run into some snags and would be slightly delayed. As he saw panic beginning to contort some faces, he explained, "No one is being sent back to Germany. You are free, of that I assure you most emphatically." He then gave us a sign to start walking.

We followed him, a motley group of about seventy to eighty people, along an icy and slippery road. Nowhere was there a sign of life. Snow-covered fields stretched wide into the horizon, and in the distance we could see snow-capped mountain peaks which we knew to be the Swiss Alps to the south.

We finally arrived in a village so completely blanketed in snow that only the rooftops and chimneys of the houses were visible. Our guide took us to a compound that looked suspiciously like three stables, U-shaped within a rectangular yard, through which a trough ran from one end to the other. There he made us stop and said apologetically that, unfortunately, Switzerland had been so overrun by refugees that no decent accommodations were available. He advised us to make ourselves as comfortable as we could in the straw in the three stables and assured us that blankets and food would be provided. With these words, he left us completely to our own devices.

Our group greeted his words and sudden departure with dismay. This, I thought, did not seem to be a great improvement over Germany; but then, of course, we were in the German part of Switzerland, and could not expect to be greeted with open arms. A murmur of complaints and even sounds of crying issued from several corners. Our new companions were mainly former concentration camp inmates and one woman, who confided to me in a trembling voice, said that the place had a disturbing aura about it, reminiscent of the barracks they had left behind. I agreed, for our new quarters reminded me of the fearsome complex at 4 Lwowska Street. Aside from the brief initial elation, the first step toward freedom had not been encouraging.

We stayed in St. Gallen for a week or so. Morale sagged, and in some cases came close to crumbling altogether as, one after another, people began to fear that we would be shipped back to Germany. The thought occurred to me, too, but I forced myself not to dwell on my suspicions. They were unthinkable and smacked of paranoia. We slept in the straw, body close to body for a little warmth in the sub-zero weather, and we washed in the trough by breaking off the icicles and melting them in our hands. The food, brought in huge pots, probably from some institutional kitchen nearby, was standard prison fare. The Swiss officers came and went, telling us each time that our miserable conditions would not last much longer. Our disappointment with our reception was so great that many of us began to suspect the Swiss to be in collusion with the Nazis.

After a time fraught with fear and a sense of hovering danger, we were awoken from our sullen state by a high-ranking Swiss official who arrived in our compound and addressed us in German. "I hope you will forgive my government for the inadequate facilities provided for you. We literally had no other place to house you. However, this last ordeal of yours will be over tomorrow morning when you will travel by train to Geneva, where you will be turned over to the right authorities." On hearing the encouraging news, even though given to us in the detested language, our mood underwent a complete turn-about and we applauded him warmly. The exchange had not been a myth: we were actually going to be repatriated.

The ride to Geneva was charged with excitement. Through the un-covered windows of our compartment we could see fairy-tale towns and villages scattered at the foot of majestic mountains. Mother, Hela and I opened our windowpane a crack and inhaled lungfuls of cold but deliciously clean air. Within the train, the atmosphere was like that of a jolly fair. Once more there was dancing, stomping, singing, crying and laughing, as all of us, one by one, knew with finality that we had escaped death by the Nazis. "Daddy," I kept repeating to my-self, "it worked. It is a miracle. We are alive and on our way to you."

I looked at Hela's face all smudged where the tar from the stables had mingled with her tears and burst out laughing. "Look at you," I said, "how do you expect to be exchanged with a face like that?"

"You don't look better yourself," Hela retorted. "We'd better clean up a bit." In the tiny washroom, fighting for a piece of the mirror, we each pulled out a hanky from our pockets, washed our faces and brushed the straw of the stables off our clothes. Feeling a bit more civilized, we rejoined Mother and wiped a few smudges off her forehead and cheeks as well. When the train slowed down and came to a stop in Geneva, we felt ready to meet our future.

As I looked down from our window, I saw several men in khaki uniforms wearing white helmets with the letters MP on them. At first, I thought they were Swiss; however, when I spotted some members of our group tumble out quickly and turn to the men with hugs and kisses, I suddenly knew these were the American Military Police, probably sent to Geneva to accompany us on the next leg of our journey. Giving in to my impulse and tripping on the steps, I jumped to the platform and held on to the nearest man by the lapels of his uniform. "You are American, aren't you? Please, let me hear you speak so that I can really believe it," I begged hysterically. "You'd better believe it," he answered, his eyes sparkling with glee. "We are as American as apple pie."

At the time, I did not understand the allusion. Yet the unique experience of words uttered in English by an American in Geneva while the war was still going on filled me with wonder and amazement akin to a profound revelation. I did not let go of him until he explained that he and his comrades had been dispatched from Marseille, through the liberated corridor of southern France, to meet the trains bringing Allied citizens for repatriation.

After the excitement had abated somewhat, we were put on board yet another train, this one heading for Marseille. During the five-hour trip, strangers were swapping stories, exchanging plans for the future and slapping one another's backs with unsuppressed joy. There was a lot of movement from compartment to compartment as people, testing their unaccustomed freedom, walked back and forth, eager not to miss a moment of the surging camaraderie that had sprung up among the passengers. It was as though a curtain had come down over the recent tragedy, and a new happy play was about to begin. Amid spells of spontaneous, uninhibited laughter, I thought that it had been a long time since I had seen Jews laugh. The sight was uplifting; it spelled an affirmation of life.

It was getting dark outside as the train started to slow down before coming to a complete stop. The MPs made the rounds of all the compartments and advised us to pull our window shades down. They explained that even though the southern part of France had been liberated and the Allied troops held all the beaches and other large parts of France, the war was still raging in pockets here and there; the German Luftwaffe had been severely crippled but there was the possibility that stray German planes might drop occasional bombs. We obeyed the instructions but greeted the announcement with recklessness. Nothing, some people sitting next to me said, could harm us now. We raised our hands in a mock salute to the Allied forces and applauded thunderously the speaker who had addressed us.

When we disembarked, I realized in the gathering dusk that the train had brought us almost right into the Marseille harbour. In front of us, obscuring the view of the Mediterranean, there was a huge canvas structure, about half the size of a circus tent, with an open entrance. We were asked to line up near it, with ample time to inspect the premises since we had waited, as usual, while some last-minute formalities were being settled.

There were several large tables arranged in two rows on either side of the tent. Men in civilian clothes were sitting behind them and spoke to others who seemed to act as their aids or messengers, walking from table to table distributing piles of papers. The area in the centre was empty. Peering at the far side where the tent ended, I noticed another opening, leading to something barely distinguishable in the dark, which looked like a ladder or a few stairs. I realized almost immediately that what I saw was the gangplank of a ship, although the ship itself was obscured by the canvas wall of the tent. The proceedings began. Each family was asked to approach the first table on the left. Extending his hand in greeting, the official sitting there scrutinized a list, and then asked the processed individuals either to move to the right side of the tent or to proceed, in turn, to each table in his row.

Mother, Hela and I were somewhere near the middle of the long line. We had prepared for inspection both our Nicaraguan and Canadian passports, remembering, with a start, that the exchange was, according to Mr. Schneider, to Central American countries. If that were true, we would probably land in Managua and would somehow have to negotiate our entry to Canada. While the line was moving slowly, we discussed that possibility which, in our initial sense of relief, we had not entertained at all. We decided that we would show our Canadian passports first. If it did not work, we concluded that we would go to Nicaragua and wait to travel to Father. In either, our freedom was assured.

I began to concentrate on what was happening inside the tent. Judging from the pattern that had begun to emerge slowly, and recognizing a few families from Liebenau, I came to the conclusion that people asked to step to the right were those with irregular or forged passports who had managed to escape the massacre at Vittel and similar murders in other places. I noticed that Mrs. Pilicz and her daughter, as well as a few others who, judging by the stoop and fragility of their bodies, must have been survivors of concentration camps had remained on the left side, and, after stopping at each table for a moment, were heading for the opening at the far end to the ship. When our turn came, I was almost sure that we belonged with the group on the left. However, I trembled a little, since the scene was somewhat evocative of the German "selections." The resemblance was obviously coincidental and illusory, but by now, every event was a parallel to my experiences under the Nazi rule. My suspicions had become a conditioned reflex.

When our turn came, the official at the first table, to whom we presented our Canadian passports looked at us with great curiosity, and then said with a smile, "You'd better go to the next table. Someone is waiting there to give you all the information you need." Well, I thought with relief, we were, so far, on the left side of the tent. When we approached the next table, a middle-aged and distinguished-looking man with greying hair rose, shook hands with each of us in turn, and said with discernible pleasure in his voice, "Well, well, at last. So you are the three Roskes ladies? Don't worry about a thing. Put away your Nicaraguan passports and keep them as a souvenir. You are going directly to your new home where I know one man who can barely wait for your arrival. My name is Cronyn, and I am a Canadian government representative sent here to accompany some eighty Canadian prisoners of war and the three of you to Montreal."

When, in my bewilderment at what I had just heard, I trusted myself to speak, I said to Mr. Cronyn, "I don't understand. This is supposed to be an exchange to Central America. At least, this is what the Germans told us."

"It is partly true," replied Mr. Cronyn, "but these repatriation transports don't ever turn out what they are initially designed to be. During the negotiations, all kinds of changes are made. If you didn't have Canadian passports, you would probably wind up with the group on the right. Those people are going on another ship to North Africa where they will be comfortably housed until they can make their way to the United States. It won't be long, for their American relatives will sponsor them and, anyway, the United States government is likely to relax their immigration laws to admit World War II refugees. When Mr. Roskes found out that Canadian prisoners of war would be included in this predominantly American transport, he got immediate permission from the government to have you on it. You left Germany as Nicaraguans, but since the change in the repatriation plans has been in your favour, you are now Canadian, going home where you belong."

After more warm handshakes, Cronyn beckoned to one of his aides who took our solitary suitcase and guided us toward the ship. Casting a backward glance to where some of our ex-fellow internees were waiting, I tried to give them a friendly smile, but they seemed glum and looked away. At first, I felt a bit like a traitor, but quickly recalling Mr. Cronyn's reassurances and remembering that we ourselves might easily have been among them, I realized that they were out of danger and in good hands. Recognizing that my guilt to which I was unusually prone was misguided and uncalled for, I followed our guide, who beckoned to us to climb the gangplank and to the ship. In a minute, we were aboard the *Gripsholm*.

All Aboard

All the lights on the ship were on, but the portholes were covered to maintain the blackout. At the upper deck level, we walked along a corridor and saw the cabin doors open. From each, two young men had emerged, as if on a signal, to stand in the doorway. They were examining us from top to toe with unabashed pleasure, and many gave a special whistling sound, the meaning of which we did not learn till considerably later. Although uninitiated, we knew that we had made a favourable impression. We smiled back at the men, responded to their waving, and self-consciously tried to straighten our nondescript clothes to appear more attractive.

Walking past all the doors, our guide volunteered detailed information about our new setup. The men we had seen were a part of an exchange transport of close to five hundred Americans and around eighty Canadians, mainly members of the air force, who had been shot down over Germany and had spent a few years in prisoner-of-war camps. Most of them were amputees or severe burn cases. There were altogether perhaps a few hundred civilians with foreign citizenship aboard, including ourselves, the Piliczes and the Schmelkes family, but this was predominantly a military exchange. Again, I could not believe our good luck. Had it not been for Mr. Cronyn's explanations about the haphazard nature of the exchanges, and the ad hoc decisions governing them, I would probably have felt that it was all another joke played on us for some unknown reason and would have agonized over its meaning.

We stopped at a cabin just below the deck. Our guide said that this would be ours for the duration of the trip. Although all cabins on the upper decks had been reserved for the military personnel, our movements on the ship would be completely unrestricted. If we needed anything, we were to ask the purser, the captain or Mr. Cronyn, who would be sailing with us. There were three dining rooms, and we were allowed to choose any one we wanted for our meals. With these words, the kindly young American official wished us good luck and was gone.

We did not leave the cabin on this, our first, night on the *Gripsholm*. We were exhausted to the point of near collapse from the events of the long day, which had begun in St. Gallen, had taken us to Geneva, and then on to Marseille and the Swedish exchange liner. After a quick and much-needed bath, we pulled out some nightclothes from our suitcase and lay down on our bunks.

I slept in short snatches, full of nightmares and waking dreams. In a kaleidoscopic succession of images, I saw, against a vast panorama of bombed-out cities, rubble, huge craters and marching troops singing "Deutschland über alles"(Germany above All), my good friends and relatives digging enormous graves, straining against the gloved hands of the SS pushing them through iron doors to gas chambers, and lying by the roadside, blood gushing from their multiple wounds. After a few hours of torment, I had to change my perspiration-soaked nightgown, and decided to forget about sleep. I put on my bedside lamp and tried to read some poems from Mrs. Vidakovic's anthology, yet even the best and my favourite ones among them could not assuage my mental anguish and depression. Is this what life would be like from now on? Had Zyga and Klara and Meyer and my grandfather and my grandmother and my aunts and uncles with their families, and all of them, taken an essential part of me with them when they went to their deaths? Would my losses block my enjoyment of reunion and freedom? What right did I have to be alive and free when all of them — many much more deserving than I — had died uselessly, in a carnage unlike any the world had ever seen? Would I always feel guilty about my survival and feel it as a betrayal? The frenzy of my self-lacerating questioning mounted, but no answers would come. I thought restlessly, while finally succumbing to drowsiness at the first light of dawn, that perhaps I had been spared to tell their story, to shout it from the rooftops if necessary, to shake up all those who did not know, or pretended not to know, and to scream into their ears — wake up, look, listen and never forget! Weakened from my nightlong struggle, I fell into a stony, dreamless sleep and did not hear the morning bell announcing that it was breakfast time.

When I awoke, I found a note from Mother and Hela that, reluctant to rouse me, they had gone out to have something to eat and to explore the ship. I dressed quickly, the shivers still running up and down my spine after my disturbing night, and went in search of them. I climbed the few steps to the upper deck and gazed with amazement when I beheld the enormous size of the *Gripsholm*. Suddenly exhilarated by the cool but fresh sea breeze, I ran excitedly from fore to aft, and several times leaned over the ship's railing to look at the blue Mediterranean, smooth and glistening like a finely polished mirror. American soldiers were all over. Some were hobbling on their crutches and others were sitting on deckchairs, enjoying the balmy day. Finally, two of them beckoned to me to sit on an empty chaise between them and I did so with alacrity.

At first, they joked and wisecracked about the pleasure of seeing women again for the first time since 1942. On a more sober note, they described their lives in the prisoner-of-war camps, saying that they had not really been maltreated. It was in the other camps nearby, those for Russian, Serbian or Polish prisoners, that life meant agony and death; this part of their story was no news to me, as I had observed the treatment of such prisoners first-hand during my stay at Liebenau. They asked me about my family's ordeals, but I was as curt and succinct about them as they were about their amputations. They were obviously unfamiliar with the Nazis' "final solution" for the Jews, and I did not feel distanced enough from the painful subject to enlighten them. As I was about to leave to have late breakfast or early lunch, one of the pilots, a handsome young amputee from California, asked me for a date later that day. I consented happily. After Meyer, there had been no men in my life, and on the *Gripsholm* I had an opportunity to feel like a woman again. Besides, I was curious to find out what a ship date under our very special circumstances would be like.

I met Mother and Hela in two different spots, each talking to American and Canadian air force men, and noticed that they were as delighted about the new and pleasant experience as I was. It was lunchtime before we could get together and disentangle ourselves from groups of men who accosted us at every step. By then, a sort of easy intimacy had been established: we, and the handful of other women on board, had obviously been given a seal of approval and we were eager to form new friendships with our unexpected shipmates with whom we shared our new freedom.

Lunch was well-prepared and filling, and we wolfed down all the courses, concentrating most on the meat and vegetables, which we had not tasted in years. We then returned to our cabin to sort out our impressions, hoping to take a brief rest. Every few minutes there was a knock on the cabin door and a soldier or officer was standing behind it, asking whether we were asleep. Absurdly, we kept answering "yes," which made each man withdraw, to be placed by another asking the same question.

Enjoying our game, we had to give up the idea of rest and left the cabin in pursuit of company. I went in search of Sergeant Brown, with whom I had my first date. He was sitting in one of the ship's lounges, his crutches leaning against the back of his chair, and his face, which I saw in profile before he spotted me, was wearing a sad and serious look. Coming upon him from behind, I laid my hand on his shoulder, and he, guessing that it was mine, held it there for a while without turning. I pulled up a chair to sit near him and noticed that the large hall was well filled with groups of air force men, each surrounding one or two women, all evidently engaged in swapping stories about how they had come to be on the *Gripsholm*.

Jim Brown's thoughts seemed far away. When I asked him whether anything was wrong (and I could have bitten my tongue after I had asked and saw again his empty and folded trouser leg), he followed my glance and said, "No, that's not it. Not anymore. The American surgeons will fit me with an artificial leg. They've got a lot of experience." A sigh escaped him and then he continued. "I left a wife and a two-month-old baby in San Francisco before I was shipped out. My thoughts about them kept me going and gave me something to live for after I landed first in a German hospital and then in a POW camp. In her last letter, my wife wrote that she was leaving me. My absence and my amputation were too much for her to take. She is asking for a divorce."

I was on the verge of saying that she might reconsider but held my tongue when I realized that the comment would sound facile. Instead, I squeezed his hand. He seemed to appreciate my silence and the fact that I did not offer any consoling clichés.

"Let's get out of here. Soon they are going to dance, and I can't bear the look of one-legged men hopping on their crutches. They look ludicrous." He took hold of his crutches and, with great dexterity, guided me out of the lounge onto the open deck. "I am not going to ask you what you've been through before coming here," he said on the way. "I have heard hair-raising rumours about the Nazis' treatment of the Jews. I guess you've been in hell and would rather not talk about it." After my nightmares of the previous night, I was not in the mood to confirm the "rumours," and was grateful for his simple statement.

We sat down in the deckchairs, covered ourselves up to our waists with warm blankets against the sunny but chilly afternoon air, and remained there for a long time without talking. All sorts of uniformed men, hobbling on their crutches, stopped in front of us and unashamedly tried to flirt with me. I dodged their advances, as my thoughts were on Jim, whom I had found one of the most attractive men aboard.

I knew that it would not be long before he would ask me to sleep with him, and I had a ready answer. Although it would be nothing more than a shipboard romance, I felt that we both needed it, both because we were attracted to each other and because it would soothe the memories and thoughts that plagued us: Jim's about the future, mine about the past. And so, when he shyly put his hand on mine and asked me whether I would accompany him to his cabin, I consented without hesitation.

Jim's cabinmate was there, stretched out on the bunk, reading *Stars and Stripes*, the first American newspaper I had ever seen. Noticing us both at the door, he murmured something about being late for the mess hall and disappeared in a flash. I was amused and touched by the men's understanding of one another's needs.

In the semi-darkness of the cabin, I undressed quickly, and so did Jim, trying to turn his amputated leg away from me. I turned him around to face me and caressed his stump. Jim's relief was visible, and there were tears in his eyes. "You needn't have worried," I whispered into his ear while he kissed my neck, "I don't mind it one bit." Tenderly and expertly, Jimmy guided my hands over his entire body. When we made love, I forgot his amputated leg. I forgot Milek, Zyga and Meyer. I even forgot Father. We made love again and again, our repressed sexuality seeking and finding total and ecstatic fulfillment. Afterward, we lay quietly side by side, our hands stroking each other's bodies, our mouths joined in long kisses, completely at peace.

From that day on, although no one said a word, I was Jim's girl. We were almost inseparable, and our sexual attraction for each other slipped into an easygoing, relaxed friendship. We made absolutely no plans for the future, as neither of us had any illusions about it. Our relationship was meant to last as long as the voyage and to add to its buoyancy. Most of the other men aboard accepted that relationship, and if they had had any designs on me previously, refrained from showing them now.

As the *Gripsholm* coasted along the Mediterranean, we were told that, since the war was not yet over, German U-boats might still be roaming the ocean. Three mine sweepers had been sent ahead to comb the Atlantic, and we would not sail past Gibraltar until they returned. Even then, we were informed, our ship would be accompanied by mine sweepers all the way to New York.

The delay did not bother my family, nor did it seem to disturb Jim. It might take another week or so, but at the end of the voyage there was Father, who knew that we were safe and on our way to him and who was waiting for us. The sea was calm beneath us, so that we felt as though we were on terra firma, and the ship seemed motionless. We prowled it from one end to the other and from top to bottom, our exhilaration knowing no bounds. We learned to eat cornflakes with cream, which we regarded as veritable manna from heaven, and scoured the *Stars and Stripes* for every detail of the imminent German defeat. We now understood clearly why Mr. Schneider and company had taken refuge in Liebenau. The American missions, flying day in, day out, had been reducing Berlin and other German cities to piles of rubble.

I read a detailed account of the Nazi defeat in Stalingrad, of which I had had only very sketchy knowledge at camp, and realized that, together with the later D-Day offensive, the two events had cracked Germany wide open. I remembered the tanks I had seen rolling through Tarnów heading east on two occasions, and visualized, as with the images I had seen of Napoleon's retreating army in 1812, the ragged soldiers, their feet bleeding and frozen, wrapped in soiled bandages, making their retreat through the same streets, beaten and lost now. There was more than poetic justice in this, but my powerful desire for revenge was only partly fulfilled. I wanted all of Germany to burn, and all the SS and Gestapo gassed in the same chambers where they had martyred my fellow Jews.

～

One day, the Rock of Gibraltar came into view, its stark planes towering darkly in the blue sky. Preceded by two mine sweepers, the *Gripsholm* left the calm sea and started out for the open ocean. Thick dark clouds loomed overhead, and the water turned choppy. The chaos on board was immediate. As the swollen tides rose high enough to spray the decks with white sea foam, they sent the ship tossing and plunging in and out of the water. It was February, and the Atlantic was battered by storms and winds of gale proportions. Many of the now familiar faces turned green. Mother could not step out of her berth. She tried to stand up once to brush her teeth but fell back on her pillow with a groan. The decks and dining rooms, except for a few hardy and intrepid souls, were deserted. Most of the passengers suffered from acute seasickness.

The violent heaving and tossing of the *Gripsholm* had no adverse effects on Hela and me. We ran around with the few brave souls who managed to stay upright, and we ate in deserted dining rooms. Jim was unaffected too. However, his roommate was incapacitated for several days — a fact that hindered our lovemaking and eventually put a stop to it. After about a week of the general gastric disturbance, the decks, hall and dining rooms began to fill again. The faces of those who had been afflicted were still of a yellowish-greenish hue, but the passengers were sufficiently better to stay up and take some nourishment. The same was true of Mother, who, with Hela's and my help, managed to keep down some food, resume, though weakly, her walks and sit on deck or in one of the ship's lounges.

Our North Atlantic voyage felt endless. The *Gripsholm* rose and descended, heaving its way through the crashing waves, and our two mine sweepers proceeded at a snail's pace. After several days the captain gave us instructions that we were to stay indoors as much as possible. We were sailing slowly, he said, because we had entered a dangerous zone where some U-boats had been spotted earlier and because this was one of the roughest months of February for that region on record. He then informed us that, with luck, we would sail into New York's harbour in about a week.

Hearing this news, my heart began to pound wildly as though it would not be contained within my rib cage. I think that everyone experienced a similar sensation, for the silence that followed the magic word "New York" was more solemn and exquisite than any verbal show of feelings would have been. We all were struck by the now irrefutable fact that soon we would all be home. And, although home must have had as many meanings and connotations as there were people on board, it had at least one common denominator: freedom.

I began to shy away from Jimmy for I did not want to dissipate my feelings, which were now centred on one person only — my father. Also, I wanted to be alone to concentrate on my particular version of home; my thoughts about it were so complex and so full of diverse visions that I was reluctant to share them with anybody. More than ever, I needed solitude and privacy. We were alone in Jim's cabin just once more, and I tried to explain to him how I felt. He understood perfectly, and he, too, was sensing a similar need. He and all the other Americans were going to a large military hospital in New York and would be sent to their homes after observation, diagnosis and recommended treatment. We said goodbye to each other without any regrets and exchanged addresses. However, we both knew that the end of the voyage would mean the end of our relationship, although our good feelings for each other would remain among our happy memories. For the rest of the trip, Jim and I were just close friends.

As the days slipped by, I ceased to pay attention to what was going on around me. For once, I did not even think of the Nazis. The miracle of our voyage across the Atlantic, before the end of the war, was too staggering to comprehend. All I knew was that somehow the three of us had survived what seemed to be certain death and were on our way to Father. Nothing else mattered.

The Reunion

One day, I noticed that the heaving of the boat had subsided and that the ocean was calmer. Although it was windy and cold, all of us, soldiers and civilians, bundled up and lined up along the ship's railings so as not to miss one precious minute of our homecoming. All at once, the Statue of Liberty appeared on the horizon.

To me, it did not resemble at all the picture postcards with their glossy reproductions. It was much taller, more statuesque than I had imagined it to be. It seemed to dwarf all the ships and barges around it. It was majestic beyond all my hopes, and it appeared to beckon to us in a gesture of grace and hospitality. After being inundated for years by Nazi symbols of death and destruction, I beheld with my own, tear-filled eyes a symbol of life and hope. I could approach it only with deep gratitude and humility. The thousand or so people on the *Gripsholm* gazed at it in reverent silence; here and there, a head was bowed in prayer.

Before my eyes could dwell on the imposing New York skyline, there was a great rush of activity in front of our ship. From behind the Statue of Liberty, circling it gracefully at first, and then streaming to line up alongside the *Gripsholm*, there emerged dozens of tugboats, all aflutter with American and Canadian flags. Standing at attention on each deck were rows of WAC (Women's Army Corps), looking trim and beautiful in their olive uniforms, their left hands waving to welcome the repatriates, their right hands raised in a salute. The reaction on the *Gripsholm* was that of a dam breaking through. Greetings from a thousand throats roared in a mighty sound of joy.

During that fairy-tale scene while the *Gripsholm* was being ceremoniously escorted to shore, the ship's purser handed us several telegrams, all from Montreal. They had been timed in Montreal to coincide with our arrival. All but one were from uncles, aunts and cousins, full of emotional welcomes and expressions of relief and affection. We read them with our hearts overflowing, but they all paled in comparison with Father's cable, which we kept for the last.

Mother, Hela and I were so overwhelmed that we tried to outshout one another. Not only were we going home, but home, at least metaphorically, had come to greet us. Father was still thinking of the most minute detail to boost our egos and build our morale. As we had done with Father's letters, the Nicaraguan and the Canadian passports, we put the telegrams to our lips in a gesture of boundless gratitude. Then, calmed somewhat, we started getting ready to disembark.

We waited a long time for our turn to leave the ship. The first to go down the gangplank were the American air force men, among whom I detected Jim waving to me. I waved back, thinking fleetingly that perhaps his wife would change her mind and stay with him when she saw him. Then came the Canadian army personnel who were whisked out of sight. We could not see what was happening on the large dock, which was surging with a throng of people and teeming with army trucks. Our turn came at last. A man took our suitcase and told us that we were actually in Jersey City and in transit only, and that we must board the train to Montreal immediately. The train must have pulled up, just as the one in Marseille had done, almost right to the dock, for it seemed as though, after taking hardly any steps, elbowing our way through the crowd, we found ourselves in a plush compartment all by ourselves. There was frantic activity in the corridor as the veteran RCAF (Royal Canadian Air Force) men hobbled back and forth, exchanging greetings, laughing, shouting joyfully, and peeking now and again into our compartment to ask whether we were comfortable.

Ours was an overnight trip. I could not help but draw parallels to all our other journeys by train during the past five and a half years — to Białystok in the spring of 1939, to Krakow, Warsaw, Liebenau, Friedrichshafen, Geneva, Marseille. Compared to all the others, marred by fears and doubts, spelling mainly separation and uncertainty on reaching our destination, the train bearing us to Montreal symbolized total fulfillment and pure happiness. Never had I felt more humble and more at peace with myself than I did during the passage of hours bringing us closer to Montreal.

We were too keyed up to sleep. Every sound of the turning wheels meant diminishing distance between ourselves and Father. Unlike so many whom I had known and loved, we were given a second chance. Would I do it justice? Would I deserve my incredibly good fortune? Would my life, wrenched from murderous attacks, have real meaning? Although I knew no answers to the multitude of questions crowding my mind, I could foresee, for the hundredth time since our inclusion in the transport was announced, that I was going to cherish and revere all the Jews I had known personally and the millions of others whom I had not known but whom I considered my blood brothers and sisters. Deeply in my wounded psyche, I vowed once again to tell anyone who would listen, and those who would not, all I knew about the Holocaust. There were to be many broken promises in my life, but this one I fulfilled conscientiously, talking to individuals, lecturing and reporting to dozens of groups and organizations, and willingly giving interviews to the media for many years.

The next morning, February 22, 1945, the train began to slow down on the outskirts of a city that the soldiers told us was Montreal. They said we were heading for the old Bonaventure station where all troop arrivals and departures had been taking place since the beginning of the war. They themselves were returning to the very same spot from which, amid emotional farewells to their families, they had been shipped out to combat, followed by years of captivity. Dirty snow was lying in mounds in the streets, and the greyness of the February morning made the city look drab and shabby. We, however, were entirely unaffected by the scenery. As the train entered the tunnel leading to the station, we stood huddled together, trembling with excitement, close to the steps that would soon be lowered to let us out on the platform.

At first, we could not distinguish individuals for the denseness of the crowd. Aside from the families of the repatriated RCAF personnel, there were all sorts of people, including a large group of reporters, scurrying to and fro, their cameras flashing, trying to approach the descending passengers. Finally, after scanning the swarming crowd anxiously, we spotted Father. He was hatless, standing with a handful of our relatives and yet detached from them. We saw one another simultaneously. As soon as our eyes met we began to run, reaching one another somewhere midway. Pushed and almost trampled by the surging crowd, we hung together, our tears and embraces intermingling, a muffled cry escaping one or another of us. In a climax of emotional outpouring, we stood, swaying together, our arms around one another, our hands feeling the contours of a long-absent face. We were glued together wordlessly as though we would never come apart. It was only after the uncles, aunts and cousins had gently touched our shoulders, and, after the reporters besieged us with a barrage of questions, that we reluctantly acknowledged the presence of others and released one another, continuing to clasp hands. Father looked gaunt and very tired. Mother would have to see to it, I thought crazily, that he get proper nourishment from now on.

Then came the jumbled, disconnected words. Father did not need a coherent account to understand and intuit the horrors we had lived through: he had known all along. Nor did we need an account of his loneliness and endless fears: we had had ample proof of his agonies.

Our love transcended it all, its flame having burned away all the dross, alight evenly at last.

Even the reporters seemed to sense that there was something magical in what they beheld. Their humanity took precedence over their professionalism. They stepped away from us, and one of them asked respectfully whether we could give them an interview as the situation was extraordinary and had no precedent: we were among the first Jewish civilians to arrive in Montreal from German-occupied territories, and this fact was highly newsworthy. It was Father who answered, asking them to please leave us alone for twenty-four hours; after that time they were invited to our hotel suite to ask questions, which, Father said, pointing to me, his daughter would be glad to answer. I nodded in agreement.

Then, embracing us again, Father told us, in a voice still shaky, that, on hearing of our release, he had bought a home for us. However, as it was not yet ready for occupancy, he had reserved a suite in the Windsor Hotel for the time being. At last, leaving the crowd on the platform, we linked hands and walked toward a taxi. All four of us squeezed into the back seat, and, half-sitting, half-crouching, stayed together, our limbs entwined, our silent tears moistening one another's faces and clothes, until we arrived at our destination.

Afterword

It has been over eighty years since the first events in my mother's memoir. As is the case for many survivor families, almost all the people my mother wrote about are gone, and there is now a robust third and a fledgling fourth generation of the Roskies family. Our family is deeply connected to Judaism, and there is no danger that World War II and the Holocaust will be forgotten by us. But the personal stories of individual members of the family are more vulnerable.

My mother's memoir tells the story not just of her own life but also the lives and feelings of many others: her sister, Hela, her mother, Ida, her father, Izak, aunts, uncles and cousins, and her friends, from just before the war years until her arrival in Canada toward the end of the war. It is an exciting and unusual story, with near-misses, lucky breaks, unflinching determination, wonderful friendships (that lasted more than one lifetime), love affairs and a fortunate outcome. I hope this book is of interest to the current generation of the Roskies family and extended families — as well as to a wider readership.

The work speaks for itself, and I worry that anything I say is at best superfluous and at worst detracting, and that the fact that anything I write necessarily presents my mother through my eyes is so limiting as to not do her justice. However, I was asked if I would write something, and I want to. I will never write a memoir of my experiences, and this is the only chance I will have of putting something in writing that captures my thoughts and feelings about my mother.

I will say something about three topics: the world my mother lived in compared to the one we do; my mother's life since 1945; and my mother's legacy.

～

Air travel, the internet, Steve Jobs and the Roomba robot vacuum notwithstanding, life in Tarnów in the 1920s and 1930s was not all that different, in some ways, from life in the Montreal suburb where I grew up in the 1950s and early 1960s — or, for that matter, in Los Angeles, New York City, Pittsburgh, Boston, San Francisco, San Diego, Portland, Edmonton, Eugene or, probably, Jerusalem, all cities where members of the Roskies family have been growing up since then. From what I know of my mother's life from the stories she told me, she and Hela had the same good things and challenges in their lives as we did and still do.

One challenge was Ida. My grandmother was not what anyone would call warm and cuddly. She knew what side the bread was buttered on and did the best she could to make sure that side was on top when it fell. I thought my grandfather Izak was the greatest thing on earth; Ida was not so sure. She once told me she only married him because all the good catches were away at the front in World War I. My mother was the first-born and very smart, and Ida was bound and determined that she should excel scholastically. She routinely rapped her daughter's knuckles with kitchen utensils when she made mistakes in her homework. Like many of her generation, my mother was taken with socialism and Zionism, joining local Zionist organizations in her teens. Ida adamantly opposed this, as she opposed anything that risked my mother's moving into upper bourgeois society. I was told that Izak used to put a ladder outside my mother's window so she could go to night meetings without Ida knowing. Even if it is apocryphal, the fact that my mother told me this story tells you pretty much all you have to know about family dynamics during her adolescence, and the scene is very familiar — parental disagreements about getting a car or going to NYC with USY anyone?

In the twilight of the pre-war years, my mother was seventeen years old, in love, debating whether to go to the Sorbonne or Edinburgh to study journalism, and planning to live in British Mandate Palestine with her boyfriend after graduation. This could be any of us postwar, anywhere.

That said, in other ways the world we live in is a vastly different place than the one my mother grew up in, and not just technologically. In 1939, the entire Roskes family lived in Europe. No more. Our family has virtually no connection with any of the places we lived in before the war. As far as we are concerned, the "lands of our fathers" are effectively gone. None of us lives in Europe — we all live in the United States, Canada and Israel. None of us speaks Polish or Russian or Romanian. None of us thinks we will ever return to Poland or Romania. None of us has relatives there. No one identifies with Russia, or Ukraine, or Poland or Romania. We don't care, or know, if there is a shortage of shoes in Moscow or if a Pole wins Olympic gold in weight-lifting. When we travel to Europe, it is to see the Uffizi, go to plays in London, eat on the Côte d'Azur. Very few of us have gone to see where our family members lived before the war. I have visited my great-aunt Mandy's apartment building in Vienna but have never been to Tarnów, and do not expect I will ever go (my aunt Hela went once with one of her daughters). Some of us tell stories at our own seders of seders before the war, and there is one rather mournful tune (I was going to say "awful," but I didn't) that was introduced at one such pre-war seder that one cousin and her family sings. A few of us — mostly my mother's surviving cousins, average age probably seventy-seven — make recipes that came from the old country. A few of us have gone to visit the reminders and memorials of the Shoah. Family members whose work is devoted to Jewish culture and literature have professional connections in Eastern Europe. That is the extent of our living connection with where we came from.

The obvious explanation for why we have no living connection to Eastern Europe is that the war was traumatic, but I don't think that's right, since Germany, the source of the horror of the war, is a comfortable and even attractive destination for many of us. I think we have no connection to this part of Europe now because we had never had any connection there before the war to anything outside the Jewish world, and that world is gone. There is now nothing of ours there with which to connect.

What connections remain are to things Jewish as they existed before the war. I am connected to Europe, both its secular culture and the experiences — good and bad — of Jews in Europe, through my mother. My extended family are all aware of the richness of pre-war Jewish religious and cultural life. The majority of us either try to experience it as much as possible through books, videos or other representations, or have it on our agenda to do so, or wish we spoke Yiddish to be more able to access it. The family who lived in Poland and elsewhere experienced this richness.

The richness of their lives before the war leads to the question — why did the Roskes family leave Europe? The obvious answer — that the Nazis were on the rise — is not good enough. Millions of Jews did not leave Poland. Many could not, of course, but many who could chose not to. There was, at the time, good reason to stay. For those with means to leave, life was stable and often good. Among major leaders, who other than Churchill saw the war coming? The *Anschluss*, Germany's annexation of Austria in 1938, had passed virtually unnoticed. Chamberlain had promised "peace for our time" after the Munich Agreement. Germany's subsequent annexation of the Sudetenland was practically ignored. The Molotov-Ribbentrop Pact, which made Germany and the Soviet Union non-belligerents and paved the way for the German invasion of Poland, was not signed until August 23, 1939. By that time, it was too late.

The Roskes did leave. My mother's memoir describes how. It begins with the discussion that took place at my great-grandfather's seder table in the spring of 1939. The decision to leave was made by the old and blind, much-revered David Roskes — after whom all three first sons born after the war were named — who told his children they had to leave Europe. He foresaw the future clearly, but the ambiguity of the situation and the ambivalence people felt about leaving can be seen in the fact that not everyone left at the time. Izak did, but Ida, Sonia and Hela stayed — to wait for things to be "set up" in the New World. It is said that Ida wanted to hear that Izak had bought a house and hired servants before she was going anywhere. (I am afraid that Ida is not coming across all that well here, and, in her defense, I want to say that my mother and Hela both told me often that she was the one who insisted the family stay together in Tarnów. Rita Ross, née Schmelkes, whose family is mentioned in the chapter "Uneasy Journeys" and who Arielle Berger, who edited this book, located and introduced me to, remembers her fondly from their time in Liebenau.)

What to do when political changes occur is discussed all the time, and the question of leaving one's home has come up since 1939. Much of the Roskies family settled in Montreal, and the question arose when the French-Canadian separatist movement became politically powerful in the 1970s. Although previous French-Canadian governments had been antisemitic, this seemed to be a new type of threat. For my mother, the events of the 1970s brought back vivid memories of the war. She often had flashbacks to Nazi broadcasts and nightmares when she heard Separatist leaders speak. She was not the only Jew who was frightened. More than twenty-five thousand Jews — 20 per cent of the Jewish population — left Quebec, including my parents who moved to Ottawa. But, as it turned out, the threat was not existential, and those who stayed lived perfectly good lives in an increasingly French province. Similarly, I remember telling family members who lived in Israel that they should take the next plane out when Saddam Hussein fired Scud missiles at Israel during the 1991 Gulf War. I recall my aunt saying, "I can't do that. This is my home. I could never belong here afterwards if I left now." Again, staying turned out to be fine. My wife and I live in Boston. We renewed our Canadian passports when Trump was elected, but we are not going anywhere. We have too much where we are. But we now have those passports.

How should one decide such things? No one knows. The retrospectoscope is an accurate but useless instrument; if a prospectoscope becomes available on Amazon, please let me know. In my view, you can never know what you would do "if." You have to be in the room where it happens. Even then, you don't get to decide, if by "decide" you mean deliberately and consciously think about the options and their probable and possible outcomes. You do get to act, partly rationally, partly not. And you get to make the best of your life after you have "chosen." Which the Roskies family did.

∽

After the war, my mother picked up where she left off. She made plans to go to McGill. She joined everything. On one occasion, she went skiing in the Laurentians with friends. That day, there happened to be a young medical student on the train who thought she was drop-dead gorgeous and that her Polish accent was sexy. They got married within a year, and I came along as soon as possible thereafter, ending my mother's academic plans.

Marriage was part of my mother's plan, and Hyman (Hy) Caplan was the best thing that could have happened to her. My father did not have the same background as most of my mother's friends. He was the first of four children born to Joseph and Ida in a cold water flat on de Bullion Street in the epicentre of the Montreal immigrant community. Joseph was a bricklayer who had lost his legs to diabetes, and my father grew up in poverty. Going into medicine was a dream. Jews were not welcome at McGill at all, let alone in McGill medical school, but he made it. (His brother, Bernard, who had better grades than he did, didn't; the Dean of Medicine told him, "One per Jewish family is enough.") He had planned to be a surgeon but thought better of it after butchering the repair of a hand wound. Instead, he became a renowned child psychiatrist, an analyst and a professor of child psychiatry at McGill. He never lost his ambition to advance in the world, but he was not a driven man. On the contrary, he was gentle, understanding, empathetic and funny. He was, as they say, a mensch. The quality of *menschlichkeit* was to be badly needed.

My parents were married in a huge wedding — 550 guests, which included many of my grandfather's business associates — at the Shaar Hashomayim, the Montreal Conservative *stadt shul*. I was born soon afterwards (this was considered a good thing at the time), and my brothers, Jerry and Martin, came two and seven years later. I was part of a large and vibrant family, with many gatherings and much love. One of my favourite stories indicates just how bonded the family was. My maternal grandfather, Izak, was a brilliant, irascible, impatient man, the least likely person you would think had anything in common with my paternal grandfather, Joseph, a legless bricklayer at the polar opposite of the economic, educational and social spectrum. But Izak routinely went to his *machatunim*'s house, got into bed with Joseph, sucked hot lemon water through sugar cubes, and the two spent hours talking to each other. About what, *wer weiss*?

My mother found herself in the young Jewish community in the Town of Mount Royal and in literary interests. She chaired the education committee of our then rapidly growing synagogue, Beth-El, where she took an active role in determining curriculum, teaching personnel and other matters. Because of her, we were extremely close to the young rabbi who led Beth-El in those formative years. She took literature courses at what was then Sir George Williams College (now Concordia University). She took me and sometimes Jerry to lectures. She hung out with budding poets at McGill. She enjoyed her family. Life was truly good.

But even then, there were signs. I cannot tell whether my mother's perfectionism stemmed from her anxiety or vice versa, but they went hand in hand. I have vivid memories of her studies. One part of her Shakespeare exam was to write short notes about lines taken from any of eleven plays that they had studied — who said the line, to whom, under what circumstances, with what import in the drama. My job was to quiz my mother, quoting any line from any of the plays to have her answer the questions. All the texts were the Pelican paperback editions. My mother reclined in her bed, and I would open any play to a random page and read a word or two, and she would say, "That's Richard III, Act II, scene 3, X telling Y about Z...." She had every play memorized to the point that she could identify lines by the place in the book that I had opened and a word or two. The day of her final, she ran a fever of 39 degrees Celsius. She came home and collapsed for two days. She still got 99 per cent, but not 100, because, as her professor said, "This isn't Math. There's no such thing as a perfect paper in English." She spent years writing three versions of an MA thesis on Matthew Arnold; she believed none were good enough to submit.

My mother had losses, many unexpected. My aunt Hela, who lived in Detroit, lost her husband very young to heart disease, leaving her to raise their three children. My parents were involved in a head-on collision, and my mother required extensive plastic surgery on her face. In 1955, her father, Izak, died. Hela's oldest son died in a car accident. Hela's oldest daughter left home and was missing for years before returning. Hela's youngest daughter developed a case of brittle juvenile diabetes and nearly died. These were terrible and difficult events, but my mother recovered. But there were four losses from which she did not.

The first, and in many ways the worst, was that my brother Martin died when he was seven years old. The circumstances were as bad as you can imagine. Martin was the oldest of a group of eight kids at a day camp who climbed a small mountain in the Laurentians. There was a forest fire lookout tower at the top of the mountain, and the two counsellors took turns bringing half the kids up to see the view. One counsellor left the trap door of the lookout platform open, and Martin fell eighty feet to a stone ledge below. My mother and father were at home in the cottage they were renting. When time passed and Martin did not come home, they decided they would go see what was keeping him. They arrived at the foot of the mountain to see ambulances, fire trucks and police. My father introduced himself as

Martin's father and a physician and asked if he could help in any way. He was told his son was dead.

We lost a good part of both Hy and Sonia that day. My father went on; at least, he went to work. He later said that being in psycho-analysis at the time saved him. But he was a changed man. Our rabbi, Morton Leifman, who was very close to the family, said he "soured." Sonia did not have work to go to. She took to her bed for what seemed to me, and what may have been, months. This was before medications that help with serious depression, and talking therapy made no dent. She eventually emerged and began to live again. She took more litera-ture courses, hung around with budding poets again, was engaged in my and Jerry's lives; many of my more intellectual friends remember her challenging them and teaching them about literature throughout high school. But something was gone.

The second was that my mother got sick. She developed bowel problems and underwent what was expected to be a simple resec-tion of a non-functioning part of her large intestine. It turned out she had Crohn's disease and eventually developed serious complications that resulted in repeated hospitalizations lasting weeks to months and then a surgery to create an ileostomy. She stabilized but could not accept living with a bag and returned for more surgery, leading to another cycle of complications, hospitalizations and an eventual permanent ileostomy, which was extremely difficult for her to accept. The entire process lasted years, during which she was never well and rarely had more than a few months between major complications.

Just as her condition stabilized a bit, my brother Jerry died in an avalanche cross-country skiing in Norway. He was thirty-three and a resident in pediatrics at Western University in London, Ontario. He had had a bit of a ragged path through life. He went to MIT and did exceptionally well in his first two years but became depressed or lost in some way and barely finished his bachelor's degree. With my father's encouragement, he had entered medicine and was making his way. The accident report said he tagged along with a group of better skiers and tried to take a shortcut to catch up and that he had been warned of avalanche danger in that area. Ten days after he died, my parents received a postcard he had mailed the day before he died. He was happy, maybe hypomanic. The note read, "It is a far, far better thing that I do, than I have ever done." My mother would have known that this was Sydney Carton about to sacrifice his life for the woman he loves at the end of Dickens's *A Tale of Two Cities* and that it is followed by "it is a far, far better rest that I go to than I have ever known."

My parents were now alone in Ottawa, where they had moved after the separatist government came to power in Quebec, and my wife and I moved to be with them in late 1979. We had six months together. In June 1980, my father died of heart failure.

Sonia lost her last effective support. She had never regained her health after her surgeries. She had experienced increasing anxiety and depression, which my father had managed to help her deal with. With him gone, her illness and losses were overwhelming. Her anxiety and depression worsened; she was treated by some of the leading psychiatrists in Ottawa with every medication known and hospitalized several times, but nothing improved her condition.

I could not cope with her sadness and worry. I had not realized how much I needed my father, both for myself and to help me deal with my mother. My marriage collapsed and in 1981, I left Ottawa for Philadelphia. An insightful marriage counsellor told me, "You think you are leaving your wife, but you are really leaving your mother."

Sonia spent her last seven years in the condominium she and Hy had moved to in 1978. In 1982, I remarried and moved to Montreal — close enough to see her but far enough not to be overwhelmed. In 1984, we had a daughter, Hilary, who my mother saw often. She rebounded, somewhat. She saw a few friends and family who lived in Ottawa. She wrote this memoir at that time. It is incredible to me that she wrote it in her physical and mental condition. Its clarity and force are a testament to how important it was for her.

~

At my mother's funeral, Rabbi Langner, who had taken over Beth-El from our beloved Rabbi Leifman, had the funeral cortège pass by the synagogue and pause in front. This honour, he said, was to remember her contributions when Beth-El began. He said she was "a force," a woman who quoted Voltaire and Rousseau at Board of Education meetings.

My mother's family is filled with very bright and very accomplished people. Izak and his brothers were successful businessmen, running a woollen mill in Huntingdon, Quebec. Many of my mother's generation went into academia and her first cousins include professors of Jewish studies at the Jewish Theological Seminary and Harvard, and a Princeton PhD in mathematical physics who co-directed the Pittsburgh Supercomputing Center; others played leadership roles in Jewish organizations (running the Montreal Jewish Public Library; at YIVO). At my mother's shiva, one of her cousins said, "Sonia was the smartest of them all." Years before her death, in a reflection of the times, her uncle Enoch paid her one the greatest compliments that could be paid to a Jewish woman. He told me, "If she had been a boy, she could have been a Gadol B'Yisroel," a great Jewish scholar.

What does a woman with these talents and vulnerabilities leave?

To her family, friends and the many people she knew, Sonia left a set of values and beliefs: that intellectual life mattered and was sustaining; that effort was important and rewarding; that there are good and beautiful things in the world. Everyone who came in contact with her left with a glimpse of how you could have a material life in a Montreal suburb and a mental life that was connected minute by minute to centuries of history and culture. People took the experience of my mother with them for their entire lives. A few years ago, one of my high school friends, now a professor of literature at Harvard, told me he remembers the books in our home and discussions with my mother about English literature.

Implicit in my mother's life was that family was the centre of everything. This was so obvious that no one ever said it, but everyone knew that my mother would never have done the things she did without her parents, Hela, aunts and uncles, cousins, children and, above all, Hy. The same has been true for all of us.

My mother lived daily with the experienced reality that life is filled with danger, disease and loss, and experienced deep depression and anxiety, and yet she believed, and showed us, that life was filled with beauty and creativity and was worth living. Most importantly, the experience of love made it worth it to bring children into the world even if she could not know what they would become or even if they would live.

The gift of these beliefs came to me, as well as to everyone touched by my mother's life. The memory of her determination and belief in the goodness of life was empowering at times when my own was in shambles. After my difficult divorce to Hilary's mother, I remarried again, and Gloria Waters is both a wonderful partner for me and an essential parent for Hilary. And life renews. As this book goes to press, Hilary and her husband, Paul, have just had a son, Sebastian, whose first initial is in memory of Sonia. For me, it is truly a miracle.

I owe my interest in language to my mother. The scientific study of language has been central to my professional life, but my more important inheritance in this regard came from her passion for literature, which has sustained and enriched my life immeasurably. My house is filled with her books. I received from her the gifts of Yeats, Eliot, Shakespeare and countless other writers. One of my most valued possessions is her copy of James Joyce's *Ulysses*, filled with the annotations she made, which I read and lightly annotated myself several times before giving it to my own daughter, Hilary, who has done the same.

My mother's life came full circle from the seder in the spring of 1939, ending on the last day of Passover in 1987. Shemini Shel Pesach is one of four days a year when Yizkor, the communal prayer to remember the departed, is recited, so Yizkor and the annual personal Kaddish (the prayer commemorating the deaths of first-degree family members) coincide for me. Because of this, I am sometimes privileged to read the Haftorah (the reading from the prophetic literature) on that day. The reading is the great messianic vision of Isaiah 10:32–12:6. Some of the verses of the Haftorah are excerpted here:

וְיָצָא חֹטֶר מִגֵּזַע יִשָׁי וְנֵצֶר מִשָּׁרָשָׁיו יִפְרֶה:

וְהָיָה צֶדֶק אֵזוֹר מָתְנָיו וְהָאֱמוּנָה אֵזוֹר חֲלָצָיו:

וְגָר זְאֵב עִם־כֶּבֶשׂ וְנָמֵר עִם־גְּדִי יִרְבָּץ וְעֵגֶל וּכְפִיר וּמְרִיא יַחְדָּו וְנַעַר קָטֹן נֹהֵג בָּם:

וּפָרָה וָדֹב תִּרְעֶינָה יַחְדָּו יִרְבְּצוּ יַלְדֵיהֶן וְאַרְיֵה כַּבָּקָר יֹאכַל־תֶּבֶן:

לֹא־יָרֵעוּ וְלֹא־יַשְׁחִיתוּ בְּכָל־הַר קָדְשִׁי כִּי־מָלְאָה הָאָרֶץ דֵּעָה אֶת־יְהֹוָה כַּמַּיִם לַיָּם מְכַסִּים: {ס}

וְנָשָׂא נֵס לַגּוֹיִם וְאָסַף נִדְחֵי יִשְׂרָאֵל וּנְפֻצוֹת יְהוּדָה יְקַבֵּץ מֵאַרְבַּע כַּנְפוֹת הָאָרֶץ:

וּשְׁאַבְתֶּם־מַיִם בְּשָׂשׂוֹן מִמַּעַיְנֵי הַיְשׁוּעָה:

צַהֲלִי וָרֹנִּי יוֹשֶׁבֶת צִיּוֹן כִּי־גָדוֹל בְּקִרְבֵּךְ קְדוֹשׁ יִשְׂרָאֵל: {ס}

But a shoot shall grow out of the stump of Jesse,
A twig shall sprout from his stock.

Justice shall be the girdle of his loins,
And faithfulness the girdle of his waist.

The wolf shall dwell with the lamb,
The leopard lie down with the kid;

The calf, the beast of prey, and the fatling together,
With a little boy to herd them.

The cow and the bear shall graze,
Their young shall lie down together;
And the lion, like the ox, shall eat straw.

In all of My sacred mount
Nothing evil or vile shall be done;
For the land shall be filled with devotion to the LORD
As water covers the sea.

He will hold up a signal to the nations
And assemble the banished of Israel,
And gather the dispersed of Judah
From the four corners of the earth.

Joyfully shall you draw water
From the fountains of triumph, …

Oh, shout for joy,
You who dwell in Zion!
For great in your midst
Is the Holy One of Israel.

My mother left an annual experience of one of the greatest expressions of hope in the world's literature.

David Caplan
2021

Glossary

Ahad Ha'am (1856–1927; Hebrew, "one of the people") The pen name of Asher Ginsberg, an influential Zionist leader and writer from Ukraine. He believed that Zionism should focus on the revival of Hebrew and on the Land of Israel as the centre of a cultural and spiritual renaissance.

Anschluss (German; union) The annexation of Austria into Germany in March 1938, as part of the Nazi plan to unite all German peoples into a Greater Germany.

Aryan A nineteenth-century anthropological term originally used to refer to the Indo-European family of languages and, by extension, the peoples who spoke them. It became a synonym for people of Nordic or Germanic descent in the theories that inspired Nazi racial ideology. "Aryan" was an official classification in Nazi racial laws to denote someone of pure Germanic blood, as opposed to "non-Aryans," such as Slavs, Jews, part-Jews, Roma, and others of supposedly inferior racial stock.

Auschwitz (German; in Polish, Oświęcim) A Nazi concentration camp complex in German-occupied Poland about 50 kilometres from Krakow, on the outskirts of the town of Oświęcim, built between 1940 and 1942. The largest camp complex established by the Nazis, Auschwitz contained three main camps: Auschwitz I, a concentration camp; Auschwitz II (Birkenau), a death camp that used gas chambers to commit mass murder; and Auschwitz III (also called Monowitz or Buna), which provided slave labour for an industrial complex. In 1942, the Nazis began to deport Jews from almost every country in Europe to Auschwitz-Birkenau, where they were selected for slave labour or for death in the gas chambers. In mid-January 1945, close to 60,000 inmates were sent on a death march, leaving behind only a few thousand inmates who were liberated by the Soviet army on January 27, 1945. It is estimated that 1.1 million people were murdered in Auschwitz, approximately 90 per cent of whom were Jewish; other victims included Polish prisoners, Roma and Soviet prisoners of war.

Bergen-Belsen A concentration camp complex in Germany comprising three sections: a prisoner-of-war camp, established in 1940; a residence camp that held Jews who were to be exchanged for German nationals or goods, established in 1943; and a prisoners' camp, which held prisoners from other camps who were brought in to build the residence camp. The residence camp was divided into a number of groups, with different rules applying to each: The "star camp" was the largest group, holding about 4,000 "exchange Jews" who were all required to do manual labour; the "neutral camp," for Jews who were citizens of neutral countries, had better conditions and the inmates didn't work; the "special camp" held Polish Jews, most of whom were deported to Auschwitz; and the "Hungarian camp" held Hungarian Jews, some of whom were eventually released to Switzerland. Toward the end of the war, thousands of prisoners from camps close to the front lines were sent on death marches to Bergen-Belsen, pushing the number of inmates from about 15,000 in December 1944 to over 55,000 by April 1945, and causing a rapid deterioration in camp conditions. British forces liberated the camp on April 15, 1945. An estimated 50,000 people died in Bergen-Belsen.

"Deutschland über alles"(German; "Germany above All") A common name for the German national anthem "Deutschlandlied"

("Song of Germany") from its first lines, which were part of the anthem from 1922 to 1945. The anthem was based on a poem written in 1841.

Geneva Conventions A set of treaties and protocols that were negotiated between 1864 and 1949 to establish an international law for the standards of humanitarian treatment of victims of war, both military and civilian. The 1929 Geneva Convention was a revision of previous provisions and specifically sought to improve the treatment of prisoners of war, such as by classifying who was a POW and regulating conditions of captivity.

Gestapo (German; abbreviation of Geheime Staatspolizei, the Secret State Police) The Nazi regime's brutal political police that operated without legal constraints to deal with its perceived enemies. The Gestapo was formed in 1933 under Hermann Göring; it was taken over by Heinrich Himmler in 1934 and became a department within the SS in 1939. During the Holocaust, the Gestapo set up offices in Nazi-occupied countries and was responsible for rounding up Jews and sending them to concentration and death camps. They also arrested, tortured and deported those who resisted Nazi policies. A number of Gestapo members also belonged to the Einsatzgruppen, the mobile killing squads responsible for mass shooting operations of Jews in the Soviet Union. In the camp system, Gestapo officials ran the Politische Abteilung (Political Department), which was responsible for prisoner registration, surveillance, investigation and interrogation.

Herzl, Theodor (1860–1904) Austro-Hungarian journalist who wrote about the need to combat antisemitism by establishing a Jewish state in the homeland of biblical Israel. In 1896, he published the political pamphlet *Der Judenstaat* (The Jewish State), in which he argues for the founding of Jewish state, and in 1902 he expands on this vision in the utopian novel *Altneuland* (The Old New Land). Herzl is credited as the founder of Zionism.

High Holidays (also High Holy Days) The period of time leading up to and including the Jewish autumn holidays of Rosh Hashanah (New Year) and Yom Kippur (Day of Atonement) that is considered a time for introspection and renewal. Rosh Hashanah is observed with synagogue services, the blowing of the shofar (ram's horn) and festive meals during which sweet foods, such as apples and honey, are eaten to symbolize and celebrate a sweet new year. Yom Kippur, a day of fasting and prayer, occurs eight days after Rosh Hashanah.

International Committee of the Red Cross *See* Red Cross.

Jewish Council (in German, Judenrat) A group of Jewish leaders appointed by the German occupiers to administer the ghettos and carry out Nazi orders. The councils tried to provide social services to the Jewish population to alleviate the harsh conditions of the ghettos and maintain a sense of community. Although the councils appeared to be self-governing entities, they were actually under complete Nazi control. The councils faced difficult and complex moral decisions under brutal conditions — they had to decide whether to cooperate with or resist Nazi demands, when refusal likely meant death, and they had to determine which actions might save some of the population and which might worsen their fates. The Jewish Councils were under extreme pressure and they remain a contentious subject.

Jewish police (in German, Ordnungsdienst; Order Service) The police force that reported to the Jewish Councils, under Nazi order. The Jewish ghetto police were armed with clubs and carried out various tasks in the ghettos, such as traffic control and guarding the ghetto gates. Eventually, some policemen also participated in rounding up Jews for forced labour and transportation to the death camps, carrying out the orders of the Nazis. There has been much debate and controversy surrounding the role of both the Jewish Councils and the Jewish police. Even though the Jewish police exercised considerable power within the ghetto, to the Nazis these policemen were still Jews and subject to the same fate as other Jews.

kashrut (Hebrew; also, kosher) Fit to eat according to Jewish dietary laws. Observant Jews follow a system of rules known as *kashrut* that regulates what can be eaten, how food is prepared and how animals are slaughtered. Food is kosher when it has been deemed fit for consumption according to this system of rules. There are several foods that are forbidden, most notably pork products and shellfish.

Liebenau Internment camp established in 1940 outside the city of Friedrichshafen, Germany, to hold non-combatant women from enemy countries as prisoners of war, including citizens from the United States, Great Britain, the Netherlands and Greece. The camp facility included a castle where an organization called the Liebenau Foundation had functioned as a home run by nuns for people with mental or physical disabilities. More than five hundred of these former inhabitants were deemed "unfit" and murdered in the Nazi T4 Euthanasia Program to make room for the camp inmates. The conditions in the camp were satisfactory, with the Red Cross providing food and other supplies to those imprisoned there. The camp operated until 1945. The Liebenau Foundation is still in existence in the area of the former site of the camp.

machatunim (Hebrew) Relatives through marriage, used to refer to a child's in-laws.

matzoh (Hebrew; also matzah) The crisp flatbread made of flour and water that is eaten during the holiday of Passover, when eating leavened foods is forbidden. Matzoh is eaten during the seder to commemorate the Israelites' slavery in Egypt and their redemption, when they left Egypt in haste and didn't have time to let their dough rise. *See also* seder; Passover.

menschlichkeit (Yiddish) Humanity. Derived from the term mensch, meaning a good, decent person; someone with honourable qualities.

Molotov-Ribbentrop Pact *See* Treaty of Non-Aggression between Germany and the USSR.

Munich Agreement An agreement signed in the early hours of September 30, 1938, in Munich, Germany, by Nazi Germany, France, Britain and Italy, giving Germany permission to annex the strategically important Sudeten region of Czechoslovakia. Czechoslovakia was not invited to participate in the crucial conference that would determine its fate, and in early October the Germans occupied the Sudetenland. Not satisfied with the agreement, Germany occupied the remaining Czech territory in March 1939.

Oberscharführer (German; senior squad leader) A senior rank in the SS.

Orthodox The religious practice of Jews for whom the observance of Judaism is rooted in the traditional rabbinical interpretations of the biblical commandments. Orthodox Jewish practice is characterized by strict observance of Jewish law and tradition, such as the prohibition to work on the Sabbath and certain dietary restrictions.

Palestine (also British Mandate Palestine, Mandatory Palestine) The area of the Middle East under British rule from 1923 to 1948 comprising present-day Israel, Jordan, the West Bank and the Gaza Strip. The Mandate was established by the League of Nations after World War I and the collapse of the Ottoman Empire; the area was given to the British to administer until a Jewish national home could be established. During this time, Jewish immigration was severely restricted, and Jews and Arabs clashed with the British and each other as they struggled to realize their national interests. The Mandate ended on May 15, 1948, after the United Nations Partition Plan for Palestine was adopted and on the same day that the State of Israel was declared.

Passover (in Hebrew, Pesach) An eight-day Jewish festival that takes place in the spring and commemorates the exodus of the Israelite slaves from Egypt. The festival begins with a lavish ritual meal called a seder, during which the story of the Exodus is told through the reading of a Jewish text called the Haggadah. During Passover, Jews refrain from eating any leavened foods. The name of the festival refers to God's "passing over" the houses of the Jews and sparing their lives during the last of the ten plagues, when the first-born sons of Egyptians were killed by God. *See also* seder.

phylacteries A pair of black leather boxes containing scrolls of parchment inscribed with Bible verses and traditionally worn by Jewish men on the arm and forehead at prescribed times of prayer as a symbol of the covenantal relationship with God.

Red Cross A humanitarian organization founded in 1863 to protect the victims of war. During World War ii, the Red Cross provided assistance to prisoners of war and civilian internees by distributing food parcels and monitoring the situation in prisoner-of-war (pow) camps and civilian internment camps, and also provided medical attention to wounded soldiers and civilians. Today, in addition to the international body, the International Committee of the Red Cross (icrc), there are national Red Cross and Red Crescent societies in almost every country in the world.

Sabbath (in Hebrew, Shabbat; in Yiddish, Shabbes, Shabbos) The weekly day of rest beginning Friday at sunset and ending Saturday at nightfall, ushered in by the lighting of candles on Friday evening and the recitation of blessings over wine and challah (egg bread). A day of celebration as well as prayer, it is customary to eat three festive meals, attend synagogue services and refrain from doing any work or travelling.

Scharführer (German; squad leader) A rank in the SS equivalent to staff sergeant.

Schutzpolizei (German; abbreviation of Schutzpolizei des Reiches; State Protection Police) Also known as the Schupo, the Schutzpolizei were a division of the German Ordnungspolizei (Order Police) and were the uniformed municipal police of most towns and cities in Germany and parts of Nazi-controlled Europe.

seder (Hebrew; order) A ritual meal celebrated at the beginning of the festival of Passover. A traditional seder involves reading the Haggadah, which tells the story of the Israelite slaves' exodus from Egypt; drinking four cups of wine; eating matzah and other symbolic foods that are arranged on a special seder plate; partaking in a festive meal; and singing traditional songs.

shiva (Hebrew; seven) In Judaism, the seven-day mourning period that is observed after the funeral of a close relative.

SS (abbreviation of Schutzstaffel; Defence Corps) The elite police force of the Nazi regime that was responsible for security and for the enforcement of Nazi racial policies, including the implementation of the "Final Solution" — a euphemistic term referring to the Nazis' plan to systematically murder Europe's Jewish population. The SS was established in 1925 as Adolf Hitler's elite bodyguard unit, and under the direction of Heinrich Himmler, its membership grew from 280 in 1929 to 52,000 when the Nazis came to power in 1933, and to nearly a quarter of a million on the eve of World War II. SS recruits were screened for their racial purity and had to prove their "Aryan" lineage. The SS ran the concentration and death camps and also established the Waffen-SS, its own military division that was independent of the German army.

stadt shul (Yiddish) Town synagogue.

Star of David (in Hebrew, *Magen David*) The six-pointed star that is the most recognizable symbol of Judaism. During World War II, Jews in Nazi-occupied areas were frequently forced to wear a badge or armband with the Star of David on it as an identifying mark of their lesser status and to single them out as targets for persecution.

Sturmscharführer (German; storm squad leader) The most senior enlisted rank in the SS, equivalent to sergeant major.

Sudetenland The name used between 1919 and the end of World War II to refer to the region of Czechoslovakia that bordered on Germany and Austria and was inhabited primarily by ethnic

Germans. The Sudetenland was annexed by Germany in October 1938 under the terms of the Munich Agreement. *See also* Munich Agreement.

tallith (Hebrew; in Yiddish, *tallis*; prayer shawl) A four-cornered ritual garment that is draped over the shoulders or head, traditionally worn by Jewish men during morning prayers and on the Day of Atonement (Yom Kippur). Fringes on the four corners of the garment are meant to remind the wearer to fulfill the biblical commandments.

Talmud (Hebrew; study) A collection of ancient rabbinic teachings compiled between the third and sixth centuries that includes explications of scriptural law in a text known as the Mishnah and deliberations about the Mishnah in a text known as the Gemara. The Talmud remains a focus of Jewish study and the basis of traditional Jewish law and practice today.

Torah (Hebrew; instruction) The first five books of the Hebrew Bible, also known as the Five Books of Moses or Chumash, the content of which is traditionally believed to have been revealed to Moses on Mount Sinai; or, the entire canon of the twenty-four books of the Hebrew Bible, referred to as the Old Testament in Christianity. Torah is also broadly used to refer to all the teachings that were given to the Jewish people through divine revelation or even through rabbinic writings (called the Oral Torah).

Treaty of Non-Aggression between Germany and the USSR The non-aggression treaty that was signed on August 23, 1939, and was colloquially known as the Molotov-Ribbentrop Pact after the names of its signatories, Soviet foreign minister Vyacheslav Molotov and German foreign minister Joachim von Ribbentrop. The main, public provision of the pact stipulated that the two countries would not go to war with each other for ten years and that they would both remain neutral if either one was attacked by a third party. A secret component of the arrangement was the division of Eastern Europe into Nazi and Soviet areas of occupation.

The Nazis breached the pact by launching a major offensive against the Soviet Union on June 22, 1941.

Untersturmführer (German; junior storm leader) A rank in the SS equivalent to second lieutenant.

USY An acronym for United Synagogue Youth.

Volksdeutscher (sing. German; pl. *Volksdeutsche*; German-folk) The term used by the Nazis to refer to the ethnic Germans living outside Germany, mostly in Eastern Europe. Nazis estimated that there were 30 million *Volksdeutsche* and used them to support their idea of a pure-blooded German race and to further their plans to expand to the east. *Volksdeutsche* were given special status and benefits, such as property that had been stolen from Jews and Poles, and many saw the Nazis as liberators. After the collapse of Nazi Germany, most *Volksdeutsche* were expelled to Germany.

wer weiss (Yiddish) Who knows.

yekkes (pl. Yiddish, also Hebrew) A term used to refer to a Jewish person from Germany or with German Jewish ancestry; or referring to the stereotypical characteristics of such a person, such as meticulousness and orderliness. The term is sometimes used derogatorily.

Zionism A movement promoted by the Viennese Jewish journalist Theodor Herzl, who argued in his 1896 book *Der Judenstaat* (The Jewish State) that the best way to resolve the problem of antisemitism and persecution of Jews in Europe was to create an independent Jewish state in the historical Jewish homeland of biblical Israel. Zionists also promoted the revival of Hebrew as a Jewish national language. *See also* Herzl, Theodor.

Documents and Photographs

Gripsholm Arrivals Describe Blood Lust of Nazis in Poland

By LOUIS V. HUNTER.

MONTREAL, Feb. 23.—(CP)— Miraculous survivors of German anti-Jewish terrorism in their home town of Tarnow in Poland, Mrs. Ida Roskes and her two attractive daughters, Sonia, 23, and Rachela, 19, today are enjoying happiness, freedom and comfort they haven't known since the day war broke out 5½ years ago—the very day they received word their papers were in order to leave for Canada.

Eye-witnesses to the cold blooded slaughter of many of their fellowmen, a fate they themselves several times expected to suffer, the Roskes reached Montreal last night after arriving earlier at New York aboard the Swedish exchange liner, Gripsholm. They were met here by Isaac Roskes, who left his family in Poland shortly before the war to go into the woollen manufacturing business with three brothers at Huntingdon, Que.

Relates Story.

Surrounded by bouquets of flowers in the Roskes suite at their hotel, Sonia, clad in a smart grey suit, chain smoked cigarettes and nibbled at chocolates as she related the story of their life under the Nazi heel.

The Roskes were unable to leave for Canada in 1939 as they planned because, Sonia explained, even though their papers were in order, there was no railway communication with Warsaw and they could not pick them up.

When the Germans first reached Tarnow, about a week after the start of the war, they shot a few people "now and then" for such crimes as stealing bread. Looting was rife, and the Germans deprived the Jews of their homes without compensation. Terrorism really didn't start until 1942.

"There were about 30,000 Jews in the town and it took the Germans about a week to dispose of 20,000 of them", Sonia said. "Some of them were sent away to the east, and those who couldn't walk—the old, the sick, the weak, the children, and pregnant women —were killed. No news ever reached us of those who were taken away."

Sonia had no idea how many Jews were killed, but those who were to be sent away, were crowded in a square in the centre of the town and made to kneel there for hours. Without shooting at anybody in particular, Sonia said the guards occasionally sprayed sections of the crowd with machine-gun and rifle fire.

"The square was all blood, and it still is covered with blood."

"They were three times to our place. One Gestapo man told us to be ready in a couple of hours. He threatened to shoot us, but he never came back. We spent a couple of horrible hours."

In June, 1942, all the remaining Jews in Tarnow were sent into a Ghetto, which consisted of three or four streets in the most unsanitary part of town. People were crowded into rooms and everyone was put to work. Mrs. Roskes and Sonia sewed shirts and Rachela made horse brushes.

The Roskes and 14 others lived in three small rooms.

"The Gestapo shot immediately without warning anyone they saw on the streets of the Ghetto while the people were supposed to be at work. Every day almost there were 10, 20, 50 people shot, but some days there was only one. I saw many of my own friends shot. Sometimes, coming home from work, we had to walk through the pools of blood."

Lauds Red Cross.

Sonia couldn't say enough about the work of the Red Cross and so grateful is she for the help it gave her family that she intends to do Red Cross work here. The American and Canadian soldiers on the Gripsholm, too, "behaved in a most admirable way to us and the others on the ship".

An article in the *Ottawa Journal* in which Sonia Roskes was interviewed about her wartime experiences. February 1945. Courtesy of City of Ottawa Archives.

INTERNMENT CAMP LIEBENAU

by

SONIA ROSKES

The following article was written for the News Sheet by a young Polish woman who recently arrived in Canada and who, with her father, mother and sister, is starting a new life in a new country. During her two years of internment at Camp Liebeneau, Miss Roskes learnt to speak English from the British women who were her comrades in captivity.

I was only half awake when after four day's journey our group, consisting of 30 women and children, arrived at the little station of Mecken-beuren about 11 miles from the Lake of Constance and only 2 miles from our final destination. It was a cold but sunny morning of New Year's Day 1943. In my complete exhaustion following the three dreary weeks I had spent in the worst German jail of Gracow, and in a peculiar state of mental apathy which usually accompanies the feeling of being cold and hungry, I had no eyes for the beauty of my new surroundings — the snow-covered pinewoods and meadows at our feet, the majestic Swiss Alps in the background.

Suddenly my consciousness was roused by a man's rough voice — it appeared to belong to one of our escorting guards — explaining to some of my companions that in our new place we would feel more at home, as it was an internment camp for British and American women. "Your own people will take care of you," he concluded with a sarcastic smile, "and I hope you will like the change."

"Your own people..." These words stirred something in our hearts some secret wish which had lain there concealed and suppressed throughout the misery of the past three years. Was it possible that the camp we were going to was not just another of the concentration camps where innocent people were being killed daily by the thousands, but a place offering a chance of survival ? Was it really true that in a couple of hours we would meet American and British women ?

After a short while we were loaded on to a huge horse-cart, including our meager hand-luggage (all we were allowed to have according to the German order on the day of our internment) and driven in the direction of Liebenau. It was noon and the snow was dazzling white under the bright sun, when we arrived in the village in the middle of which was a block of two-storied buildings and a double-towered church which was separated from three neighbouring cottages by a high stone fence. An iron gate was flung open by an elderly German policeman, and our wagon rolled past a small guards-house to come to a standstill in front of one of the three buildings.

In a second we found ourselves surrounded by a large group of women of all ages, whose eyes smiled at us in a warm welcome and whose numberless questions, asked in about ten different languages, we in vain tried to answer. All we gathered from the chaotic conversation was that we had nothing to be afraid of any more, that as subjects of enemy countries we fell under Geneva Conventions which secured protection for prisoners of war and civilian internees on German territory, and that, though life was pretty tough and miserable in camp at times (which we would find out ourselves very soon), the worst part of our internment was over. The appearance of of the women who were gathered around our cart confirmed their reassuring words : there was nothing about them to remind us of the haunted looks of all those many thousand of underfed and persecuted beings we had known so well in Poland: their clothes, consisting in most cases of slacks and thick woollen pullovers, were in a fairly good condition and except for a trace of bitterness in their voices whenever they spoke about 'being locked up in a cage" they did not sound too depressed.

It was only in the evening when, after my first bath and supper I lay down in the first clean bed I had known for many a month, that I became aware of the change in my life. "However hard it may be to live for months and perhaps years under a lock," I said to myself, "however gloomy and monotonous it may become to be herded with different people under the same roof, I shall try to make the best of it; the main thing is that my mother, sister and myself are alive and that we shall not know the fear of a German bullet, the fear which became a part of our inner selves in Poland, any more."

It took me about a month to become acquainted with the daily routine of camp life, to learn something about my fellow internees and to come into closer contact with some girls of my own age. In another few weeks' time it seemed to me that I had been there for many years — so familiar appeared every face, every voice, every room.

Liebenau became an internment camp for women, holders of British and American passports who happened to live in various European countries before the outbreak of the war. Originally an asylum for mentally deficient German children and grown-ups, with an adjacent convent of German nuns in charge of the sick, it contained at the time of my internment over 600 interned women and children — a number which by far exceeded the usual capacity of the place. The mentally deficient Germans (or "lunies" in the slang of the internees) still occupied a few wings of the camp buildings. Employed by the German nuns at field and garden work, they were a common sight within the camp boundaries; their disfigured bodies and faces did not make the prison atmosphere any brighter.

In the three years previous to my arrival, the camp had gradually developed into a fairly well organized community. In order to keep the necessary discipline and to carry on all the official negotiations, a camp captain had been elected. That 60 year old Englishwoman, who enjoyed the greatest respect and confidence of all the internees, performed her duties with iron energy and never-failing efficiency. Mrs Violet Froom, camp captain, was always ready to solve difficult problems, to give advice and to step in whenever intervention was necessary. Assisted by six floor captains, each chosen by the members of her floor, she ran the administration, registered newcomers, reported them to the Swiss Legation — the Protective Power over all the Allied prison camps in Germany — and arranged the distribution of Red Cross food

and clothing parcels. It was due to her great character, broad-minded attitude towards all the problems of the world and to her sincerely democratic ideas that a couple of hundred women, all coming from different countries, speaking different languages and having different habits of their own, could lead a relatively peaceful community life under extraordinary circumstances.

The floor-captains' main duty was to keep order on their floors. As internees were supposed to perform all the domestic task within the camp, they compiled special working lists, all the instructions of which had to be followed strictly. The harder jobs, such as cleaning corridors, carrying food from the German kitchen, and being air raid wardens in case of raids, were done by young and strong girls; others had to keep diningrooms and bathroom tidy, to wash up dishes and attend to the boilers — our only source of tea water. Some of the most reliable and the professionally trained internees were given more responsible work; they became the organizers of schools and educational courses, shows and other small entertainments, discussion circles, and groups of literature lovers.

The head of the camp's Educational Committee was another English-woman, Mrs. Vidakovic, formerly a professor of English at the University of Belgrade, Yougoslavia. With the help of a large group of voluntary teachers and librarians, untired in her efforts to give every internee the possibility of studies and warmly interested in each individual case, she was the soul of the spiritual life within the camp — the inspiration of various courses in English and other lagnuages, the supervisor of the library and the adviser in all matters concerning general education.

The more official part of the administration was carried out by the Germans. The six German guards gave us our mail, next-of-kin parcels and German newspapers (the only source of our political information); every evening they made roll-calls in all the rooms occupied by the internees who were not allowed out of doors after 6 p.m. They escorted the daily afternoon walks in the surroundings. An old German paymaster who had his office in one of the camp buildings dealt with money questions, received various petitions and inflicted all kinds of punishment on those who broke "the law." A staff of German nuns supervised the food.

It is when speaking about the food provided by the German that I am approaching the subject of the most important factor in our camp life. Though our living accommodations and sanitary conditions were a great deal better than those in other prisoner-of-war and civilian internment camps in Germany, the food received from the Germans would not have been sufficient to prevent us from starvation. Breakfast consisted of a slice of sticky and often mouldy bread, jam and an absolutely undrinkable coffee substitute; lunch of thin soup and some vegetables floating in a dark gravy; supper of a few potatoes, the same sticky bread and an identical "coffee".

This is where the Red Cross comes in. Big consignments of Red Cross parcels, British and American, would arrive in the camp at frequent intervals, where they would be unloaded and unpacked with enthusiasm by the internees. Their regular weekly distribution by the camp captain secured our food situation and shut off the danger of hunger. Besides food parcels the Red Cross provided us with various clothing articles. Many an English or American woman who had been dragged out of her house by the Germans at a moment's notice without being allowed to take the most essential items, was, after some time, dressed from top to toe in clothes sent by the Red Cross. The foundation and constant increase of our liberty was rendered possible by Red Cross book supplies. The chool for the 60 interned children could function systematically and successfully thanks to the Red Cross delivery of text-books and stationery, games and toys for the Kindergarten and various instruction leaflets for the teachers of the camp. Shows and other performances could be put up from time to time in our more than primitive theatre hall, because the Red Cross always responded to our artists' requests for theatrical costumes, paints for the scenery, and musical instruments. Many women who, not having anything particular to do, would have broken down

as a result of boredom and lack of occupation, were kept busy knitting and doing all kinds of other handwork, owing to the Red Cross delivery of knitting wool, cotton and embroidery silk. Health service in the camp, naturally handicapped by shortage of trained nurses and the utter ignorance of an old German doctor, would have been ever more inadequate had it not been for the regular supply of Red Cross invalid comfort parcels and all the medicines required.

The two years which elapsed between my arrival in Liebenau and my final release from the camp were marked in the history of the place as abounding in happenings and extraordinary events. In fall 1943, when the monotony of camp life was becoming unbearable and when phrases like "I am fed up," "I am bored stiff," and "I wish to Goodness something would happen" were inseparable from our daily vocabulary, a great change took place. A department of the German Foreign Office arrived in the camp, where it made its permanent residence.

The cowardly officials who had fled from Berlin where they were exposed to the daily danger of becoming the victims of Allied bombs and who hid shamelessly under the protection of internees who were relatively safe from this fear, took possession of one of the buildings by removing all the internees from it. We were shaking with helpless rage and indignation when, after being crowded in our small rooms more than ever before, we began to suffer from al the restrictions made by "Berlin across the garden path" as we ironically nicknamed the Foreign Office. The small amount of freedom which had been our greatest treasure up to that period was considerably cut down : two gardens, one behind and the other in front of the camp buildings, were closed to the internees; only three walks weekly were permitted; room arrests, stopping of mail, and even deportations to other camps became a frequent punishment for crimes like picking apples on country roads, waving at the Allied planes flying over Liebenau, attemps to offer a package of cigarettes to Serbian prisoners-of-war working in the village, or not greeting the German guards.

General depression and even feelings of hopelessness reached their climax in 1944 when first exchange transports on a larger scale began to leave the camp.

The first one to take place was an American repatriation transport, in February 144, including about 80 U.S.A. citizens from our camp. Anxious speculations and wild rumors as to who was going to be chosen — the usual symptoms in every internment and P.O.W. camp whenever "something is in the air" — were put an end to by the publication of the official list of names, accompanied by a notice signed by the departmental chief of the Foreign Office to the effect that the names listed had been received from Washington. How great was our indignation when, about half an hour after the publication of the first one, another list of about 20 persons was added ! It was then that we realized how great was the power the Germans had over us; for it was the German Foreign Office that had selected the people for exchange, and from which the repatriation of each one of us depended. Complaints addressed to the Swiss Legation in Berlin were censored by the German paymaster; and if he disapproved of their contents, our letters ended in his wastepaper basket.

During the next four repatriate transports which took place successively throughout the same year we had to experience yet another injustice. Whenever a number of repatriates, whether to England or the United States, was about to leave the camp, only a very few of our internees were included. The Germans completed the number they were supposed to give in exchange for their own prisoners by taking people from outside the camp, people who had been free all during the time the 600 Liebenau internees were losing their physical and mental strength in the long years of captivity. A few days before the departure of a transport dozens of these "outsiders" would stream in; and by a special order of the Foreign Office they had to be treated like guests, which meant that they were free from all the duties we had to perform and not compelled to obey the regulations we were subjected to.

At the close of the year the atmosphere in the camp became gloomier and our spirits lower than ever before. As there was a big American exchange in sight, and the small rooms could not hold any more persons, all the dining rooms where we used to gather for meetings, to study, and to take our meals, were turned into bedrooms for the "guests"; on account of bad railway connections within Germany and the Allied successes threatening the Ruhr district, our usual supply of coal was cut down, so that we were forced to pick wood on our walks in order to have boiling water at least once daily; a few weeks running not one letter reached the camp, and even the German newspaper stopped arriving regularly. The schoolroom was half empty in the hours set for adults' educational courses : the internees, for many of whom it was the fifth Christmas away from their homes, lost all their

desire for the continuation of their studies and their power of concentration over books.

It was soon after New Year 1945, that the rumours about a great repatriation transport to the U.S.A. which had been very persistent for some weeks past, were officially confirmed. On January 19th a list of about 115 persons included in the exchange was put op on the notice board. Three days later, just before the transport was about to leave Liebenau to go via Switzerland to Marseilles and sail from there on the "Gripsholm" an additional list of names was published, my mother's, sister's and my own among them.

The happiness which filled my heart at the moment I saw our names on the list was beyond control. All jobs that remained to be done in the last day of my internment, the hectic packing, ceding my duties to some of my remaining friends, taking our luggage down to the canteen, to be searched and sealed, I performed without being conscious of what I was doing. My heart was singing with mad joy while I was saying to myself, "It is really, undeniably true; it is true that in a month's time I shall be in a free country which does not know the Gestapo and the German methods of cruel persecution; it is true that at last the misery of three and half war years in Poland and the two years of internment are over; it is true that our family has been granted the happiness of survival."

Over 300 British women have remained in Liebenau. It was when I was saying goodbye to these less fortunate friends of mine at the gate of the camp that I suddenly knew my happiness would never be complete until they were/ finally released, too; it was then that I felt, with an intensity I had never known before, how deeply attached I had become to each one of them and how much their friendship had meant to me in the period of my greatest need for human understanding.

On board the Gripsholm, which we took in Marseilles and where we met American and Canadian wounded soldiers being, like ourselves, on their way home after long years of captivity, I once exchanged my experiences with a Canadian ex-prisoner-of-war. "I don't agree with those who maintain that happiness makes one forget past sorrows and worries," he said. "Happy as I am to have left the gloom and hardships of my prison years behind me, and to go back to the ones I love, I know that for a long while yet I shall not be able to tear the memories of the camp out of my mind and heart. Only when I hear that all my fellow-prisoners, who still have to go through the ordeals of this final war stage in Germany, have safely reached the shores of Canada, will these memories give way to an undisturbed enjoyment of my new freedom."

The Gripsholm landed in New York on Jan. 21st; on the day following her disembarkment our family arrived in Canada. In the first six weeks which I have spent in this splendid free country, the broadminded, generous-harted people of which I have already learned to love, I have often recalled the words of that wounded Canadian soldier. All I can add to them is that though Internment Camp Liebenau belongs to the past, I shall always remember the lesson I was taught there that — in order to become a useful member of any community one has to develop an attitude towards one's fellow-creatures based on understanding and goodwill; not on selfishness and prejudice !

P.O.W. AT KOBE
Air Raid Precautions

Air Raid Precautions have been taken at the Prisoner of War Hospital at Kobe, in Japan, which was visited by the International Red Cross Delegate on 18th August of this year. The report of the Delegate's visit has just reached Australia.

The hospital is attached to the Osaka Group of camps on the main island of Japan, Honshu. At the time of the visit there were altogether 101 patients, of whom 15 were Australians and there were three Australians on the Hospital, but not Medical, Staff.

Location is said to be on a quiet, sunny hillside, in seven foreign-style wooden buildings with tiled roofs. Ventilation, drainage, water supply are reported to be adequate.

Bedding consists of straw mats 'on a wooden floor with five blankets for each patient, and pyjamas. Food consists mainly of rice, barley and vegetables, with very little meat and fish. There are no eggs, milk, fat, cheese, sweets, coffee or canned foods. The kitchen equipment seemed adequate, reported the delegate, but there was no refrigerator or ice-box.

(*Australian P.O.W. Magazine*)

AID FOR BRITONS IN FRANCE

A new Red Cross and St. John Sub-Commission has been set up in Paris to care for British civilians, particularly children and the sick and aged, who need help in France. A considerable number of Christmas parcels as well as clothing and blankets have already been issued.

Persons eligible to receive relief include all children under 18 with British fathers and dependants of all men killed or captured while serving with the British forces. Distribution arrangements for the children include a system whereby they can be referred to the out-patients department of the Hettford Hospital, Paris, for future preventative treatment against such diseases as tuberculosis and rickets. This hospital, which will shortly be reopened by the Red Cross and St. John, will receive supplies for this purpose of cod liver oil and Adexolin from Great Britain. The British Consuls in Lyons, Bordeaux, Nantes and Rouen have been asked to supply lists of all British subjects in their care, especially of children and aged and sick persons, so that appropriate supplies can be sent for distribution. Relief parcels have already been sent to Marseilles and Nice.

Colonel Gielgud, who has a long and intimate knowledge of the country, is at present touring France in the hope of tracking down all British subjects in the country who may be in need of help. Opportunities for extending this relief work for the British in France are also being examined.

A similiar organisation to help Canadian citizens has been set up in Paris by the Canadian Red Cross, while civilians from other dominions and Colonies will come within the scope of the British scheme.

PRAISE FOR FPRISONERS OF WAR WORK

Mr. H. B. Burdekin, who is the examiner in Accountancy subjects at New Zealand University, has written to London saying :

"I am in the middle of my University exam. marking again. Curiously enough the best ones I am getting are coming from members of the armed Forces. Three batches that I had towards the end of last year from prisoner of war camps in Germany were all of high quality, some very good indeed."

(*Kincardineshire Branch B.R.C.S.*)

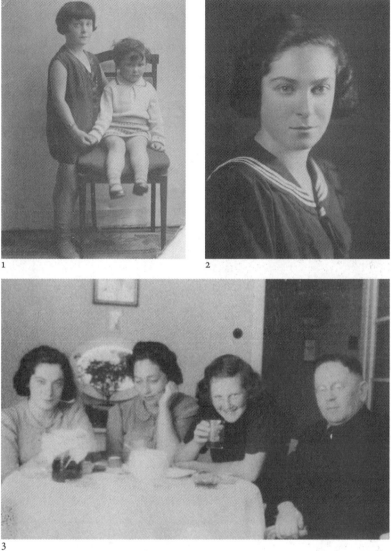

1 Sonia (left) with her sister, Hela. Tarnów, Poland, circa 1930.
2 Sonia's high school graduation photo. Tarnów, 1938.
3 Sonia with her family, before her father's departure from Poland. From left to right: Sonia, her mother, Ida, her sister, Hela, and her father, Izak. Tarnów, 1938 or 1939.

1 Sonia's grandfather, David Roskes. Białystok, Poland, date unknown.

2 Sonia with her father (left), her uncle Leo (right) and her grandfather, David (front). Białystok, circa 1939.

3 Sonia with her extended family before the war. In back is her uncle Moishe and Aunt Pola. In front (left to right): her aunt Masza, her grandfather, David, her cousin Benjamin (Benjie) and Sonia. Białystok, circa 1939.

1 Sonia's family at her grandfather's home. In back is her father, Izak (left), and her
  uncle Enoch (right). In front (left to right): Sonia's aunt Pola, her grandfather,
  David, and her uncle Owsej. Białystok, circa 1939.

2 Sonia's uncle Enoch (left) and aunt Mandy with her father, Izak (right), after they
  all arrived in Canada. Montreal, late 1939.

1 Sonia. Tarnów, 1939.

2 Sonia wearing a coat made for her to go to the Sorbonne in Paris. Tarnów, early 1939.

3 Sonia in Krakow, 1939.

1   Sonia (left) with her friend Meyer Taub at a spa town in the summer of 1938. The
    name of the person on the right is not known. Krynica (now Krynica-Zdrój),
    Poland, August 1938.
2   Israel Schmuckler, Hela's boyfriend during the war, who helped Hela, Sonia and
    their mother survive in the Tarnów ghetto. Tarnów, 1939.

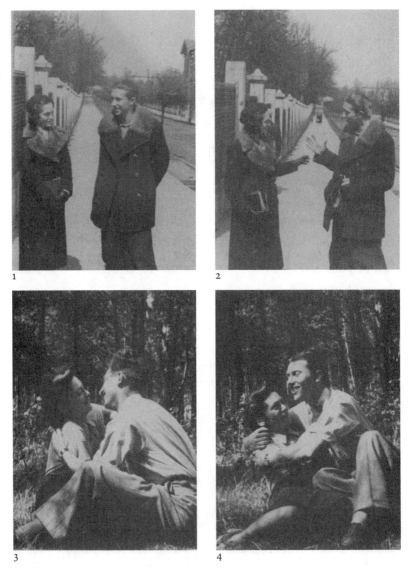

1–4 Sonia and her boyfriend, Milek Korn, before the war. Tarnów, Poland, 1937–1939.

1–3 Passport photographs of Ida, Sonia and Hela, circa 1940.
4 The cover page of Sonia's Nicaraguan passport.

1 The first pages inside Sonia's passport, indicating the date and that it will remain valid for one year.

2 The next pages of the passport, stamped and signed by the consul general of Nicaragua in New York, N.A. Portocarrero. The text in Spanish indicates that the passport has been granted to Sonia and asks the civil and military authorities of the countries through which she passes to not hinder her and to provide her with help and protection if necessary.

1 The last page of the passport with type on it, listing Sonia's nationality, age, address, place of birth, that she is single and a student, and various other descriptive features.

2 Prisoner card of Sonia (here spelled as Sonja) Roskes from the Liebenau internment camp, January 1, 1943. The columns indicate debits, credits and balance, and the handwriting at bottom right indicates that she was exchanged to America on January 25, 1945. Courtesy of ITS Digital Archives, Arolsen Archives.

1   Sonia (left), with her mother, Ida (centre), and her sister, Hela (right), at the Liebenau internment camp. Meckenbeuren, Germany, circa 1943.

2   Sonia (left) with her friend Linka Gold at Liebenau. Meckenbeuren, July 1944.

3   Sonia (seated, second from left) with her sister, Hela (front, crouching), and a group of friends at the Liebenau internment camp. Meckenbeuren, March 1943.

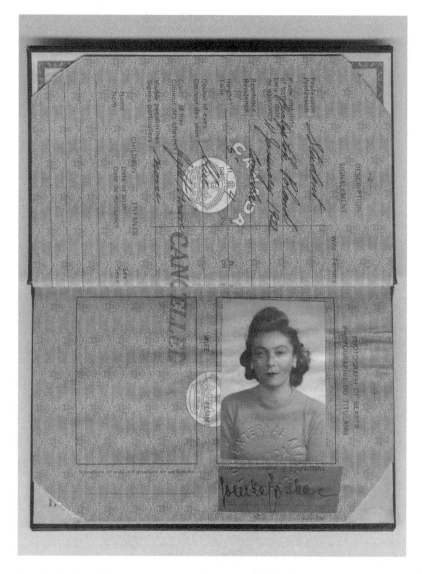

Sonia's first Canadian passport, sent to her in 1944 while she was interned in Liebenau.

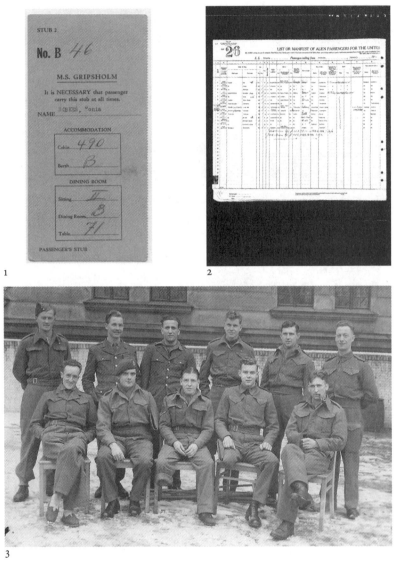

1 Sonia's passenger ticket stub from the MS *Gripsholm*.

2 Part of the ship manifest for the MS *Gripsholm*, showing the Roskes family name. Courtesy of Arolsen Archives, ITS Digital Archives.

3 A group of the soldiers who had previously been POWs and were aboard the *Gripsholm* with Sonia. The photograph was sent to either Hela or Sonia as a memento after the voyage.

Ida, Hela and Sonia (left to right) on the day of their arrival, at the Windsor Hotel. Montreal, February 1945.

1 On arrival day with family at the Windsor Hotel. In front (left to right): Hela, cousin Ruth, Ida and Sonia. In back: Sonia's father, Izak, her uncle Leo, uncle Owsej and aunt Mandy. Montreal, February 1945.

2 Sonia and her family in front of the château they went to in the summers. From left to right: Sonia, Ida, Izak and Hela. Huntingdon, Quebec, circa 1946.

Sonia and Hy's wedding. Montreal, 1946.

Sonia. Montreal, circa 1949.

1 Sonia's parents, Ida and Izak, on a vacation. Miami Beach, Florida, circa 1949.

2 Hela and Ida. Quebec, late 1940s.

3 & 4 Sonia and Hy. Montreal, early 1950s.

1 Sonia with her newborn son David. Montreal, 1947.

2 Sonia with her newborn son Jerry. Montreal, 1949.

3 Sonia (front, left) with her mother-in-law, Ida Caplan, her husband, Hy, and their children Jerry (left) and David (right). Montreal, circa 1952.

4 Sonia's three sons. David (left), Martin (centre) and Jerry (right). Montreal, circa 1955.

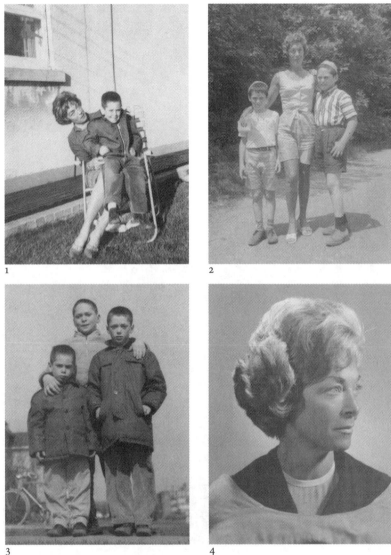

1 Sonia with her son Martin. Montreal, circa 1960.
2 Sonia with her sons Jerry (left) and David (right). Montreal, circa 1960.
3 Sonia's sons, David, Martin and Jerry. Montreal, circa 1960.
4 Sonia's graduation photo from Sir George Williams College (now Concordia University). Montreal, 1962.

1 Sonia. Ottawa, 1980.

2 Sonia's sister, Hela, at the summit of Larch Mountain. Corbett, Oregon, circa 2003.

3 Sonia and Hela's mother, Ida (right), with their aunt Masza. Montreal, late-1980s.

1 Second, third and fourth generations. Sonia's son David Caplan (far right) with his family. From left to right: David's son-in-law, Paul; David's daughter, Hilary, holding her newborn son, Sebastian (named in memory of Sonia); David's wife, Gloria; and David. Elk Island National Park, Alberta, September 2021.

2 Paul, Hilary and their son, Sebastian. Edmonton, Alberta, August 2021.

Index

youth, 4, 5, 8, 9, 14, 15, 19; factory work, 102, 103, 104, 136, 138–139; German occupation, life under, 38, 39, 51–52, 57, 58; Gestapo, picked up by, 65–67; Ghetto B, hiding in, 138–140; leave-taking from father, 22–23; life in Canada, 211, 216; preparations for leaving Poland, 24–25; relationship with mother, 8, 23. See also *Gripsholm, MS; Liebenau internment camp; Montelupich prison; repatriation; Schmuckler, Israel; Tarnów; Tarnów ghetto; "three or none"*

Roskes, Ruth (cousin), 12

Ross, Rita B., 146n1, 213. *See also* Schmelkes, Mrs., and family

Running from Home (Ross), 146n1

Rzeszów, 145

Safah Berurah (Tarbut school), xxi, 5, 6

Schenkel, Wolf, xxiii

Schmelkes, Mrs., and family, 146, 146n1, 167, 181, 193, 213

Schmuckler, Israel, xxiii, 52–53, 66, 116–117, 123, 127–128, 130–133

Schnabel, Artur, 146n1

Schneider, Herr (Foreign Office head), 166, 167, 176–177, 179–180, 199

Schutzpolizei, 56, 58, 90

Sebastian (great-grandson), 220

selections, 90, 116

Shaar Hashomayim *stadt shul,* 215

SS, xxvii, 36, 41–42, 91–92. See also *Aktionen* (deportations and executions); antisemitic measures; atrocities; Gestapo

Stalingrad, 164, 199

Stanisławów (now Ivano-Frankvisk, Ukraine), xix

Stars and Stripes, 198, 199

Statue of Liberty, 203

Stitzinger, Ludwig, xxii

Streicher, Julius, 62

survival, seeking means of: "Aryan" papers, 54, 69, 79–80, 97, 105; bunkers, 111–115, 122, 123–124, 130; forged passports, 105, 146, 147–148, 166–167; going into hiding, 71, 81–82, 105; legitimate foreign passports, xviii, xxviii; refugees, becoming, xxii, 30–31, 33, 77. *See also* Canada; Caplan, Sonia (née Roskes), under Nazi rule; Nicaraguan passports

survival, Sonia's reflections on, xv, 171, 174, 183, 194–195, 205

Sweden, 45, 46, 87, 101

Switzerland, xxviii, xxix, 158, 159, 185–188

Szebnie forced labour camp, xxix

Tarbut coeducational gymnasium (Safah Berurah), xxi, 5, 6

Tarnów: appearance in spring 1939, 1–2; chaos after German invasion, 29, 33; German occupation of, xxii, 35; Grabówka, xxv; Jewish community in, xvi, xix–xx, 2–4, 5, 8; Krakowska

The Azrieli Foundation was established in 1989 to realize and extend the philanthropic vision of David J. Azrieli, C.M., C.Q., M.Arch. The Foundation's mission is to support a wide spectrum of initiatives in education and research. The Azrieli Foundation is an active supporter of programs in the fields of education, the education of architects, scientific and medical research, and the arts. The Azrieli Foundation's many initiatives include: the Holocaust Survivor Memoirs Program, which collects, preserves, publishes and distributes the written memoirs of survivors in Canada; the Azrieli Institute for Educational Empowerment, an innovative program successfully working to keep at-risk youth in school; the Azrieli Fellows Program, which promotes academic excellence and leadership on the graduate level at Israeli universities; the Azrieli Music Project, which celebrates and fosters the creation of high-quality new Jewish orchestral music; and the Azrieli Neurodevelopmental Research Program, which supports advanced research on neurodevelopmental disorders, particularly Fragile X and Autism Spectrum Disorders.